ONE

SOUFFLÉ

AT A

TIME

ONE
SOUFFLÉ
AT A
TIME

A Memoir of Food and France

ANNE WILLAN

with Amy Friedman

ST. MARTIN'S PRESS ❧ NEW YORK

ONE SOUFFLÉ AT A TIME. Copyright © 2013 by Anne Willan Inc. All rights reserved. Printed in the United States of America. For information, address St. Martin's Press, 175 Fifth Avenue, New York, N.Y. 10010.

www.stmartins.com

Design by Steven Seighman

Library of Congress Cataloging-in-Publication Data

Willan, Anne.
    One soufflé at a time : a memoir of food and France / Anne Willan ; with Amy Friedman.
        pages cm
    ISBN 978-0-312-64217-4 (hardcover)
    ISBN 978-1-4668-3702-7 (e-book)
 1. Willan, Anne.   2. Cooks—England—Biography.   3. Cooks—United States—Biography.   4. Cooking, French.   I. Friedman, Amy.   II. Title.
    TX649.W55A3 2013
    641.5092—dc23
    [B]

                                                                            2013004043

St. Martin's Press books may be purchased for educational, business, or promotional use. For information on bulk purchases, please contact Macmillan Corporate and Premium Sales Department at 1-800-221-7945, extension 5442, or write special markets@macmillan.com.

First Edition: September 2013

10 9 8 7 6 5 4 3 2 1

James Scherer

This book is for my dearest husband, Mark Cherniavsky, and our two children, Simon and Emma. May they, and their children and their children's children, prosper long and happily.

Contents

....

Acknowledgments

·······················

This book would not have been possible without Amy Friedman, who has become my second voice and a close friend who knows more about me than I do myself.

Warmest thanks to:

Emma, my daughter, who first suggested the project.

Elizabeth Beier, my outstanding editor at St. Martin's Press, who took a bet that *One Soufflé at a Time* would rise high.

Lisa Ekus, my agent, whose warmth and wise counsel brought us all so close.

Jenn Garbee, who worked on our book proposal and found the title.

Todd Schulkin, tireless advisor, manager, and on-the-spot editor, who also happens to be my son-in-law.

Elizabeth Weinstein, whose editorial insights kept us on the right track.

Susan Broussard, who, with Nicole Quessenberry and Angel Liu, tested the recipes.

And to editor Jim Burns, longtime friend who pulled the final recipes into shape.

Things I've Smuggled in My Suitcase

....

- Ginger biscuits for a midnight feast at my boarding school
- Exotic fruits and vegetables from Manaus on the Amazon, confiscated in Miami
- Fresh truffles for Julia Child, packed with camphor balls to distract sniffer dogs
- American bacon for the French chefs at La Varenne—so much crispier, they said
- Trunks of American flour to France for testing recipes
- French Mars bars to the United States for the best hot chocolate sauce for the children
- Christmas gingerbread houses from America to France; if the roof collapses it still tastes the same
- *Ypocras,* a medieval spiced wine, labeled "Spiced Vinegar" so it can cross the state line
- A vinegar "mother" from Italy for our U.S. kitchen

ONE

......

SOUFFLÉ

....

AT A

......

TIME

At La Varenne in the early days, Chef Michel Marolleau and I worked hard together.

Chapter One

. . . .

UPSTAIRS IN PARIS

If you can't stand the heat, get out of the kitchen.
—Harry S. Truman

On a chilly November morning I rushed out of our apartment over-looking the Eiffel Tower. Just a few months earlier, in the summer of 1975, my husband, Mark, and I, with our two small children, Simon and Emma, had moved to Paris. I'd already taken this twenty-minute walk dozens of times, a straight path east along the Rue Saint Dominique, on my way to my cookery school that was, after years of planning, nearly ready to open. This was the day Craig Claiborne, the renowned restaurant critic of *The New York Times* and the most important fixture on the American food scene, was coming to see the school. That he was coming at all was a great compliment, but a mention in *The Times* could make all the difference, since his words could make or break our reputation.

I hurried past top-class food stores—a poulterer and several bakeries. I had already picked out "my" café, the place I stopped every morning to drink a café crème and read the *Herald Tribune;* from the first day the server knew my order without asking. But that day I didn't stop. I swept past commanding historic buildings and across the gray gravel then fronting Les Invalides, the vast complex of military-themed museums and Napoléon's tomb. I spotted our sign painted in crisp black letters on a cream background: LA VARENNE ÉCOLE DE CUISINE and felt a shiver of pride at the sight of it and of our window boxes with their cheerful geraniums.

Keeper of the keys, I climbed the back stairs and turned the ancient, crabby lock, releasing the heavy sidewalk door, which surely dated from the 1930s. Our French business partner and landlord, Sofitel, had helped us find this old bistro beside one of their hotels in the heart of Paris. Finding the right place had not been easy. Restaurants in Paris were doing very well, and French law demanded that any premises in which there would be cooking had to have a restaurant license. But this 150-year-old building with its stone-vaulted cellar naturally insulated for a *chambre froide,* a walk-in cold room with meat hooks, was just right. By that day in November we had spent months remodeling—one classroom on the ground floor for the morning hands-on practical classes, with another upstairs to double as a practical kitchen and a space for afternoon demonstrations that would, like the cinema, welcome drop-ins. Now I hoped to lure some students.

Our chef, Michel Marolleau, arrived at nine on the dot. Marolleau had been recommended by Sofitel and was the image of what I'd imagined as the La Varenne chef with his good looks, neatly combed hair, and pencil-perfect moustache. He was young—just twenty-nine to my thirty-seven. Although he had not one word of English, he did have solid cooking experience. That morning as he changed into his starched chef's whites in the cubbyhole behind the upstairs office, I busied myself with last-minute preparations. I noticed the loose telephone wires still about but consoled myself that at least the main demonstration bench and crucial overhead mirror lined with Mylar reflecting plastic were installed. I smiled up at that mirror, envisioning a showman chef who might flambé with too much enthusiasm and scorch a hole in the Mylar—and later did just that.

All that summer and into fall had been a flurry of activity, but I was fortunate to have the support not only of the family but also of so many lights of the food world. Simone Beck—better known as Simca and Julia Child's co-author—had gone with me to the frenetic Salon des Arts Ménagers, where I purchased equipment for the school. Simca's energy was astounding; in her toy-sized car, also called a Simca, she drove me around the Place de l'Étoile never looking left or right. Armed with her wisdom and keen eye, I decided on appliances that combined economy with toughness. We could not afford the robust German makes, let alone anything American, which was the wrong image anyway. My mission was to teach real French cooking, but so many of the French appliances were of poor quality, so we finally decided on the French-made Arthur Martin as a good compromise. At the school the utilitarian brown floor was shiny clean. The sight of the curtains I had made myself from the expensive chintz fabric printed with herbs, an opening gift from my mother, gave me a rush of pride. I'd wanted to add a touch of hominess to temper all that cold stainless steel of the bench and ovens.

I had spent many days preparing for this particular morning. At my request, Chef Marolleau had made his signature apple tart and chewy almond cookies called *financiers* because they are the color and shape of gold bars. I'd also instructed him to be prepared to serve lunch, though I couldn't be certain Craig would stay. I fussed over every detail, lastly my clothes, the flared black wool skirt my mother had bought for me on Rue du Faubourg Saint-Honoré and my favorite red-patterned shirt. My mother had insisted I dress well for such an occasion—so much was at stake.

For nearly eighty years the Cordon Bleu had been *the* cooking school in France for professionals from other countries. But in the 1960s when I was a student at the school in Paris I'd been frustrated by the fact that while we learned a great deal, none of it was on paper. That was the way I had always been taught, especially at Cambridge University, where I had earned my degree in economics. At Cambridge one was always hearing: "If it's interesting, write it down," but at the Cordon Bleu nothing was, and there also was only one cantankerous old chef. Although he was good, he flatly refused to discuss anything. I always had questions—"Chef, why are you cooking this so fast?" or, "Chef, what exactly does it mean to sauté something?" or, "Chef, how do I know when something's done?" Whenever anyone dared ask anything, the chef snarled, "Don't bother me."

So we learned by inference—we had to watch how the chef cooked. That's what I did. And I took copious notes. Every night of my months there I went to my room and typed the recipes on three-by-five cards. When I began to prepare to open my own cooking school, some of these recipes became the inspiration of the curriculum. Behind all this was my belief that we must look at cooking the way the French look at it: Cooking has a structure, a particular way of doing things. For instance, roasting involves dry heat, moderately high but sometimes very high temperatures, so you know certain techniques are involved in the process. If you know that structure, you can roast anything. Everything has a structure—the basic sauces, the stocks, the *crème pâtissière*. And with technique, you build. Even a simple dish such as fillets of sole Provençale provided a good lesson in lifting the four skinny fillets from a whole fish, then sautéing them briskly, but not too fast, in butter, with a tablespoon of oil to discourage scorching. The tomatoes (fresh only) must be peeled and seeded, and the seasonal garlic of late spring is best.

FILLETS OF SOLE PROVENÇALE

Any whitefish fillets are good cooked this way and this is a last-minute dish, best served at once. Add a wedge of lemon to each plate.

Serves 4

4–8 fillets whitefish (1½ pounds/675 g total)
2 medium tomatoes
4–5 tablespoons/30–40 g flour
Salt and pepper
4 tablespoons/60 g butter, plus more if needed
1 tablespoon/15 ml vegetable oil, plus more if needed
2 shallots, finely chopped
2 cloves garlic, finely chopped
1 tablespoon chopped fresh parsley

Rinse and dry the fish fillets on paper towels and cut large fillets in half, lengthwise. Core the tomatoes and cut them in half crosswise. To remove the seeds, squeeze the halves in your fist so the seeds pop out; then coarsely chop the tomato flesh.

Spread the flour on a sheet of paper towel and sprinkle with salt and pepper. Press each side of a fish fillet on the flour; lift and pat it with your hands to form an even coating. Coat the remaining fillets. Heat half the butter with the oil in a large frying pan over medium-high heat. When the butter stops sputtering, add half the fish fillets, skin side upward. Sauté briskly until browned, 2 to 3 minutes, turn, and brown the other side. Transfer the fillets to two warm serving plates and keep warm. Add more butter and oil to the pan if needed, and sauté the remaining fillets to fill two more plates.

Wipe out the pan. Melt the remaining 2 tablespoons butter and sauté the shallots until translucent, 1 to 2 minutes. Stir in the garlic and cook until fragrant, 1 more minute. Stir in the tomato and cook briefly, stirring, until very warm, about another minute. Stir in the parsley, take from the heat, and spoon over the fish fillets. Serve at once.

With La Varenne, I wanted to bring the best cooking in the world—French cooking—to a wider audience. That had always meant I had to open the school in Paris, where I could find world-class chefs and where students would have an opportunity to dine and eventually work in the finest restaurants. It was my mission to make it easy for the students to learn. The school would be bilingual, which at that time the Cordon Bleu in Paris most emphatically was not. Despite the fact that I understood the chefs rarely followed written recipes, students would receive paper copies. Eventually, to deal with grumbling from students discovering an incongruity between the written recipe and what the chef was actually doing, we added a caveat: "Since each chef may prepare his own version of this recipe, please consider the above as a starting point for your own notes."

I wanted to make everyone feel at home. Because I was born English, I knew what it felt like to be a stranger in France. I wanted our school to allow for national tastes and to incorporate ingredients from afar. For years I lugged American flour from the United States to Paris in my red valise so that anyone returning to the United States could succeed at making butter puff pastry the French way at home. I insisted on putting hand to dough—*la main à la pâte,* as the French would say. I understood that good food is food without pretension, food that delights by surprise, food that appeals to every sense. That was the understanding I hoped to instill in our students. Details mattered. My Grand Diplôme from the Paris Cordon Bleu, dated March 27, 1964, misspelled my name—Anne Willian—although we had fewer than twenty students in our class and I had been there for eighteen months. Not only did that feel insulting, but it was the kind of indifference to students I was determined not to allow at La Varenne.

For two years before we opened, our family had lived in Luxembourg, where my husband worked at the European Investment Bank. It was in Luxembourg that the idea for the school began to take real shape. From a gastronomic viewpoint, the two years in Luxembourg were a dead end—"mountain trout" came from the hatchery; game seemed to have fled over the border into the French and Belgian Ardennes. Luckily, France was not far away and Mark, my éminence grise in so many things, kept reassuring me we would move back to Paris and I would open a school.

But other than Mark and my friends Julia Child and Simca Beck, few people understood my idea. Whenever Mark and I talked about the idea with English friends, they were nonplussed. How could anybody, particularly a foreigner, open a cookery school in Paris? They wanted to know. They thought we were mad even to imagine the idea. American friends outside the food world found the idea entrepreneurial, an inverted form of the American dream. But they asked things like, "Do you speak French?" or, "Will the Paris chefs help you?" They actually had no idea.

Indeed, as I was quickly coming to understand, neither did I. The previous months had been an orgy of preparation. We had been busy moving the family and finding a nanny and schools for the children, who were three and five, and also working hard to raise sufficient funds for the school. Our early investors included many in the food world who had been so welcoming—Julia and Paul Child, James Beard, Simca Beck, as well as our good friend Nick Brown. But I quickly discovered it is a quantum leap from cooking professionally and writing about food—both of which I had been doing for more than a decade—to organizing and running a school. Julia was great from the start, offering not just financial help but also ideas and friends and friends of friends—people who made yearly pilgrimages to the three-star restaurants; people who played tennis with the Troisgros brothers, famed restaurateurs; people who fermented their own crème fraîche for Lutèce; cookbook authors and editors who led to yet more friends.

Julia and Simca had arranged for me to teach six weeks of classes at the fabled Gritti Palace hotel in Venice in the early summer of 1975. There I would be introduced to a wider audience. Julia also introduced us to her lawyer, William Peter Kosmas, whom we liked immediately. It was Bill who worked out a partnership contract with Sofitel and he who had found us a woman to help with promotion. "Yanou Collart," he told us, "represents Paul Bocuse." Bocuse, whose restaurant l'Auberge du Pont de Collonges near Lyon was one of a small number in France to receive the *Guide Michelin* three-star rating, was one of the most prominent chefs in the world. So although we had no experience with publicists, naturally we contacted Yanou.

Yanou was big and matronly. Though I couldn't be sure, she was apparently a lesbian who was open about her sexuality at a time when that was rare. And her advice was priceless. "What you have to do," she told me, "is hold classes and invite anybody and everybody. Then we'll get journalists to come and write about the classes. . . ." I didn't think for one moment of ignoring her advice. I knew good press would be vital. Still, in late September, six weeks before opening, we had just one registered student. I was apprehensive.

Before Luxembourg, we had lived in Washington, D.C., where I worked as food editor at *The Washington Star,* and I had learned there that fake photo setups look artificial. So instead of making a pretense, I rounded up just a few friends to provide animation for our demonstration. I carefully prepared the menu—Marolleau seemed willing to turn his hand to anything. On our dry run one week earlier for a freelance journalist, everything had gone beautifully. I felt confident all would go well that day, too. Besides, I hoped Craig wouldn't have bothered to agree to come unless he had positive feelings about the school.

Small, slightly plump, and cherubic-faced, Craig arrived promptly on time, but when he walked in he tripped slightly over those telephone wires. Thankfully, he didn't take a spill. He had less than an hour, he explained as we hurried up the stairs for a look around. He was on a tight schedule. For a moment I was disappointed, but I understood that a visit to an infant cooking school could not be a high priority for the most famous cookery journalist in America. Looking back, I understand still better: That very week he and his longtime friend Chef Pierre Franey embarked on an adventure at the prominent Paris restaurant Chez Denis, a meal that became an unfortunate cause célèbre, a $4,000 tab on a thirty-one-course meal. Readers lambasted him for the extravagance in a time when so many in the world were dying of hunger.

Still, I was honored to have him at La Varenne, and as I showed him around I handed him copies of many of the nearly one thousand recipes I'd spent the last several years writing, and more information about the school Yanou insisted I give him. I led him in to observe Marolleau's demonstration, which I translated, opening by articulating my idea behind La Varenne. "We intend to instruct in every facet of French cooking—sauces, roasts, fish cookery, pastry and dessert making, soups, hors d'oeuvre . . ."

The rest of that hour is a blur.

By the time Craig left it was scarcely lunchtime, yet I felt as if a whole day had passed. Exhausted, Marolleau and I sat down and ate his *gigot d'agneau de sept heures* and nibbled on the financiers. I'd deliberately chosen the slowly braised lamb to be reheatable. Thank heaven no French meal is complete without a glass, or two, of wine.

SEVEN-HOUR LEG OF LAMB

This recipe was once intended for tough mutton, but today's tender meat takes only 4 to 5 hours to cook. A few small boiled potatoes are the only accompaniment needed.

Serves 6 to 8

A leg of mature lamb (about 6 pounds/2.7 kg)
2 cloves garlic, cut in slivers
A large bouquet garni of parsley stems, 3 bay leaves, and several
    stems of thyme
Salt and pepper
4 quarts/4 liters water, plus more if needed
3 carrots
3 small turnips
3 medium leeks
2 small celery roots
3 medium onions
10–12 cloves garlic, chopped

Cheesecloth; string; large casserole or heavy roasting pan

Heat the oven to 275°F/140°C and set a shelf low down. Trim the lamb of excess fat and stud the meat with the slivers of garlic, poking small holes with the point of a knife. Wrap the meat in cheesecloth and tie it tightly with string (it will shrink during cooking). Put it in the casserole with the bouquet garni, a pinch of salt, and enough water to cover it by three-quarters. Bring the water slowly to a boil on top of the stove and skim it well.

Cover the casserole, transfer it to the oven, and cook for 2 hours. The water should scarcely simmer, so if necessary turn down the heat. Turn over the meat after 2 hours and continue cooking another hour. Meanwhile, trim, peel, and cut the carrots, turnips, leeks, celery roots, and onions into ⅜-inch/1-cm slices. Mix them with the chopped garlic, salt, and pepper.

After 3 hours, lift out the meat, add the vegetables in the casserole, and replace the meat on top. If necessary, add more water so that the meat is half-covered. Replace the lid and continue cooking until the meat is very tender indeed and would fall off the bone if not wrapped, 1 to 1½ more hours.

Remove the meat to a warm place and cover it loosely with foil. If the vegetables are not very tender, continue simmering them, uncovered, on top of the stove until they almost collapse into a fragrant mélange. Transfer them with a slotted spoon to a deep platter, discarding the bouquet garni. Cover and keep warm. Increase the heat so the cooking liquid boils and reduces.

Discard the cheesecloth and strings from the lamb, lift it carefully onto the vegetables, cover, and keep the platter warm. Continue reducing the cooking liquid to about 3 cups/750 ml of concentrated broth to serve as gravy—this may take up to 20 minutes. Taste it and adjust the seasoning. Serve the vegetables and meat in shallow bowls—the meat will fall apart without being carved. Spoon over a little of the broth, passing the rest separately in a bowl.

On November 5, 1975, just five days before our official opening, Craig's glowing piece about La Varenne appeared in *The New York Times*. Although he mentioned those trailing wires, he also remarked on the "far from unpleasant mingling of odors—roast meat with the good smell of game, celery, apples and fresh paint." He wrote about the brightly lighted room, the spotless modern range, and our young chef applying himself to "multiple good things including . . . a caramelized tarte Tatin." He quoted my mission, and at the end came a paragraph about our opening on Monday, November 10. We were off.

Our earliest days of press coverage assured me I was on to something. Even France's *Le Figaro* described what we were doing as an alliance "of American bonhomie and the French art of the table." I remained confident that we were offering something different from, and better than, the Cordon Bleu of those days. It is true that a soufflé that would rise in the Paris Cordon Bleu basement kitchen in their ovens with no thermostat would rise anywhere. But I wanted something much better, and I believed we had set the stage.

We had problems early on—primarily staff, or rather the lack of it. I was on the front line, not only translating demonstrations and classes but also welcoming walk-in visitors and cleaning up after class. Marolleau reported full-time, as was required by French law, but also under French labor law, chefs do not wash up. We paid him handsomely, though most of the time he was lolling around, because into December we had only a trickle of students. He spent mornings in the basement organizing his *mise en place* for the afternoon class in case a few students did show up. Every day at 2:30 I would walk downstairs to the front door and peek outside to see if anyone happened to be waiting on the sidewalk for the drop-in class. Many days there was no one there.

Just the week before Christmas our first full paid student came, Abby Mandel from Chicago. Several months earlier at a cooking demonstration for a benefit in Illinois that Julia gave, she had talked up the school. So Abby, who had persuaded Julia to do the demonstration, decided to come. Abby eventually brought the first sustainable farmer's market to Chicago and was one of the first of many La Varenne students to go on to stellar careers in food. But in those early days besides Abby we had only the dentist's wife, everybody and anybody's secretary or cousin, whomever we could persuade to come.

In mid-December Yanou arranged for a journalist, Susan Heller Anderson, to visit. Susan came to one class, then to a second, and when she asked if she could come a third time I thought, *Well, honestly . . .* , because those classes were costing us money. But I held my tongue. This time she asked if she could bring along a photographer. Looking back, I suppose I should have known that was a sign things were going places, but I was too busy to notice.

On the day Susan came with the photographer, he happened to catch a freak photo. Michel was making *chaud-froid de poulet,* and I was animatedly translating, pointing at the dish. The photographer happened to catch a picture of us at the moment that Marolleau, in his chef's hat, was making precisely the same gesture as I was. At the end of the day, Susan said, "I think I've sold a story about the school to *Time* magazine."

That night I told Mark, and we agreed it would likely be one of those two-sentence paragraphs. We thought nothing more about it as we closed up the school for the holidays. Christmas is always an important gathering time for our family, and there was no question that we would close. We celebrated during the lull until the New Year. Then, at the start of 1976, the new *Time* came in the mail, and when we opened it we were speechless. There was an enthusiastic story with a two-column-wide photograph occupying half a page.

What sets La Varenne apart from any other school of *la cuisine classique* in France is that it is run—efficiently—by an Englishwoman, Anne Willan—and it is the first full-scale school to offer lessons in English as well as French. Without mincing any *mots*, the well-financed academy has set out to challenge the haughty Cordon Bleu, the 80-year-old citadel of French culinary tradition that has become a synonym for distinguished cookery. ["Modern Living: A Franglais Challenge to Cordon Bleu," *Time*, January 5, 1976.]

Susan described me as an unflappable practical cook with the Grand Diplôme from the Paris Cordon Bleu and other credentials—like the twenty-volume *Grand Diplôme Cooking Course* I had edited back in the early seventies in America. And, she wrote, "she has a well-traveled palate." I loved that description. In the second week of January when we reopened, the phone lines began to ring off the hook. From having no students, by the third week of January we had one full class of ten and another half-filled. Suddenly I was translating two practical classes and five demonstrations each week and Marolleau was on his feet all day. I understood we had created a living, breathing animal.

So much of cooking is indefinable, a question of instinct. In France, unlike America and England in those days, children were brought up thinking about what they eat. From a very early age they were aware of the importance of how something should taste. Questions followed: "Does this have enough salt?" "Wouldn't this be nice with tarragon?" "This sauce has just the right balance of this and that . . ." From infancy, children in France hear people talking this way. I wanted our students to pick up the French custom of appraising what they ate, just the way I had learned from a family I lived with while I was at the Paris Cordon Bleu in the early 1960s.

The Charpentiers, with their seven children, followed a program of discipline that I'm certain went back generations. Each day Monsieur, a wealthy industrialist, came home for a two-hour lunch at which all the children were expected to behave impeccably. The food was plain—dried salami sausage, celery root rémoulade, radishes with butter, followed by roast meat and a single vegetable, fish on Fridays, then cheese and fruit. I was impressed by the way the whole family talked about food. The youngest child was born while I was living there, the oldest was twelve, and they grew up with an "I always cross Paris to get the best chickens on Sunday" attitude. Their chickens came from a special poulterer, the finest in Paris. The Charpentiers were upper bourgeoisie, but even in ordinary restaurants in France I saw parents and their children relishing food, tasting, say, *steak frites,* saying things like, "Oh, these *frites* are not as good as last week's."

Back then every self-respecting Frenchwoman had her special chocolate cake, though sometimes it did seem the only dish well-to-do Frenchwomen could cook. Most French families seemed to have hidden a plump little old lady in the kitchen, a fact that had prompted Julia to comment of the elegant mesdames out front in the salon, "Frenchwomen can't cook!" But Marielle Charpentier was different. The Charpentier house was a paradise of good wine and food, and dessert was a festival of tastes—fritters with honey or snow eggs of meringue floating in vanilla custard and topped with crisp caramel. Marielle had a small repertoire, but each dish was perfection.

Her chocolate snowball has toured the world with me, greeted everywhere with acclaim. How can you miss with more or less equal weights of chocolate, butter, sugar, and eggs in a cloud of whipped cream?

CHOCOLATE SNOWBALL

For me, the darker the chocolate, the better this dessert will be.

Serves 8

4 eggs
8 ounces/225 g dark sweet chocolate, chopped
¾ cup/175 ml espresso coffee
1 cup/225 g unsalted butter, cut into pieces
1 cup/200 g sugar

For the Chantilly cream

1 cup/250 ml heavy cream, chilled
1 tablespoon sugar
1 tablespoon/15 ml cognac or ½ teaspoon vanilla
Fresh mint sprigs or candied violets

1-quart/1-liter charlotte mold or deep metal bowl; pastry bag and small star tip; heavy-duty aluminum foil

Line the mold with a large sheet of aluminum foil, pressing it down into the base and up the sides as smoothly as possible without poking a hole. Preheat the oven to 350°F/180°C. Whisk the eggs in a bowl until mixed.

In a medium saucepan, melt the chocolate over low heat with the coffee, stirring until melted. Cook the mixture, stirring constantly, until it is thick but still falls easily from the spoon, 2 to 3 minutes. Add the butter and sugar, and keep stirring over the heat until both are melted. Bring the mixture almost to a boil and take from the heat. Stir in the eggs a little at a time: the retained heat will cook the eggs and thicken the mixture slightly.

Work the mixture through a strainer into the lined mold. Set the mold on a baking sheet and bake in the oven until a thick crust forms on top, 45 to 55 minutes. The mixture will rise slightly, then fall again as it cools. Cover and chill in the refrigerator at least 24 hours. The chocolate snowball can be kept up to a week and the flavor will mellow.

To finish: Not more than 2 hours before serving, run a knife around the mold, turn the snowball onto a serving plate, and peel off the foil. (The mixture tends to stick and look messy; do not worry.) For the Chantilly cream, whisk the chilled cream in a cold bowl until it holds soft peaks. Add the sugar and cognac or vanilla, and continue whisking until stiff peaks form, 30 seconds to 1 minute. Scoop the cream into the pastry bag with the star tip, and pipe small rosettes all over the chocolate mixture to cover it completely. Top the center of the mold with a single large rosette. Decorate with mint sprigs or candied violets, and chill until serving. Serve the snowball by cutting in wedges like a cake.

I hadn't found such appreciation of food in England, and in America there was even less of a habit of analyzing the food on the plate. It's different now, but in the sixties and seventies that approach didn't exist. For the cook there are two parts to tasting. One is the intellectual side: what the natural combinations are—like nutmeg with milk and cream, or lemon with fish. Just the knowledge of that entering your consciousness forever is part of the underlying grasp of cooking. And there's the actual physical side, where you should taste everything at every stage—testing the boiling water for salt even before you drop in the greens.

The most difficult skill to teach is how to taste. A cook must learn not only how to judge flavor but also to test it all the time, and even those who enjoy cooking and are good at it find that difficult. After tasting the water you need to taste the cooked spinach, then taste again when you reheat it with a bit of butter. As for those complex sauces? You taste the stock, then the sauce itself half a dozen times as it simmers and deepens over the hours. Tasting is part of a chef's instinct, the part that's difficult to ingrain in students and so hard to explain.

With thirty students and three full classes, straightaway I could tell who had the instinct. I could tell whether or not a student felt at ease in the kitchen, and it wasn't necessarily a matter of experience. Those who felt at home did not need to be told to do things like pick up dirty pots and take them to wash up; without being taught they trimmed their onions just right before starting to slice or dice them. I began to understand it was like a sport—some people pick up that physical side quickly and some never do; some people have a good palate, and some do not.

Our son, Simon, was only five when La Varenne opened, but he already had a good food memory and could recognize the taste of his scoop of nameless white sorbet—apple, pear, lemon, or grapefruit. Later, in his teens, he would recognize flavors within a complex sauce that had eight different ingredients—"ah, that's cumin," he'd say, "not coriander." And Marielle Charpentier had that kind of palate, able to compete with the sommelier at La Tour d'Argent with its world-renowned cellar. At La Varenne, I began to see that in a class of ten students eight would be in the middle; I knew half of those were likely to emerge as pretty good chefs. There was always, sadly, the one student who was prone to disaster—burning things or making sauces that tasted of raw flour. And the tenth, with luck, would be a real natural who had what it takes in the head and in the hands.

In the first few years of La Varenne's existence, I was lucky enough to find just the right chefs, while thousands of cooking enthusiasts walked through our doors—restaurateurs, caterers, chefs, cooking teachers, food writers, and some complete amateurs. Just a small handful—perhaps a dozen a year—became *stagiaires,* interns who followed a program that eventually emerged as a nine-month work program covering over one thousand recipes.

But in those first months I wasn't thinking of what our future would be. I was rushing about handling what I had created out of my imagination and learning again that great cooking is so much more than recipes. Memorable cooking is like great music, with balance and sureness of touch that goes straight to the heart. At École de Cuisine La Varenne we gathered brilliant teachers and eager students, who roamed through recipes on the page and in the kitchen, and I remained determined that everyone who came to us should feel touched by the magic of success. I wanted people to leave saying what one student early on remarked: "When I go home I will never look at food the same way again."

From earliest childhood I loved the Yorkshire Dales where my father was born, and you can see that I was already a strong-minded child.

Chapter Two

. . . .

GOING MY OWN WAY

My living in Yorkshire was so far out of the way, that it was eleven miles away from a lemon.

—Sydney Smith

In early 1941, when I turned three, my mother and Nanny and I lived for a year at my paternal grandparents' home in North Yorkshire. My father was away at the War, and up there in the wilds of Wensleydale my mother was forever termed a far-offer, considered a foreigner despite having been born and bred in Yorkshire and despite having married into a family that dated back in the rural hamlet of Appersett to the seventeenth century. But Nanny was a Daleswoman who came from somewhere near there, and as a little girl I was accepted as a local. It was Nanny who told family and friends that year that the only time I didn't cry was when I was allowed to eat as much as I wanted. As far as I'm concerned, that simply means I was always a sensible child. Often eating as much as I wanted led to a double portion of whatever was on hand, so it's no surprise that I grew to become sturdy—never fat, but always solid. I never cared that later I required the biggest horse for my riding lessons, and although I'm certain I must have had some cheek-blushing moments among my diminutive schoolmates, I recall only a joyful childhood, and a delicious one.

I was born on January 26, 1938, in Newcastle, along the river Tyne. Not far away, in North Yorkshire, in the country part of the "shire" (not West Yorkshire, which was given over to—ugh—manufacturing), was the house my mother's father built for my parents when they married in 1935. The house of brick and pebbledash sat atop a hill with a terrace all around. It wasn't a grand house, but it had an expansive view of the Yorkshire country-side, a 180-degree view all the way to the Pennine hills in the blue distance. It had four bedrooms and servants' quarters at the back, for it was built for the days when well-to-do families had live-in cooks and housemaids. From our terrace I could see not only my mother's exquisite garden that surrounded the house but also the lush Yorkshire fields dotted with cattle, wheat fields, church towers, and farmhouses. One of those was the family farm where my grandmother and my aunt had been born. When the wind was right, we could hear the church bells chime. Sometimes those hills sent downslope winds racing our way, and to the east rose the North Yorkshire Moors. Often for days at a time we were enveloped in dense fog. Each morning my mother would tap her weatherglass and make a pronouncement on the days to come, good or ill (no television forecast in those days, and radio was unreliable).

For my first two years, I lived with Mummy and Daddy, my beloved Nanny, and Emily, our stout, voluble cook who arrived when my parents mar-ried. Looking back, I suspect Emily first inspired my love of cooking, for some of my earliest memories take me to our ample house alone with Emily and my mother. This was because when I was just two my father was drafted and left for the south of England, where, throughout World War II, he ran an RAF station. The kitchen was, from early days, the center of my universe. It was warm, perfumed with cakes baking and pinecones crackling in the open fire. I loved to eat just about everything but especially fish cakes with crispy browned outsides, kippers, and almost anything fried—like the chitterlings from the dead pig that arrived in pieces in bloody bowls twice a year at our house.

The pig was one of many things my mother, Joyce, and her sister, Aunt Louie, shared. It was up to Auntie Louie's husband, Uncle Tommie, and Emily to divide that pig. As I recall, Emily always won the contest hands down, so our family had the largest, fattest chops, most of the head, and far more than half the precious fat, which Emily rendered down to supplement our meager rations—this was, after all, the War. Emily called the chitterlings crappings, and I stole these from the larder, along with other delicacies like cheese, which I have always adored. Emily must have known about my theft, but she never betrayed me. I was brought up on bacon and egg pie and was amused to later find this popular Yorkshire food changed its name to quiche.

Despite rations, we were never actually hungry during the War, and my childhood memories are chock-full of food. In the north-facing storage room there was always a ham and a slab of bacon hanging from the ceiling, swathed in cheesecloth to keep out the flies. When the hens stopped laying, my mother preserved eggs in a curious slimy liquid called isinglass, made with dried sturgeon bladder, which sealed the shells so they kept for a couple of months or more. At the end the actual egg tasted slightly peculiar but was not rotten. The only challenge was to vary our diet, particularly in winter when the only greens were cabbages, leeks, and Brussels sprouts. Our apples and pears were stored in another cool, airy storehouse on slatted shelves so they did not touch one another, but after a month or two they would wither, or in a wet year they would rot. Drying fruit was not an option in that damp climate and freezers did not exist, and anyway electricity was unreliable. In summer I helped Mummy shell fresh peas that in a wet year would be invaded with crawly maggots.

When I think of the War years and Yorkshire, I think of the kippers and smoked haddock we ate in the morning—among the few things that weren't rationed. My mother and I would share a kipper. For a few years she prepared it for me, carefully detaching the backbone to include all the bones attached, but one day she was late to breakfast and I was hungry, so I deboned my own and sat down and began to eat. When she came downstairs and saw me, she was cross, for she dearly hated doing it. "Why didn't you tell me you knew how?" With few exceptions she did not much like anything having to do with preparing meals, and from then on I did it myself.

Even with rationing, a few treats came from the nearby market town of Northallerton. "In the north of England there's no grocery the equal of Lewis and Cooper," my mother would declare about the store that had opened in 1899 and had, in my grandmother's time, offered free tea and scones for customers on Wednesday, market day. It was indeed a wonder that our little country town of only fifteen thousand inhabitants hid a world-class gourmet store that in 1970 stocked twenty-six thousand items, something for everyone—like the Punt e Mes, a bitter Italian aperitif for the local vicar, caviar from Russia, South African biltong, and an American pasta sauce.

For Christmas my mother would buy a whole Stilton cheese that weighed at least fifteen pounds and arrived in October to finish maturing in our cold larder. Twice each week Mummy turned it, and from time to time she cut a sample from the center with an apple corer, replacing it after inspection to see if it was aging to creamy, blue-veined perfection. If a trace of rancid acidity suddenly developed, to save its life we ate that Stilton long before the holiday, disguising its shortcomings in recipes like cheese ramekins. I can still taste them.

Although my mother much preferred her garden to the kitchen, she recognized that food was important and took pride in a few savory specialties such as oxtail stew and steak and kidney pie. I have her old cookbook, and rather to my surprise I discovered it included two recipes for what we would call ginger cookies. The first is called "Ginger Biscuits" and comes from her family home. The recipe is dated 1935, the year my parents married, and the quantities bear witness to the constant stream of my grandfather's visitors. When my father was away during the War, our little household of three would sit around the kitchen fire at elevenses (the sacrosanct British mid-morning break) with mugs of strong, milky tea for dunking the crisp biscuits. At the time this habit was not socially acceptable, so we all had a pleasant tingle of sin as we dipped. Only one biscuit each was allowed, but sometimes, if I was a good girl, my mother would share hers.

GINGER BISCUITS

The dough is quite soft, so it needs to rest in the refrigerator a half hour before rolling. You'll find that trimmings are popular, as the dough tastes just as good raw as when it is baked and crisp!

Makes 3 dozen 4-inch/10 cm cookies

1 cup/400 g golden syrup
10 tablespoons/150 g butter, plus more for the baking sheet
4 cups/500 g flour, more for rolling
2 tablespoons ground ginger
1 teaspoon ground allspice
¼ teaspoon baking soda

4-inch/10-cm cookie cutter

To make the cookie dough: Heat the golden syrup and butter in a pan until melted, stir to mix them, and set aside to cool. Sift the flour, ginger, allspice, and baking soda into a bowl and make a well in the center. Add the cooled golden syrup and stir with your hand to make a smooth dough—it will be quite soft, but if it is sticky work in a little more flour. Cover the dough and chill it about 30 minutes—this makes it easier to handle.

Heat the oven to 400°F/200°C and set a shelf near the center. Butter a baking sheet. Turn the dough onto a floured work surface and cut it in half. Roll one half to about ⅛ inch/3 mm thickness. Stamp out rounds with the cookie cutter and set them on the baking sheet. Chill them in the freezer until firm, 10 to 15 minutes. Meanwhile press the trimmings into the remaining dough, roll, and shape more cookies.

Bake the cookies until golden brown around the edges, 7 to 8 minutes. Transfer them to a rack to cool. Ginger biscuits do well in an airtight container for up to a week.

Not only was I physically solid, but I also had a sturdy temperament. I was an only child and once, after the War, my mother said, "In wartime was no world for more children." And Nanny would have told anyone who asked that even at six months old I was my own person. My mother often read to me, and Beatrix Potter's Mr. McGregor was part of my real fantasy world, for we were forever waging war against wild rabbits. In vain we fortified my mother's beloved garden with chicken wire, and in vain did Old Metcalfe, the mole catcher, set snares to catch those rabbits that gamboled on our front lawn, undaunted by the wire. Sometimes my mother rose early to take pot shots with a rifle from her bedroom window, but the rabbits had a sixth sense and scampered away just as she was taking her sights. I had no idea that forty years later and five hundred miles to the south in rural Burgundy I would once again live amid an abundance of rabbits.

In fact, it seemed certain I would live my whole life in northern England, just as my family always had. My father and his father were country solicitors. My father, a serious and loving man, had a top brain, an extraordinary memory, and an immense respect for learning. His mother's family was Quaker, from Liverpool, and my grandmother had an austerity about her that pervaded that whole family. My father grew up with four siblings in Appersett. Sadly, his favorite sister died very young of rheumatic fever and two younger brothers drowned in a flash flood in the stream that flowed behind their house. Daddy tried to save them, and I still have the medal he was awarded for bravery. But the local clergyman refused to bury the boys in hallowed ground because as Quakers they had not been baptized. My grandfather was so angry, deservedly so, he never again went into the church. The boys were buried with the non-believers way up a hill behind the church. That left on my father's side only Aunt Esther, who married an Italian and settled in Florence. Her Italian-speaking daughter is my only cousin and living in Italy has played very little part in my life.

I loved both my parents, deeply, but it is my mother's spirit that most inhabits me. Mummy's background and temperament and family contrasted sharply with Daddy's. Her life had been quite exotic for someone who came from a small, rural village. Her father, John Todd, was illegitimate, and when he was born it was arranged for his mother to have a rented farm. (We still do not know who his father was.) So he was brought up a farm boy who raised calves for himself. But John Todd never sat still. Ambition led him to take the calves to the nearest auction mart, and by the time he was twenty-five he had bought the mart itself. By forty he was dealing in property all over England. His specialty became buying up big estates—various ancestral homes whose families were going broke during the Depression—and selling off bits one by one. Family legend has it that these estates included the home of Elizabeth Bowes-Lyon, the queen consort to be and later Queen Mother to the present Queen.

When I was older my mother told me that she had found it awful to see her father breaking up these magnificent properties. I sometimes think that perhaps subconsciously, when I was grown and my husband, Mark, and I bought Château du Feÿ in Burgundy, I was trying to rehabilitate just such an old property. I certainly inherited Grandfather Todd's love of antique furniture—we still have a few pieces of his, including a magnificent grandfather clock more than three hundred years old that keeps time to within five minutes each week, chiming exactly on the hour. And I inherited as well his love of adventure.

Grandfather Todd made a great deal of money, and my aunt and my mother had an easy life and a rather glamorous one. By the time my mother was born, the family had moved from the farm where Auntie Louie was born and they frequently traveled, as far away as Ceylon. Every winter they stayed for several months in smart hotels in the south of France. By the time I was born my mother had been to Italy, Egypt, and Palestine. The money my grandfather made deeply affected my mother's life, and later mine. Indeed, it was Grandfather's money and properties that gave me, always, the kind of security that allows one to travel and do slightly crazy things—you can get sick in the knowledge that you will be rescued. That security made many of my later adventures possible.

But my mother did not get on with her father. He was the consummate businessman, and he was also a classic little Napoleon, a bully who quarreled with his business partners and shouted at his children. Auntie Louie was enormously fond of him and they always got along well, but my mother was, herself, enterprising and strong-minded (she once told me she would have liked to have had an independent career as a fashion designer). She loved her mother, who she felt kept the family together while my grandfather traveled and undertook vast projects. Sadly, my grandmother died quite young of breast cancer.

Mummy told me that when my father was courting her they were not permitted to be left alone and so my mother's grandmother Louisa Young Clark, who was born in 1849 and lived until I was seven, would sit in the room while Mummy and Daddy canoodled on the sofa. They survived that and throughout their lives remained devoted to each other. Although my mother had a strong mind, she chose to devote herself to my father's outlook and opinions. As it turned out, that suited her wonderfully, for she did not much like to socialize.

Back then most fortunate Englishwomen got along well with their gardens while kitchen work was reserved for the household cook, and my mother felt very deeply that all women should take more kindly to potting soil than to pummeling butter in a bowl. Handsome, fair-skinned, stylish even in Wellington boots, she spent as much time as she could outdoors in her garden, never mind rain or cold—and that hillside where we lived could get frigid. She cleared the garden of its unpropitious heavy clay and grew not only beautiful flowers but during the War also most of our produce—peas and beans, root artichokes, potatoes, carrots, cabbages, and Brussels sprouts, with mint, sage, and parsley the only herbs. Her traditional English border of flowering plants was hell to clear of weeds, but like all creative gardeners, every year or two she expanded the flower beds. She grew glorious raspberry bushes that lined the vegetable garden in August and bright green onion shoots that in spring peeked out of the soil among the rose beds, her literal response to the popular wartime slogan "Dig for Victory!"

Mummy was also exceedingly fashionable, with an eye for dress I never inherited. She had couture clothes made at the fashionable Worth's in London until they closed, and she had a few pieces of stunning Cartier jewelry. Even in the garden she dressed fashionably in tweed skirts and thick stockings. She had great style and distinction, always a good figure. It took me until I was an adult, but eventually I did come to realize how alike she and I were. Not only did we look almost exactly alike, but we were similar in character. True, we navigated the world on reverse sides of the coin—she in her garden, me in the kitchen—but we both were passionate about our particular worlds and the people in them whom we loved.

Northallerton was surrounded by half a dozen quite large RAF bases (airfields), where the bombers took off for Germany, and every night during the War I heard them circling in an angry buzz around the rendezvous before they flew off. The War was very real and affected all of us deeply. Army trucks were common on the roads. I recall one day when my mother was weaving her little car in and out of a long convoy of armored tanks. I was terrified by the menace looming over us, and when we reached home my mother said, "I'm sorry darling. I would have stopped if I had known you were so frightened." The British government was nervous about a German invasion, and that is why at the start of the War Mummy, Nanny, and I were evacuated to live with my father's parents up remote Wensleydale.

I loved it up there, huddled at the head of the valley and surrounded by sheep. The atmosphere of the place enlivened me—the hills, the sense of timelessness. When it was sunny outside, which was rare, amazing shadows played in the dips and rolling hills. The walls were ancient, freestanding stones and pack roads that dated to the Middle Ages and ran straight up into the high hills. Also, despite my paternal grandmother's intellectual austerity, she liked to cook, and one simple specialty of hers has stayed in the family, treacle tart.

TREACLE TART

Treacle, otherwise known as golden syrup, looks like thick, golden honey and is formed during the refining of sugar. Be sure to get the genuine golden syrup, not the squeezable version that is thinner and has less taste. Grandma made her pastry with lard, but shortening or more butter can be substituted in the recipe. Treacle tart should be thin like a pizza, and I use a shallow pizza plate. Treacle tart is perfect topped with vanilla ice cream. Somehow, Grandma could always find it in the wilds of Yorkshire shortly after World War II.

Serves 8

For the pie pastry
2½ cups/300 g flour
½ teaspoon baking powder
½ teaspoon salt
6 tablespoons/90 g butter, plus more for the plate
6 tablespoons/90 g lard
4 tablespoons/60 ml water, plus more if needed

For the filling
1 slice white bread
½ cup/200 g golden syrup
Finely grated zest and juice of ½ lemon

10-inch/25-cm heatproof pizza pan or shallow pie pan

For the pie pastry: Sift the flour with the baking powder and salt into a bowl. Cut the butter and lard in small cubes and add to the flour. Rub the fats into the flour with your fingertips to form crumbs. Stir in the water with a fork to make sticky crumbs, adding more water, if necessary. Press the dough together with your fist to make a ball, wrap it in plastic wrap, and chill until firm, 15 to 20 minutes.

For the filling: Cube the bread, spread it on a baking sheet, and freeze until firm, about 30 minutes. Grind the frozen bread cubes in a processor, using the pulse button. Measure the golden syrup into a bowl; stir in the lemon zest and juice, then the crumbs. Butter the pizza pan.

To assemble the tart: Cut off and set aside about a quarter of the pastry dough. Roll out the rest on a floured board to a 12-inch/30 cm round (the dough will be about ¼ inch/5 mm thick). Line the pan with the dough round, leaving a 1-inch/2.5-cm border overlapping as an edge. Roll the remaining dough with the trimmings to a long strip and cut it in ribbons about ¾ inch/2 cm wide. Pour the filling into the pan and spread it with the back of a spoon almost to the edge. Lay a diagonal lattice of pastry ribbons over the filling and trim the ends. Fold the dough edge over the ribbon ends and press down with the tines of a fork to neaten them. Chill the tart until the pastry is firm, 15 to 20 minutes.

Set a baking sheet on a shelf in the center of the oven and heat it to 375°F/190°C. Set the tart on the hot baking sheet, and bake until the pastry and filling are browned, 25 to 30 minutes. Serve warm, topping each slice with a scoop of ice cream, if you like.

———————————

Some memories of those early War years are vivid. I especially recall Nanny pushing me home in my pram from my grandparents' house to the village of Gayle, about a mile and a half away, explaining about the stars overhead. I remember the black of the bridge as we rolled beneath it, and perhaps I recall that moment so vividly because I adored Nanny. In those days I felt closer to her than I did to my mother, for kind as she always was, Mummy did not go in much for cuddles and hugs and let's-sit-on-the-sofa-and-listen-to-the-wireless or anything of that sort. It was Nanny who was affectionate. It was also Nanny who was wonderful at sewing. She made me classic smocked dresses with puffed sleeves and little collars, a new dress each year. Always farsighted, before things went on ration my mother had bought six bolts of raw silk, as well as tins of butter we kept for the Christmas cake. Each year she allowed me to choose the color I would like best to have for my dress for that year; in those days little girls did not wear trousers.

After the year with my grandparents, when I was four and a half, Mummy and I returned to Northallerton and Nanny had to leave us, for she was drafted. I remember clearly the day my mother was loading up the car. She handed me a little tin box in which she had hoarded some chocolate—always strictly rationed. "Go next door and eat that chocolate with Betty Ned," she told me. I was feeling sad because Nanny was gone, but I walked next door to sit with Betty Ned, who was an old, old man; his mother had been called Betty, and so he was forever Betty Ned. I remember us sitting side by side on those cold stone steps eating chocolate while my mother maneuvered the ironing board through the car window.

In wartime most things were rationed, among them petrol, and though Auntie Louie—beloved Auntie Louie—lived in Hurworth not far from our house, she came over just once a week. Auntie Louie was ten years older than my mother and a wonderful, generous woman. She never had her own children, so she treated me as if I were a daughter. She was always full of hugs. Also in contrast to Mummy, Louie was what we now would call plump. Our family would laugh about her figure. Not long ago, in an old album of hers I found an exercise regimen she had cut out of *The Daily Telegraph*. Like my mother she wore expensive clothes, though she was the shape of the Queen Mother and wore those same floating dresses. She was a grande dame in other ways as well—she knew everyone in the village and always organized the village fête. When she drove up the street, she would wave with a regal bow. Auntie Louie was famous for her luck at the tombola, a raffle popular in Great Britain (she once won a diamond brooch, which I still possess), and for her cocktail parties, powered by vicious gin martinis and sharp little cheese balls that exploded into crumbs if you tried to bite them. Auntie's sense of hospitality, her instant welcome to anyone who came to the house, her sheer joy of life, taught me a lot.

AUNT LOUIE'S CHEESE BALLS

Makes about 30 balls

1¼ cups/150 g flour
1¼ cups/150 g finely grated Parmesan cheese
½ teaspoon salt
½ teaspoon pepper
½ teaspoon dry mustard, plus more to taste
½ cup/110 g melted butter, plus more if needed

Mix the flour in a bowl with the Parmesan cheese, salt, pepper, and dry mustard. Stir in the melted butter so the mixture forms crumbs.

Kneading with your hands, press it into balls the size of small walnuts—
a half-tablespoon measuring spoon as a mold can be a help here. If
the mixture is very dry and crumbly, add a bit more melted butter.
Set the balls on a buttered baking sheet and chill about 15 minutes.
Heat the oven to 375°F/190°C.

Bake the cheese balls in the oven until browned, 35 to 45 minutes.
Test for doneness by cutting into a ball; it should not be doughy in the
center. Transfer the cheese balls to a rack to cool. They can be stored
in an airtight container for up to a week, and I always have a backup
supply in the freezer.

Of the important women in my life in those days there were Nanny,
Mummy, and Louie and there was Emily, our cook, who overflowed the
edges of her kitchen stool. She tried to contain her bulk in peach-colored
whalebone corsets, which she laced with a grimace each morning (she had no
false modesty in front of me). Her hair was crimped into marcel waves with
giant, awe-inspiring bulldog clips. Emily was famous for her malapropisms—
"he died of the Te Deums," she said of one bloke in the village when she
meant the DTs, and she often referred to the "Roaming Catholics." But
more than those malapropisms, I remember Thursdays, baking day.

Best of all, Emily allowed me into her kitchen. On baking day she woke
at dawn to stoke the oven that had no thermostat—if the flue was open the
oven got hotter, and when it was closed the oven slowly cooled. She baked us
the week's jam tarts and maids-of-honor, tarts topped with frangipane made
with ground rice instead of almonds when food was short. I still have Emily's
rolling pin. I loved her ribbon cake, swirling with chocolate, egg yolk yellow,
and cochineal pink (from beetles, the original red food coloring and not nearly
so bad as it sounds). The chocolate bit was best.

Emily placed the little cakes and scones that baked quickly into the oven
first, and then came larger cakes like sponge cake and currant loaf, and finally,
as the oven cooled, the slow-baked fruitcakes, puddings, and custard tart.
Officially I wasn't permitted to taste any of these treats until Friday—Emily
had her firm beliefs, and one of these was that fresh cakes were bad for diges-
tion. Thus she squirreled them away as soon as they cooled. I must have been
at least ten before I realized how good cake fresh from the oven tasted. I would
stand watching Emily line up these aromatic treats to cool, and my mouth
watered with desire.

My great-grandmother, my mother's grandmother, lived in a cottage a mile away from us where two elderly cousins looked after her. She and I were fast friends and would take little walks together—the pace of our footsteps was ideally suited, for she was ninety years older than me. She was a figure from another age, white hair piled on top and wearing black from head to foot except for a froth of white lace at the neck. Her husband had owned the village grain mill and had died at thirty-seven, so she brought up her daughter, my grandmother, single-handedly as a tenant on what later became the family farm. I often stayed for tea with Granny. She would put on her best apron of black satin embroidered with pink roses.

Most of our food at home was rather plain—Yorkshire food is straightforward, appetizing food that tastes of what it is. After the War, on Sundays we would have a large roast, then cold meat for lunch on Monday and successive days until it was all gone. We always had boiled roots—potatoes, red beets, carrots, and turnips or swedes, as we called the giant roots that the farmers grew for the cattle. Until well into the 1950s but for our farmhouse Stilton there was only one kind of cheese, an industrial Cheddar referred to as "mousetrap." Only later could we enjoy real artisan Wensleydale cheese, once world renowned, for which milk was curdled with rennet and pressed into molds, with the whey going to the pigs. A few fresh curds would be reserved for curd tarts, a local version of cheesecake. Our family liked oddities like cold pickled beef tongue, oxtail (my mother would make a wonderful soup), and kidneys for steak and kidney pie. Almost every week we would have pies from the pork butcher, squat tubs of thick crust "raised" with melted lard and filled with the anonymous chewy trimmings left when cutting up a pig, seasoned with salt and pepper and possibly a bit of sage. Alf the butcher looked a bit like a pig himself, with lively little black eyes in a doughy face.

My father loved game-bird hunting, shooting, as it is called in England. He had hunting rights over half a dozen farms and would ask a group of friends on Saturdays in the fall to join him in an elaborate charade of pheasant and partridge shooting. The birds would be driven by beaters, men from the village who shouted and catcalled, banging tree trunks with sticks and urging on their dogs so that the birds flew toward the quiet line of hunters, half-hidden in the autumn mist. The wait was exciting. Suddenly there would be a volley of shots and a couple of birds would flop down. They would be hung near the kitchen, in a close-meshed wire cage to keep out flies, as long as a couple of weeks to develop the gamey flavor in cold weather. In the season we ate pheasant three times a week; I got tired of it, for Emily always cooked it the same way, thoroughly roasted until rather dry, served with gravy, my favorite fried bread crumbs, white onion sauce thickened with bread crumbs, and red currant jelly.

It would be years before I learned that Emily's recipes were in fact from my mother's modest, cloth-bound school exercise book that served as her cook-book. It offers little evidence as to how hard Mummy worked to keep our household together in those difficult years. It was my mother who hung out the clothes to dry on wash day, my mother who chopped the logs for the fires and grew our food. She also canned tomatoes—sixty jars each year; much later she told me she did this so that I would have enough vitamin C in my diet. She tried, with little success, to nurture apple and pear trees, but often strong winds swept across our hillside and nipped away the early blossoms. When these days I read my mother's recipes, I am struck by their simplicity, so differ-ent from a French or American recipe. Few sweets have frostings or fillings. The cookies are complete in themselves, and the cakes stand alone or, some-times, with a dusting of sugar. When sliced, the batter often is a decoration in itself as in her multi-colored ribbon cake I so loved. Her breads were studded with raisins and currants and candied fruits, but spices were limited to nutmeg, allspice, cinnamon, and the almost ubiquitous ginger, an English favorite since medieval times.

Our household, while not emotional, was far from repressed. We always talked about whatever we wanted to talk about, though my parents' views were rather old-fashioned. Mark said when he met them that they seemed in many ways to have stepped off the world in 1939 when the War began, and as I look back it seems to me their youth and early married years must have been the high point of their lives. Their values—of duty and trust and integrity, sometimes to the nth degree—were typical of those who lived in the countryside in rela-tive isolation. Because taxation in early post-War England took away most of what my father could earn, he retired from his work as a solicitor when he was forty, and after that he never took an active and outgoing role that might have kept him more in touch with social changes.

Daddy often helped me with the homework from the school I attended until I was ten—Mrs. Lord's School in Northallerton, a Dame School as it was known, the name associated with the time of Charles Dickens. In this case, Mrs. Lord was the Dame and the school was a place for those children whose parents wanted their daughters (and a few sons, too) somewhat pampered. The school was in Mrs. Lord's private home, and she ran it in military-style. I liked school. I rapidly mastered the elegant, looped copperplate handwriting that was soon to go out of fashion, and I was always doing things like dressmaking, knitting, and crocheting, which I was good at and had taught myself since Mummy hated it. I could darn socks and there was something called the rag bag that had bits of leftover fabric and I made clothes for my dollies with those scraps. Someone at the Dame School must have taught me to make them. At home I spent my time knitting and reading, and I bought a book on lace making and taught myself three or four kinds: needlepoint, Limerick lace embroidered on a net background, even bobbin lace, a particular skill still practiced on the streets of Bruges. I collected nineteenth-century lace bobbins, too, and one of these had "Thomas loves Anne" inscribed on its handle.

One day prizes were being given at the school and my parents were sitting in the audience as it was announced that I had won the prize for being top of the class. Of course I was proud, and so, I thought, were my parents. I ran off with quite a lot of the prizes that year, and one of those was the French Prize. Back home that evening my father let me know he was appalled. It was he who had helped me with much of my French homework. "Anne, why didn't you tell me there would be a prize for French? I never would have let you take credit for what was supposed to be your work," he admonished me. I never forgot that, and it may well have been his anger that inspired me, much later when I was writing books, to make sure always to give full credit to everyone who worked with me.

Another thing that upset my father terribly was a report from the Dame School that I was lazy. I was brighter than the other girls, but quite often I just "switched off." When my weekly report was bad, my father drove me to the school in our bull-nosed Morris Minor and all the way there he would give me an unpleasant ticking off about laziness. My father was a very serious man, and when he was upset his anger felt like a slap in the face. It certainly had the desired effect. I worked harder.

Although it was against my father's nature to be extreme, we always celebrated Christmas with lavish gifts. Daddy could see everyone was having a grand time and he loved that, so he went along with it. Auntie Louie was in charge of Christmas Eve. Mark was amazed when he saw how the family had stocked up on treats during the War—the leftover bottles of gin and cigars that he smoked in the 1960s; the Yorkshire closet had proved a perfect humidor. My family would go to her house, where the menu never varied—that whole Stilton we brought with us and furmenty, a curious porridge of whole wheat berries flavored with cassia that dates back to medieval times. It took Auntie two or three days to make it, and I still remember that ancient, musty taste. Sometimes a slice of ham was substituted for my father, who regarded porridge as infant's pap. We'd also, of course, have my aunt's Yule bread; pairing cheese with something sweet is a Yorkshire habit—for instance, Wensleydale cheese with fruit chutney in a ploughman's lunch.

Auntie Louie would have begun the Yule bread at least a month early, toward the end of November when the new dried fruits of the season appeared. She assembled mountainous quantities of dark raisins, tiny piquant dried currants, and luscious candied orange peel. Baking day began early, for her Aga had to be fired up to achieve a generous but not scorching heat. The bread dough, raised with yeast, could take three hours to double in bulk on the gentle warmth of the stovetop. Meanwhile I helped pick over the fruits, discarding the occasional stalk, then tossing in flour so they would cling when mixed with the sticky dough. Our target: at least a dozen loaves. I would plunge my arms to my elbows in the fragrant, yeasty dough, so warm it felt alive, first helping to mix and knead and then squishing in the fruits with my fists. My aunt, her hair firmly anchored with pins and her tweed skirt wreathed in a white apron, shaped the loaves, patting out a portion of dough and rolling it to a cylinder before lowering it carefully into the buttered pan. Auntie Louie estimated oven temperature by the time it took to brown a piece of newspaper she thrust into the oven (one minute was the aim). She adjusted the shelves, just right. During cooking, pans had to be rotated for even browning, working fast so as not to lose the precious heat. And toward the end of baking, my aunt applied the classic test, tapping the bottom of each loaf with her knuckles—I quickly learned to recognize the hollow echo of the perfectly cooked loaf.

When the brown loaves were cool, we wrapped them in brown paper bags and left them to mature and be deliciously moist. Finally, just before Christmas, Auntie Louie and I would wrap them and pile into the car to start our tour of knocking on doors. People expected us. There would be cups of tea, scones or currant buns, an exchange of parcels, and always one for me. I still follow tradition, baking Yule loaves for the neighbors and keeping a couple for our children who visit at holidays.

AUNT LOUIE'S YULE BREAD

We enjoy Yule bread for breakfast, toasted or plain and spread with butter, though in its native Yorkshire it is served for afternoon tea.

Makes 1 large loaf to serve 8

1½ cups/375 ml water
⅔ cup/120 g raisins
⅔ cup/120 g dried currants
4 cups/500 g flour, plus more if needed
1 teaspoon salt
1 teaspoon ground cinnamon
1 teaspoon ground cloves
⅔ cup/140 g sugar
2 teaspoons/7 g dry yeast
2 eggs
½ cup/110 g butter, creamed
⅓ cup/60 g chopped candied orange peel
1 tablespoon sugar dissolved in 2 tablespoons warm milk (for glaze)

9×5×4-inch loaf pan

Bring the water to a boil, pour half over the raisins and currants, and leave to soak. Let the remaining water cool to tepid. Sift the flour into a bowl with the salt, cinnamon, and cloves and stir in the sugar. Make a well in the center and add the tepid water, with the water drained from the fruits. Crumble or sprinkle the yeast over the water and leave 5 minutes or until dissolved. Add the eggs and, with your hand, gradually mix in the flour. If necessary, add more flour to form a smooth dough that is soft but not sticky.

Knead the dough on a floured board by hand, or transfer it to an electric mixer and knead until elastic using the dough hook, 5 to 7 minutes. Put the dough in an oiled bowl, turning it so the top is oiled. Cover the bowl with plastic wrap and leave it in a warm place until doubled in bulk, 2 to 3 hours.

Butter the loaf pan. Add the creamed butter to the raised dough in the bowl and work with your hand until the butter is incorporated. Alternatively, beat in the electric mixer with the dough hook at medium speed until butter is mixed and the dough is smooth, 1 to 2 minutes. Add the soaked fruit and candied peel and mix into the dough until evenly distributed.

To shape the loaf, turn the dough onto a floured work surface. Pat it out with your fist to a rectangle 9 inches wide. Roll the dough into a cylinder, pinch the edge to seal, then drop it carefully into the loaf pan, seam side down. Cover loosely and leave to rise until the pan is full, 1½ to 2 hours.

Heat the oven to 400°F/200°C. Brush the loaf with the glaze and bake for 20 minutes. Brush again, lower the heat to 350°F/180°C, and continue baking until the loaf sounds hollow when unmolded and tapped on the bottom, 30 to 40 minutes. Transfer it to a rack to cool. Yule bread can be stored in an airtight container for up to a month, and the flavor matures. It can also be frozen.

———————————

Back home preparations would have started months before with the ultra-rich Christmas cake. Emily would rise before dawn to stoke the wood-burning fire. Meanwhile the flour was spread on a baking sheet set before the fire, stirred from time to time to dry out the all-pervasive Yorkshire damp. The whites of our farm eggs had fertilized threads in them, so they needed to be strained. Dried fruits and nuts were picked over, rinsed, and drained. The cake pan was lined with more newspaper for insulation, then with a layer of buttered parchment. And at last the mixing began. First the butter: I curved my hand like a spoon and beat the butter to a cream, then added the sugar and worked it again until fluffy. Next came the eggs, beaten into the butter and sugar one by one. By now muscle power was needed and Emily would take over, beating rhythmically and taking turns with each hand. She would beat in the flour with no effete nonsense about "folding as lightly as possible." Finally the fruits, and once the cake was in the oven we crept about the house lest a banging door create a draft on the fire, causing the cake to fall. When the Christmas cake falls, so the superstition goes, there will be a death in the family. Indeed, in 1945 the cake fell and the next year Granny died. The family blamed the cake, and I still blame it. I'm superstitious that way. I think you want to watch it.

CHRISTMAS CAKE

Despite this precedent, for more than forty years, ever since Mark and I married, I have made a Christmas cake, baking it at least a year ahead, basting it occasionally with sherry and Cognac so the dried fruits mellow and absorb the alcohol. Citron is a fragrant type of citrus, particularly juicy when candied.

Makes one 10-inch/25-cm cake to serve 12 to 16

3 cups/390 g flour
3 cups/420 g raisins
3 cups/420 g dried currants
½ cup/125 g chopped candied orange peel
½ cup/125 g chopped candied citron peel
½ teaspoon salt
½ teaspoon grated nutmeg
½ teaspoon ground allspice
¾ cup/170 g butter
1½ cups/300 g sugar
6 eggs, at room temperature
½ cup/75 g slivered almonds
3 tablespoons/45 ml Cognac
6–8 tablespoons/90–120 ml sweet sherry, port wine, or Cognac
    (for basting)

10-inch/25-cm cake pan with removable base; cheesecloth

Heat the oven to 300°F/150°C and set the shelf low down. Butter the pan, line the base and sides with a double layer of parchment paper, and butter the paper. Mix a few teaspoons of the flour with the raisins, currants, and candied peels in a bowl, and toss until the fruits are well coated and do not cling together when mixed with the batter. Sift the remaining flour with the salt, nutmeg, and allspice.

Cream the butter by hand or with an electric mixer fitted with the whisk attachment. Beat in the sugar and continue beating until soft and light, 4 to 5 minutes. Add the eggs one by one, beating thoroughly after each addition. Using your hand or a metal spoon, stir in the flour in two or three batches, then stir in the dried fruit and almonds. Finally stir in the Cognac.

Spoon the batter into the prepared pan and smooth the top, leaving the center slightly hollow so the cake rises to be flat rather than peaked. Tap the pan on the countertop to knock out any air bubbles. Bake the cake in the oven, rotating the pan once or twice, until the cake is browned and starts to pull from the sides of the pan, 1¾ to 2¼ hours. A metal skewer inserted in the center should come out clean, not sticky. If the cake browns too much during cooking, cover the top loosely with foil.

Leave the cake to cool in the pan, then unmold it and peel off the paper. Baste the top with 2–3 tablespoons of sherry, wrap the cake in cheesecloth soaked in sherry, and store in an airtight container for at least one month, and a year or more if you wish. Baste the cake with sherry, port wine, or Cognac from time to time and the flavor will immeasurably improve.

Our house was on two or three acres on a hill, with a dip in front, and beyond that, half a mile away on another hill, stood the family farm, one of my favorite places. After my great-grandmother died when I was seven, most afternoons I wandered over there, scrambling through the hedges and ditches to visit the Wilkinsons, who ran the farm. In those days we never thought of closed doors. The view from the ancient farmhouse was almost 360 degrees, even wider than the airy view of the world from home. Mrs. Wilkinson was a wonderful cook, and her Yorkshire tea spread out on the ample white-clothed table was a joy. Years later, our own children had the same reaction when Keith Wilkinson, who was eight or ten years older than I, began to run the farm with his wife, Audrey, as his father had before him and his grandfather before that. These days Keith's son Paul continues the tradition. But times have changed. Paul musters a hundred or more cows, while his father began with less than half that number.

Although my mother was never short of money, to the end of her life she was terrified of being left poverty-stricken, and one of her favorite axioms was "Pride in Poverty." She felt strongly that people, whatever their level of wealth or poverty, must maintain standards and ideals. It was more than just putting a brave face on it. Like most Yorkshire people, my mother knew what she liked and didn't like. So did my father. Both of them always imagined, as did I, that I would get a good education, but they also both imagined, and so did I, that I would marry a fine Yorkshireman and have lots of children.

In those days I didn't think much beyond that. Still, although unusual for that time, my parents and I also took it for granted that I would have a job, even a career before I married. In the 1940s and '50s there were not many obvious openings for girls—law, medicine, teaching, government employment, and nursing. Even before I chose to take a different way, my father often said to me, "Oh, Anne, you're bloody obstinate, going your own way again." Yorkshire people are famous for calling a spade a spade. I might not have known it then, but he was quite right. Perhaps that is why when I did come upon the path I wanted to follow I recognized it so clearly.

Family Archive

Still plump with puppy fat, I went with my parents to a country wedding in Northallerton wearing my first smart dress.

Chapter Three

....

A MERCIFUL BLUR

An apple pie without the cheese / Is like a kiss without the squeeze.

—Yorkshire adage

In the old days in England as soon as a woman of a certain class got pregnant, she registered her child at Eton and then waited to see if it was a boy. But it was different for girls. In Northallerton, I was the only girl whose parents planned from the start to send their daughter to boarding school. It was, simply, expected of me. When I was ten, they sent me away to prep school at Bredenbury Court, near Shrewsbury in the Welsh foothills. My mother drove me on her own in the elderly Morris (my father had very bad arthritis all his life, so my mother was the one who was often at the wheel). I had no idea what this was going to be like as I waved good-bye to Mummy and watched her pull away.

Right away I was desperately homesick, and it was three days before I could do anything but weep. We lived in small dormitories with three or four girls in each, and every minute we were told what to do and how to do it. Looking back, I see that even by ten I was, in a way, a small adult. At home I did what I wanted, and because I was an only child often I was the center of attention. I had never learned about pecking order or sibling rivalry. But the real misery at Bredenbury was in losing my solitude. I tried to make friends by sharing my ginger biscuits, smuggled in from home, but biscuits didn't seem to make much difference.

Eventually I settled in. Many children there came from a similar background to mine, and it was the first time I was in classes with girls who were better students than I was. In classes I did reasonably well, but I learned rapidly that not only was I no good at sports, I also seriously disliked them. We played hockey and lacrosse and tennis and I was introduced to horses—my parents really wanted me to ride because they always thought I would go home to Yorkshire and, by definition, if you live in country Yorkshire you're good at riding. I always had to have the biggest, heaviest horse, Nugget, a golden color and rather obstinate, and I was hopeless. Years earlier, when I was small, my parents had tried to put me on a pony on a cold day, and I vividly remember sniffling and dark clouds coming down on me. Here they were again.

I should have moved to my main boarding school when I was eleven, but I'd been at Bredenbury just one year and needed another to get up to academic speed and take the entrance test. My father once had been head boy at his school, and the headmaster, who had retired to Cheltenham, told him there was only one boarding school for me, "the best in England, Cheltenham Ladies' College." At Bredenbury I was always second top in my class, and when time came to take the tests for acceptance at Cheltenham people told me I was sure to get in. It's true I was always pretty good at most things, but I was not outstanding at anything—a good skill for taking such multi-subject exams. I had no difficulty being accepted.

Cheltenham Ladies' College was founded in 1853, a place of ivy-clad buildings and a ninety-five-meter marble corridor and more stained-glass windows than most cathedrals. One head teacher described Cheltenham as having a reputation for developing English roses—"not exotic ones, just the sort you'd find in country gardens." And so my parents hoped. In its history the school had few scandals, though it is reputed to have originated the term "chav" (Cheltenham average), a snooty word for the less-than-eligible men of the town. Unluckily for me, the school seemed to be run by women who didn't much like young people.

By the time I reached Cheltenham, my contemporaries had been there for a year, and right from the beginning it all went wrong. First, I ended up arriving twenty-four hours after the other girls because I'd got the flu and had to leave home later than planned. The school was a six-hour train ride away from home, with one, possibly two, changes. Alone at twelve, I sat on the train and thought about my big black steamer trunk full of everything we had to have—sports equipment, a goddamn hockey stick, and my uniforms, an unbecoming drab green, with skirts that had to be a certain length, and both woolen knickers and knicker linings (the housemistress lifted our skirts to check). Our shoes were flat, button or lace-ups, and we wore porkpie hats with the classic brim up at the back and down in front to the Anglican church we had to attend every Sunday.

The Ladies' College was a big Gothic place in the center of town, with eight hundred girls in sixteen houses, all very Jane Eyre. Its morality was clear: We were not to be too conspicuous. We were supposed to be all about team spirit, and the message was always, "Don't be too good at anything other than lessons and sport." I quickly learned that anything I enjoyed was either something we didn't have time to do, or it was a sin. I loved needlework, but there was never time and it wasn't intellectual enough. The same was true for cooking. In those days an enthusiasm for food was considered ill-bred and was linked in with greed. There was a lot of talk about sins at Cheltenham, and good eating was one of them.

There were about fifty girls in my house, Bunwell, one of those nice old houses, a bit later than Regency-style. There was a lot of rivalry between the houses, and because of that each house had a different school tie. Ours was hideous—black with a pink stripe. The school's main building was very large, with high Gothic brick hallways. To reach it from Bunwell, we had to walk right through town near Queen's Parade, a magnificent Regency avenue. We girls had a special walk, a kind of gallop because we couldn't be late. All day long we moved, quickly, from one end of the building to the other, lugging our school books in a satchel. Like cars on the road, we had to keep to one side of the corridor, and as a result my spine has a permanent list to the left from carrying my bag.

When I arrived, I still had a strong Yorkshire accent, picked up at the local Dame school, and immediately was roundly teased for it. In France, on the whole, you can have a regional accent and it doesn't matter, but in England a Yorkshire accent was emphatically unacceptable—it meant "Commercial" or "West Riding," with its legacy of woolen mills and big money, a place where people made a fortune and then lost the lot. There's a Yorkshire expression that says, "Muck [mud] to muck i' three generations." I decided to lose my accent, fast, and I did. But most of the girls had already settled in and made their own social structure the year before, and there seemed little room for me.

In the first months the girls' hostility took a rather nasty, active form. I slept in a dormitory with six beds, and every morning we had to strip our beds and roll up our mattresses. The others made me lie on the bare metal springs, and they sprayed me with cold water. I felt as if I'd gone to prison, and even after it was discovered and the active torture ended I never integrated completely, though in England we're taught right from the beginning when you're dealing with unpleasant things you have to simply focus on your inner self and keep going. We knew when we fell down and bruised our knees to get up without flinching. "You're just fine." So much so, that when one girl broke her ankle at hockey practice she was made to walk home and only the next day was the doctor called. Her parents removed her from the school. Since there was so much that was unpleasant at school, I learned to simply focus on something else.

So I turned to what I loved, and one of those things was my sewing. Mostly, though, we were made to do all sorts of things I didn't like, like the runs we had to take every morning around the square park out front of Bunwell. We all hated it. Many mornings a little old man on a bicycle would follow us, and when we talked about it afterward the school stopped our running. Instead they made us skip with a skipping rope in the basement.

The matron of the school for some reason I don't know really hated me, and "hate" is not too strong a word. She picked on me, made me take my socks off and put on a different pair, made me lift my skirts. She shared a bed with our housemistress—an early encounter for me with lesbianism—and it was the housemistress who managed the budget. She wanted to spend money on furnishings and left a minimum amount for food that was truly appalling. We ate huge quantities of potatoes, often twice a day, and root vegetables, though never leeks or celery because they probably cost too much. Sometimes we had things like cottage pie, and there were plenty of baked beans on toast. Boiled herring was considered a treat. Most of the time we ate cheap, fatty beef, which yielded drippings we smeared on our bread. For birthday parties we were allowed to have special food dispatched by our parents, so I had a lot of stuff sent. It was at Cheltenham that I first became conscious that I could eat more than anyone else, and the girls teased me about it. Everybody had to have a nickname, and because my name was Willan they changed that to Woolen and that led them to Fuzzy. "Oh, Fuzzy," they'd say. "You're still eating!"

But the thing was, if you ate fast enough, you could eat as much as you wanted, and because we were always exercising, we were always hungry. Usually there weren't second helpings, but there was a sort of endless supply of bread, so often I ate ten slices of bread with a scraping of something on top at supper. The fresh bread was not bad, but the two days in between were awful. We were given butter balls, actually balls of margarine, on a plate we passed around. You absolutely could not take the biggest ball, nor did you have to take the smallest. You could safely take the middle, so the luckiest people were those at the end of the chain, because the biggest ball was always there last.

At home our family rarely drank alcohol at table. Water from the tap (no ice) was our standard beverage, and the only times I had tasted wine I hadn't really liked it. But at Cheltenham, a Church of England school, by the time I was fifteen I had been confirmed and had to go to communion every second week. This entailed both fasting and getting up an hour earlier on Sunday, both of which I resented. So at the altar rail I would take an extra-large slurp of the communion wine, which was not bad, resembling port and properly alcoholic. It was one of my small pleasures.

There was also this notion at Cheltenham that one shouldn't really waste too much time on reading for leisure. There was a good library, and I always had a book or two in hand, which was great, but the books were always "appropriate." I read all the Victorian novels and Elizabeth Bowen, that kind of thing, but the "sin" of mystery novels, which I still read to this day, was not available to us. There was not much acting, which I had always loved. Right from the beginning, even when I was a child, I had two sides: I enormously enjoyed being on my own, reading a book and closing in, but I could switch on, and in kindergarten at Mrs. Lord's I was invariably cast as the male lead (there was a shortage of little boys).

Acting wasn't exactly sinful at Cheltenham, but it did have that touch of "you're making too much of yourself." Also, my mother could be trenchant about many things; she could not stand religion, particularly parsons, and she often said, "Actors are parsons, and parsons are no more than bad actors who like to show off." She never discouraged me from acting, but she certainly wasn't interested in hearing me practice my lines. So I took the private lessons in elocution for which I earned a gold medal when I was sixteen, acting out the mad scene of Lady Macbeth, baring my stocking feet to avoid the drag of heavy school shoes.

On the whole, the teaching at Cheltenham was good. If you were behind on your work, you had to go back to the school in the afternoon instead of going to sport. Most people thought that simply terrible, but I was delighted by the idea. Unfortunately, I wasn't usually behind, but when you were in trouble you were called all alone into this huge great hall where you stood at the front and the head teacher stood on a step in front of you. Then she would tell you what a miserable little worm you were, though her tone was not, "I'm here to help you," or, "I think you have a little bit of trouble, dear. . . ." That was your form teacher's job. This woman was there to bawl you out. That happened to me once, and it worked like a charm. I worked harder.

I was in what was called Ordinary Level, taking eight subjects—a spread of English literature, English grammar, French, geometry, calculus, history, physics, and chemistry. By the time I was fifteen and a half we all had to specialize, and I wanted to do mathematics. Our math teacher had told us about infinity—explaining that things can be tiny, tiny, tiny, but never nothing. These days, of course, such a concept is common, but back then the average teacher did not offer her students such ideas and I was intrigued by the notion of things being infinitely large or infinitely small. I liked mathematics because I liked the process of deduction and the excitement of getting a precise result. I liked seeing structure in things. For me the great thing about math was that if you saw it you got it. Math was truth because it could be proved. All or nothing. You were either one hundred percent right or plain wrong. The school said I didn't have a mathematical mind, but then I got a

96 on the exam, which was almost unheard of, and thankfully my father stuck up for me.

My parents knew I hated the place. My first letters home had tears on them—we all used fountain pens then. "Please take me away," I wrote. "I hate it." And in the same letter: "Please send my bedroom slippers. I forgot them." My mother felt bad. She hadn't really wanted me to go to boarding school, because she had been sent away and hated it, too. But my father was adamant; I was the rising hope of the family. There was no question I was staying, and ultimately it created a kind of stoicism in me (a stoicism people have sometimes mistaken for lack of emotion). But until the moment I went away to school, I remember nothing but a childhood of happiness.

And there was one saving grace in Cheltenham. My father had a friend from the airfield during the War, a man called John Rickards, who had a farm just five miles from school. Once each term (all that was permitted by the school authorities) I visited the Rickardses' lovely old house where their two sons, at least ten years older than me, let me drive the tractor and do the farm work that reminded me of Yorkshire. That sort of thing cheered me and John's mother was a great cook, so for lunch we had lovely roast beef and runner (pole) beans and Yorkshire pudding. It was Mrs. Rickards who made meringues and first showed me how to whisk egg whites into froth with a fork—an agile wrist was the trick.

ROAST BEEF WITH YORKSHIRE PUDDING AND GRAVY

For roast beef, Mrs. Rickards taught me to choose a heavily marbled rib roast on the bone or, better still, a sirloin roast—ribs with a portion of fillet under the bones—the favorite cut in England. You can find sirloin roast here in the United States (not to be confused with sirloin steak) at specialty butchers, if you order it ahead. The pudding from my native Yorkshire is a crispy puff resembling a popover, but with more taste added by drippings from the roast. A hot oven is key to Yorkshire pudding, and so it can bake together with the meat I always roast my beef fast. The outside is slightly charred and the inside rosy red. This produces lots of browned drippings for the gravy, too. When making the gravy, beef stock is best or water from boiling vegetables adds flavor providing it is not too salty. My mother's beef gravy was always thickened, and so is mine.

Serves 6 to 8

4–5 pounds/about 2.25 kg rib roast, on the bone
2–3 tablespoons/30–45 ml lard or vegetable oil
Salt and pepper
3 tablespoons/22 g flour
3 cups/750 ml light beef stock

For the Yorkshire pudding

1 cup/125 g flour
½ teaspoon salt
Large pinch ground black pepper
2 eggs
¾ cup/175 ml milk
½ cup/125 ml water, plus more if needed

Roasting pan; tray of standard muffin tins

Heat the oven to 450°F/230°C and set one shelf low down and another in the middle of the oven. Trim excess fat from the roast, but leave a generous layer and score it to encourage crispness. Set the meat, ribs down, in the roasting pan, spread it with lard or vegetable oil, and sprinkle with salt and pepper.

Put the roast in the oven on the upper shelf and sear at this high heat for 15 minutes, until the fat starts to brown and the melted fat sizzles. Turn down the heat to 375°F/190°C and roast the beef, basting with drippings every 15 minutes until done to your liking. Allow 12 to 15 minutes per pound for rare meat (125°F/52°C internal temperature) or 15 to 18 minutes for medium (145°F/63°C).

Meanwhile, make the puddings: Put the flour, salt, and pepper in a bowl and make a well in the center. Add the eggs and milk to the well and whisk until mixed. Gradually stir in the flour to make a smooth batter; stir in half the water. Cover and let the batter stand at room temperature for about 30 minutes.

Using a bulb baster or a spoon, pour 1 to 2 teaspoons of the drippings from the roast into each cup of the muffin tins. Put the tins in the oven on the empty rack and heat until very hot, about 7 to 10 minutes. If the batter is thicker than heavy cream, stir in a little more water.

Using a pitcher, pour batter into the hot tins, filling them about a third full—test first with a few drops of batter to be sure they sizzle in the hot fat. Return the tins to the oven and bake until the puddings are puffed, browned, and crisp, 25 to 30 minutes. They are best served hot out of the oven but can be kept warm for about 15 minutes.

When the beef is done, transfer it to a platter or carving board, setting its ribs sideways, ready to carve. Cover it loosely with foil and keep it in a warm place to rest while making the gravy. Pour off all but about 2 tablespoons of the pan fat, leaving the juices, which may already have caramelized. If not, heat the pan on top of the stove until the juices darken, 1 to 2 minutes. Stir in the flour and cook, stirring with a metal spoon, until the flour is a deep golden brown, 1 to 2 minutes. Gradually stir in the stock, stirring hard so the gravy thickens without forming lumps. Bring to a boil and simmer until the gravy lightly coats the back of a spoon, 5 to 7 minutes. Taste, adjust the seasoning, and strain the gravy into a gravy boat. Pile the Yorkshire pudding around the beef and take it to the table for carving. Serve the gravy separately.

———————————

Parents were allowed to visit school at half term. My mother and father always came, though we couldn't travel far because on Sundays we had to attend the local church. My mother loathed church, but Daddy didn't want me to be ashamed and he made her go. But I did have four weeks home at Christmas, the same at Easter, and the two summer months. I loved these holidays. I was never bored. At home I spent most of my time alone, taking long walks, doing a lot of needlework. And we traveled a bit.

Many summers we took the boat across to Ireland. My parents, like everyone else, had been totally stuck during the War years—you couldn't travel as my mother in her childhood had become used to doing. After the War, almost the only place you could go was southern Ireland, because it was part of the sterling area, so there were no foreign currency exchange problems. Ireland seemed a land of plenty. We stayed in a series of former railroad hotels on the coast, and the first grand dinner of my life was at Jammet's restaurant in Dublin. I was astonished by the choice of dishes, and I chose fillet of plaice (a bit like flounder) sautéed in butter. In the countryside food was simpler but no less abundant for those who could pay.

In those days I always got nervous about journeys, and before we left I would get sick and throw up. Journey proud, my parents called it, but once there I enjoyed myself. One of the places we visited often in Ireland from the time I was nine until I was eighteen was a very remote village where the people lived off fishing. In the little village, every other house was a bar where the locals made bootleg liquor, potheen. Nothing much happened there. The hotel had a golf course, and my father and uncle played golf while my aunt, my mother, and I took walks. I took a few golf lessons, and to everyone's surprise I was rather good at it. I swam in the sea, and we took long drives, though gas was rationed. At night there was backgammon and dancing.

Ireland was my first glimpse of the outside world and of staying in hotels. I remember at a hotel on the west coast in a large country town on market day stepping into the musty warmth of Guinness and stale cigars. The high Georgian dining room was set with huge white-clothed tables occupied by other diners, many in tweeds. My parents grew impatient. Everything in Ireland was late. They sighed when a bowl of boiled potatoes and turnips, wet cabbage, and thick slices of reheated mutton in gravy finally appeared. But I liked it, especially the hefty helping of pudding and custard for dessert. And the fish in Ireland was very good, especially the lobsters, so good, in fact, that my mother ate lobster every single day. She couldn't think why she was feeling dizzy and nauseous, but when we went home, with no more lobsters, she was fine. After that she could never eat any shellfish, and she became allergic to wine, too, anything to do with the grape. Thank heaven I didn't inherit her gastronomic sensitivities.

Since everything in England was on ration, in Ireland my mother and aunt would buy up the stores—lengths of handmade tweed, silk underwear, and cashmere sweaters. My aunt always bought two or three handbags, too. Then of course we would have to drive across the border into Northern Ireland, and my aunt had this strange belief that if you wore something it was yours and didn't count for customs purposes. Because she was plump anyway, she would put on layers and layers of clothing. My parents were goggle-eyed at the sight, but Auntie Louie simply tottered into customs dressed in all her new clothes, carrying on her arm three handbags—one in crocodile—and she was never stopped. My parents never smuggled—my father wouldn't let my mother, for he felt it wasn't moral.

One winter we traveled to Switzerland, where I fell on the ice and managed to pull the skating pro who was giving me a lesson to his knees. Auntie Louie consoled me with a bag of candied cherries, an unheard-of treat in post-War England. My first visit to France was when I was about fourteen. We took the boat over to Cherbourg and drove down western France. They were repairing the roads, and getting anywhere took a long time. I was miserably uncomfortable, and this would be the only visit to France I did not enjoy. Even the food was a disappointment on that trip—all those freshly gathered mussels and oysters and langoustes were too much. I didn't care for the salads that constituted lunch. Coffee and croissants were inadequate substitutes for bacon and eggs.

But even on that trip a few meals stood out. One day we stopped in Libourne, one of those wonderful old fortified towns. I was still young enough to have supper on my own (my parents ate much later), and when this strange piece of something arrived on a white plate I tasted it and thought it the most delicious ham I had ever had. I later learned it was in fact goose confit, forever memorable. On that trip we also stopped at a restaurant just south of Bordeaux in Les Landes, the strange sandy, pine-rooted strip that runs along the Atlantic coast. It turned out to be Chef Raymond Oliver's mother's place in a backwater called Langon; later Oliver became the owner of Le Grand Véfour in Paris, with three Michelin stars, where celebrities were regulars. But back then my father was quite savvy about restaurants; I have no doubt we had the *Guide Michelin,* so perhaps Langon was noted and maybe Oliver was even there. All I remember is the Dover sole meunière on the bone I had and delicious *fraises des bois* with something on them that turned out to be Armagnac.

On that trip we mostly stayed in a cheap seaside pension near Biarritz because we could bring only fifty pounds each out of England and had to pay everything in cash. My father bought tiny gray shrimps in the market, terrible little things to peel; I peeled them for him, and he gave me ten centimes for each shrimp. Afterward I had swimming lessons, and then came the treat—a daily visit to the pâtisserie, where I went straight to the large rum babas. The pâtissier sprinkled a bit of neat rum on my warm pastry—you needed that little bit of fresh alcohol, for the rest would have evaporated—and I ate it, the same thing every day, dripping with syrup. My habits are still the same; if I really like something I want it again and again. It was many years later, after we opened La Varenne, that Chef Fernand Chambrette gave me his definitive recipe for babas. At his restaurant he would bake the little castle-shaped cakes days ahead so they dried out and therefore absorbed a maximum of syrup.

RUM BABAS

Small bucket-shaped molds, sometimes called timbales, are essential for babas. They are presented tipped on their sides, brushed with apricot glaze to keep them moist, and decorated, if you like, with flowers formed of almond slices and a center of candied cherry.

Makes 12 medium babas

2 teaspoons/7 g dried yeast
3 tablespoons/45 ml lukewarm water
2 cups/250 g flour
1 teaspoon/7 g salt
1 tablespoon/15 g sugar
3 eggs, beaten to mix
¾ cup/110 g dried currants
3 tablespoons/45 ml dark rum
½ cup/110 g butter, plus more for the molds

For the rum syrup
2 cups/390 g sugar
3 cups/750 ml water
½ cup/125 ml dark rum, plus more to taste

For decoration
½ cup/120 g apricot jam with 2–3 tablespoons/30 ml water (for glaze)
3–4 candied cherries
4–5 tablespoons sliced almonds

12 baba molds (7-tablespoon/100-ml capacity)

Sprinkle the yeast over the warm water in a bowl, and let it stand until dissolved, about 5 minutes. Sift the flour, salt, and sugar into a warmed bowl, make a well in the center, and add the yeast mixture and eggs to the well. With your hand, mix the central ingredients, then gradually draw in the flour to make a smooth dough. It should be very soft. Cup your hand and work the dough in a slapping motion against the side of the bowl. Continue until it is very shiny and smooth, about 5 minutes. Alternatively, mix and knead the dough in an electric mixer fitted with the dough hook. Cover the bowl with a damp cloth and leave to rise in a warm place until doubled in bulk, about an hour. Meanwhile, soak the currants in the rum.

Generously butter the molds, chill in the freezer until set, and butter a second time. When the dough has risen, knead it lightly to knock out the air. Add the softened butter and continue beating with your hand until the butter is incorporated, 1 to 2 minutes. Beat the currants and rum into the dough. Using 2 teaspoons, drop the dough into the prepared molds, filling them about half-full and without getting drips on the sides. Set the babas on a baking sheet, cover them with a dry cloth, and leave them to rise in a warm place until the molds are full, 30 to 45 minutes. Heat the oven to 400°F/200°C.

Bake the babas until they are golden brown and begin to shrink from the sides of the molds, 20 to 25 minutes. Unmold them onto a rack and let them cool. If you can bake them a day ahead and leave them uncovered overnight, so much the better. They will dry and absorb more syrup.

For the syrup, heat the sugar and water in a sauté pan or wide, shallow saucepan over medium heat, stirring occasionally until the sugar is dissolved. Bring the syrup to a boil and boil rapidly for 2 to 3 minutes. Turn off the heat and stir in ¼ cup/60 ml of the rum. Drop the babas into the hot syrup. Turn and baste them so they absorb as much as possible, almost doubling their original size. Transfer them to a platter or individual plates with a draining spoon, laying them on their sides. If you need to soak the babas in two batches, reheat the syrup before adding the second batch. Reserve any leftover syrup. The babas may be soaked 4 to 6 hours ahead and kept tightly covered at room temperature.

To finish: Melt the apricot jam in a pan with 2 to 3 tablespoons water. Work it through a sieve to form a glaze and melt again in the pan. Sprinkle a teaspoon of neat rum on each baba to add fresh flavor, brush with glaze, and top with an almond and cherry flower. If any syrup is left, lace it with a bit more rum and serve it in a pitcher with the babas.

In my final year at Cheltenham, I took the exams for entering Cambridge University. For someone with a scientific bent to my mind, I always did well in English, but the applied mathematics exam was one of those magical moments. There were only three of us in the little room that day, and when I looked at the exam papers I knew I could do it. Every question seemed to lead to a conclusion. I remember coming out and walking down the stairs and outside into bright sunshine and knowing in a blinding flash of happiness that I'd got it all right.

After that I waited to hear if I'd got an interview. The chances were pretty slim, as it was rumored that only one candidate out of three hundred female applicants would actually get a place at the University. Throughout the 1950s, the remnants of War were prominent, and one of the major remnants—one I would come to understand only later thanks to Mark—was that as a generation we were quite conformist. Our parents had had their lives shattered, so we felt that we were just so lucky. The feeling was more subconscious than conscious, but we were looking for lives our parents would approve of—like going to Oxford or Cambridge and not some liberal, experimental place or refusing to go to university at all. I did get an interview at Cambridge and while there I had another piece of amazing luck of the sort I've had all my life. I was talking to an intellectual woman, a professor, who was clearly bored by interviewing all these nice girls. She was looking at building blueprints on her desk, and she looked up at me and said rather casually, "Are you interested in plans? I see you are very good in applied mathematics. . . ." That was the sort of thing I enjoyed, so I said yes, and she went on to ask if I'd seen King's College Chapel, and I told her I had. Luckily, just the day before I had walked past that miraculous monument.

"Do you know how it's held up?" she asked. I told her I had an idea, that there were flying buttresses, the fans of the vaulting were very important, leaving space for the windows with their stone tracery, and the pinnacles gave a downward thrust to counterbalance the buttresses and the outward thrust of the arched roof. I obviously made a mark, because she said, "I really don't think we have a place for you here, but I know Marjorie Holland at Girton College is looking for a girl to do economics. I see you're good at English as well as math; would you like to meet her?"

Girton was one of thirty-one colleges at Cambridge at the time, three of them for women, and it had been England's first residential university college for women. The main site was about three miles from the university, a cluster of redbrick Victorian buildings spread out on thirty-three acres. I went to see Professor Holland, who looked very vague behind her eyeglasses with her hair slipping out of its combs. She seemed unable to think of any questions to ask me. "Do you know what economics is?" she asked. I didn't, not really, and I'm not sure how I answered.

I returned to Cheltenham, and by the end of term, my last term, many of the other girls had heard from university, yes or no. I hadn't yet been contacted when it was time to go home. I collected my trunk and took the by-then familiar train journey to Northallerton. I climbed out onto the platform, a stretch especially long because it's where they used to test express trains for speed. Far down at the end of the windy platform I saw my parents waiting for me. They came toward me, and as my father hauled out my school trunk for the last time he said casually, "Have you heard from Girton?"

"No," I said, "I haven't." I had a lump in my throat.

"We have," he said. "You're in."

And with that short sentence my life was transformed.

The night I was accepted at Cambridge my mother, who hated to cook, made my favorite braised oxtail and my father brought out a twenty-year-old bottle of Champagne. To this day I am fond of Champagne that is over the hill and has lost its bubbles.

MY MOTHER'S BRAISED OXTAIL

It takes many hours of cooking for oxtail's tough, gelatinous joints to dissolve and form a rich sauce, and the smaller, tail-end ones will be done before the rest. Beef ribs can be cooked the same way and will take less time, 2 to 3 hours. A whole grain, such as barley or wild rice, makes the ideal accompaniment.

Serves 5 to 6

2 tablespoons/30 ml vegetable oil
About 5 pounds/2.25 kg oxtail, cut between the vertebrae
2–3 large onions, thinly sliced
2–3 medium carrots, sliced
3 stalks celery, sliced
¼ cup/30 g flour
3 cups/750 ml beef stock, plus more if needed
½ bottle (375 ml) fruity red wine such as Merlot
One 1-pound/450-g can of chopped tomatoes
Large bouquet garni of parsley stems, 2 bay leaves, and 2 sprigs thyme
Salt and pepper

Heat the oven to 300°F/150°C and set a shelf low down. Heat the oil in a casserole or sauté pan wide enough for all the oxtail pieces to sit on the bottom. Add the oxtail pieces a few at a time and brown them on all sides—take time to brown them thoroughly, as this adds flavor to the stew. Set the pieces aside and discard all but about 3 tablespoons of the fat from the pot.

Add the onions, carrots, and celery, and cook gently, stirring often, until lightly browned. Stir in the flour and cook gently, stirring, until it and the vegetables are well browned. Stir in the beef stock, wine, tomatoes, bouquet garni, salt, and pepper, and bring to a boil, stirring until the sauce thickens.

Return the oxtails to the soup, cover the casserole, and cook in the oven about 3 hours or until the meat is falling from the bones when poked with a two-pronged fork. Turn the oxtails from time to time during cooking, and add more stock if the sauce evaporates rapidly. At the end of cooking, the sauce should be rich and dark but not too thick. The smaller oxtail joints will cook first, so remove them and let the others cook for longer.

If necessary, at the end of cooking simmer the oxtail sauce to reduce it until rich. Skim off as much excess fat as you can. Discard the bouquet garni, taste, and adjust the seasoning. The stew will mellow if you refrigerate it for a day or two, and fat will solidify so it is easier to skim.

For the next three years, I would be trained to apply my mind to a subject I had no idea about. I would be outnumbered by men in the proportion of eleven to one, and though I didn't realize it at the time, my social horizons would infinitely expand. Right then, of course, I'd had no concept of what I might have done if I hadn't been accepted. I honestly think my parents hadn't thought beyond what a rejection might mean. I knew, absolutely knew, I wanted to go to Cambridge, even more so since seeing the beauty of the place. At school, long after the lights were out, I'd read under a night-light Dorothy Sayers's *Gaudy Night* about Oxford, and Harriet Vane, the main character, had become a kind of archetype for me. The story is a murder mystery and in the end Harriet gets engaged to Peter Wimsey, but the underlying theme of the book was a kind of women's liberation, and it led me to realize that the whole way those at top universities look at things was appealing to me—the respect and honor given to intellect, to history, to old books, to old buildings, to tradition, and to achievement. That was for me.

In my mother's overcoat, holding my father's shotgun; this is the woman my parents wished I had become.

Chapter Four

. . . .

IT'S ANOTHER ADVENTURE

No mean woman can cook well. It calls for a generous spirit, a light hand and a large heart.

—Eden Phillpotts

As a graduation gift my parents sent me that summer to Winkfield, Constance Spry's cookery and finishing school an hour from London in the depths of Windsor Forest. Spry was one of the very first female entrepreneurs, her motto "I aspire to perfection!" and her school was a classic finishing school where plain, gawky girls learned they could be much helped by a good hairdo or by losing a bit of weight or learning to walk in high heels. It was an especially good place for those girls who hadn't been happy at home or whose parents were overseas, which was common in England when the Empire was still on the go.

But for me Winkfield was the place where I could do what I loved, a reward for having stuck it out all those years at Cheltenham. Before I left Northallerton, it suddenly dawned on me that no longer would every minute of every day be programmed. Now I could make up my own mind about whether or not to do something, and Winkfield opened up the real world. Constance Spry was an inspiration. Born in 1886, she was the same era and type as Elizabeth Arden and keen on women's accomplishments. Spry had had a varied life—as secretary of the Dublin Red Cross, a welfare supervisor, head of women's staff of the civil service, and headmistress of day schools in East London. When she married her second husband, Henry Spry, she opened a flower shop in Mayfair and employed seventy people with prestigious clients such as the Duke and Duchess of Windsor. When the War started Spry began teaching again, along with her good friend Rosemary Hume, an accomplished cook and founder of the Cordon Bleu School in London, and in 1946 Spry opened Winkfield.

Ten years later I was living with fifty other girls in a great old white stucco house that was creatively furnished with all sorts of hand-me-downs—a sofa with one leg gone and grand vases and chandeliers missing a dangle or two. My mother was so fussy about caring for her old things, it was quite a surprise that some people did not seem to mind. We had cooking classes every day, and I was plunged into a world I found compelling and the three months went by far too fast. One day Constance Spry had us all in and read the huge cookbook she'd just written, *The Constance Spry Cookery Book*. Mrs. Spry was vivid and glowing pink, holding this neon pink tome, utterly captivating. I still have my signed copy of the first edition.

In the fall of that year, at eighteen and a half I went off to Cambridge. I was twenty-one when I graduated from the University, and those three years passed in a kind of idyll. I studied economics, but in my typical style, I didn't really know what would be next. I've never been one for five-year plans. Others around me were studying to become economists who would do merchant banking or go into the family business; a very few had plans to stay on to teach. Some of my fellow students became top British civil servants—mandarins—and a few went into business. At the University, the ratio of male to female students was eleven to one, and after the first year only two of us women were still studying economics. The other women, among them my closest friend, Fiona Mill, went off into another stream and pursued law or English. So Gay Hazelden, a beautiful, bright woman, and I were the only two women in a class of one hundred.

During our first year Fiona and Gay and I, along with three hundred others, lived in dear old Girton, the Victorian Gothic college campus built three miles outside of Cambridge as a way of keeping girls safe. This meant we had to travel to go to classes and, because I had never learned to ride a bicycle, I had to take a twenty-minute bus ride. My parents gave me a little allowance, which meant that unlike many of the others, I could afford to do things once in a while, like buy myself a sausage roll and lentil soup in the cheap café in town. Our big treat, especially on cold days, was to have tea and a bun in the café. Buns were the big things, especially rock buns that look like rocks, but when you bit into them they crumbled. The good ones were delicious, tasty, and filling.

One of the finest things about Cambridge was that each week we had tutorials with either a graduate student or a professor. My subject advisor, Marjorie Holland of the flyaway hair and glasses, was hopeless as a supervisor. Her subject was international trade. She was also a don and had one of those Julia Child–like voices, so she should have been a good lecturer. For her first lecture she had been assigned a room that wasn't very large, and there wasn't room for all the students. The next week she reserved one of the great halls, but this time only half a dozen students were there because her lectures were so dull. Out of loyalty to our advisor, Gay and I had to attend every single one, but they were deadly boring. Marjorie did have a magnificent ancient Rolls-Royce and occasionally drove us back and forth to Girton, but Mill Lane, where the lecture halls were, was always jammed with bikes, and as Marjorie drove she would ramble on, brushing aside the bikes before her. She was married to a don in Trinity, one of the great colleges—the one you see in *Chariots of Fire* in the Trinity Run around Great Court. Her husband had rooms in the magnificent Wren Court, and once each year we would be invited to his rooms. We ate melon sorbet from the Trinity kitchens where crème brûlée was invented. (It was originally an English, not a French, dish.) Of course Christ Church, Oxford, which Mark attended, always claimed it was they who had invented crème brûlée, but Mark never came across it as an undergraduate. Oxford and Cambridge had rivalries over everything. At Oxford, Cambridge is still referred to by the faculty as "the other place."

Walking into those colleges and climbing the medieval staircases was lovely, and my second tutor, Peter Bauer, turned out to be a role model of sophistication, one of those small, lively-eyed, compact men, intense and full of energy. He was brilliant, fluent in many languages, with an astonishing photographic memory. Bauer was born in Budapest and studied law there before embarking for England in the thirties to study economics. When he had taken his Ph.D. exams, he would remember page by page what John Stuart Mill had written and quoted slews of stuff, totally accurately, infuriating the examiners. After that, for a while Bauer worked in a London-based merchant house that conducted business in the Far East and he was at Cambridge for just a few years before moving on to the London School of Economics, where he had a long, distinguished teaching career and was appointed to the House of Lords. Gay and I were lucky to have him as our tutor, chosen, I suspect, not for our academic attainments but because it amused him to tutor the only two women in the class.

Professor Bauer once invited Gay and me to dinner in his paneled rooms in Gonville and Caius, the college next door to King's. His walls were lined with bookshelves. He had also invited a younger colleague to join us who seemed bemused by the whole experience. We had a delicious, rather grand dinner because, among its other perks, Gonville and Caius had notable wine cellars and chefs, the sort of thing C. P. Snow, chronicler of Cambridge life, wrote about. Bauer gave me a fine glimpse of civilization and helped me realize the importance of the values that my parents had instilled in me. He talked about fine music and painting, and we shared a love of architecture.

Peter Bauer was scrupulously polite. Only later, after I was no longer his student, did he give me yet another lesson, this one about personal relationships. He took me to lunch in London, and over an excellent meal he told me I had been one of his most appealing students in a long time. Then he said that one of the two of us—meaning Gay and me—was quite a good economist; he didn't say which. I was certain it wasn't me, and I'm sure I sort of looked at him waiting for the next line, but he didn't say another word about academics. He went on, putting it all sideways, but in a sophisticated and rational way, that he would like to take me to bed. In those days "nice girls" didn't jump into bed with people—the consequences could be dire. But after that, whenever anyone else tried the maneuver I knew I'd heard it all before, and far more temptingly expressed.

The summer after my first year at Cambridge I took a job as a live-in au pair girl in the London suburbs. I learned a lot about who is the boss when you get paid. I cleaned the house and cooked under supervision, and I think this is when I really discovered how much I loved to be in the kitchen. It was then that I discovered that heavenly butterscotch sauce is made simply with butter and sugar cooked to a caramel. I experimented with recipes from *The Constance Spry Cookery Book*, including the two famous cold chicken dishes that Rosemary Hume had created for the young Queen Elizabeth's coronation. As Rosemary describes it, "The luncheon was for about 350 people, the largest party to be seated in the Great Hall of Westminster School. . . . By two o'clock the guests would be very hungry and probably cold. There would be many nationalities, some of whom would eat no meat. We knew the kitchen was too small to serve hot food beyond soup and coffee." The result was two recipes for chicken, one with spicy mayonnaise called Chicken Elizabeth, the other, Chicken Philippe, topped with mushrooms in port wine vinaigrette. Both recipes are very much of the time, when chicken was a luxury, before battery production. Button mushrooms and cherry tomatoes were a comparative rarity, too, while a mayonnaise flavored with curry powder and apricot jam seemed quite exotic. Both are what I would call granny food and right back in style!

CORONATION CHICKEN ELIZABETH

This chicken always transports me back to the early 1950s. Today I like to use olive oil for the cheerful tomato salad that accompanies the chicken, though a mild vegetable oil would have been standard in England at the time. Be sure to serve the salad at room temperature, not chilled.

Serves 4

3–4 pounds/about 1.5 kg whole chicken

To poach the chicken
1 onion, quartered
1 carrot, quartered
2 stalks celery
2 bay leaves
1 teaspoon whole peppercorns
2 teaspoons/15 g salt
Water

For the curry mayonnaise

1 tablespoon vegetable oil

1 small onion, finely chopped

2 teaspoons/15 g curry powder

¼ cup/60 ml tomato juice

¼ cup/60 ml red wine

2 tablespoons/30 g apricot jam

1¼ cups/300 ml mayonnaise

Salt and pepper

For the cherry tomato salad

1 pound/450 g cherry tomatoes

Vinaigrette dressing made with 2 tablespoons/30 ml lemon juice, 1
    teaspoon Dijon mustard, ½ cup/125 ml olive oil, salt, and pepper

Paprika, for sprinkling

2 tablespoons chopped fresh tarragon

String for tying

To poach the chicken: Truss the bird and set it on its back in a deep pan. Add the onion, carrot, celery, bay leaves, peppercorns, salt, and enough water to cover the bird. Bring to a boil, skimming occasionally. Cover the pan and simmer until the bird is tender and the juices no longer run pink when the thigh is pricked with a skewer, 1 to 1¼ hours. Let the chicken cool to tepid in the broth, then drain it. Keep the broth for soup.

Meanwhile, make the curry mayonnaise: Heat the oil in a small saucepan and sauté the onion over medium heat until soft but not brown. Add the curry powder and cook, stirring, until fragrant, about 1 minute. Add the tomato juice and red wine and simmer until the mixture is pasty, 2 to 3 minutes. Stir in the apricot jam and work the mixture through a sieve into a bowl (I often don't bother to sieve, as I like the extra texture). Whisk in the mayonnaise. The sauce should coat the back of an upturned spoon. Taste and adjust the seasoning; cover and set it aside.

For the tomato salad: To peel the tomatoes, slash the skin of each one with a knife and put them in a bowl. Cover them generously with boiling water and leave until the skin starts to split, 5 to 10 seconds depending on ripeness. Drain them and cover with cold water. Peel the tomatoes and put them in a bowl. Make the vinaigrette dressing and toss with the tomatoes. Taste, adjust the seasoning, cover, and chill the salad.

To finish, discard the trussing string from the chicken and carve it into 8 pieces, discarding the skin. Arrange the chicken along one side of an oval platter and coat the pieces with the mayonnaise. Sprinkle them lightly with paprika. Stir the tarragon into the tomatoes, taste again for seasoning, and pile them beside the chicken.

During my second year at Cambridge I moved and lived, along with Fiona, in the big old Victorian building in the main college that housed nearly three hundred women. This was much more fun than living off campus, despite the lack of central heating. Cambridge is famous for its winds that we always said swept down from Russia and raced across the flat Fens, but I'd become accustomed to winter from my days up north and the cold never bothered me. People were constantly dropping into our rooms for coffee—instant, that was the drink. As for cooking, we ate most of our meals together in the Great Hall. Food was firmly institutional, only a modest improvement on Spartan boarding school. There were far too many steam trays of watery boiled potatoes, cottage pie, and boiled mutton (as lamb was always called). Breakfast was the best meal—meaty bacon, grilled tomatoes, slightly overcooked scrambled eggs, and more of those delicious buns, yeasty ones with raisins.

Down the hall from my rooms (I was lucky enough to have grabbed a corner suite) we had a kitchen with two gas rings on a corridor for thirty students. Of course roasting or baking anything was impossible, but each autumn I was spurred to action by the arrival of a brace of pheasants in full plumage sent by my father. He packed them in special cartons supplied by the Country Gentlemen's Association (only the English could have such an organization) and sent them down, express, on the train. After the excitement of opening the package, I set to figuring out what to do to improve on Emily's recipe, without the ability to roast. I developed a pheasant casserole I cooked on one of those two little burners, and on the second ring I steamed caramel custard over a galvanized tin laundry bucket. This would prove to be excellent training for adventures I still didn't know lay ahead.

MY FATHER'S PHEASANT CASSEROLE

My father's pheasants were wild, of course, dark-fleshed birds that would serve at most two people. The raised pheasants that are quite widely available now in U.S. specialty markets are plumper, serving three or even four diners—allow a pound on the bone per person. Over the years, I've used this recipe as a starter kit, for example substituting Cornish game hen for pheasant, diced root celery for mushrooms, and white wine for red.

Serves 6 to 8

2–3 whole pheasants (2–3 pounds/about 1.25 kg each)
1 tablespoon/15 ml vegetable oil
2 tablespoons/30 g butter
8 shallots, peeled, halved if large
1 pound/450 g button mushrooms, quartered
5–6 slices thickly cut bacon, diced
4 tablespoons/30 g flour
½ bottle/375 ml robust red wine such as Cabernet
3 cups/750 ml chicken stock, plus more if needed
2 garlic cloves, chopped
Bouquet garni of parsley stems, 2–3 sprigs thyme, and 2 bay leaves
Salt and pepper

Cut the legs from the pheasants. Cut each pheasant in half through the breastbone, then trim away and discard the backbones (they make excellent broth). Trim off the wingtips. If the pheasant breasts are large, cut them diagonally in half including the bone; if small, leave the breasts whole.

Heat the oil and butter in a casserole over medium heat and brown the pheasant pieces on all sides, a few at a time. Remove them, add the shallots, and brown them also, 3 to 5 minutes. Take them out, add the mushrooms, and cook until wilted, 2 to 3 minutes. Set them aside also, add the bacon to the pan, and brown it, too, 1 to 2 minutes.

Discard all but about 3 tablespoons fat from the pan, stir the flour into the bacon and cook, stirring all the time, until the flour browns, 1 to 2 minutes. Stir in the wine, bring to a boil, and simmer 1 minute. Add the stock, garlic, bouquet garni, and a little salt and pepper. Replace the pheasant pieces, pushing them down under the liquid—they should be almost covered—and, if necessary, add more stock.

Cover the casserole and simmer on top of the stove, or cook it in a 325°F/160°C oven until the pheasant is very tender when pierced with a two-pronged fork, 1 to 1½ hours. Stir from time to time, especially if you are cooking on top of the stove, and add more stock if the sauce begins to stick. The legs may cook before the wings and breast pieces, and, if so, take them out, cover, and set them aside.

About 15 minutes before the end of cooking, when the last pieces of pheasant are nearly done, add the shallots and mushrooms to the pot, stirring them into the sauce. Continue cooking until the shallots and mushrooms are tender and all the pheasant pieces are done.

Remove the remaining pheasant pieces and vegetables with a draining spoon, and add to the rest. Discard the bouquet garni and taste the sauce for seasoning; it should be rich but not sticky. If necessary, simmer a thin sauce on top of the stove without the lid for a few minutes, or add a few spoons of stock to a thick sauce. Replace the pheasant pieces and vegetables. Pheasant casserole will mellow and improve if you refrigerate it for a day or two. Reheat it in the casserole on top of the stove.

Besides our studies, sometimes Fiona, Gay, and I and a few others would get together after lunch in one or another of our rooms and listen to show tunes like those from *My Fair Lady* and *Salad Days*. Alas, I'm one of those people who cannot sing; if I open my mouth, those beside me are thrown off tune. On the other hand, at school I had quite often been asked to recite, or to read the lesson in church. I was still sewing, splurging a part of my modest allowance on lovely crisp silks from Liberty's. My favorite color in those days was turquoise blue, but somewhere along the way I switched to bright red—the color of life, as Mark said when we first met. I made rather beautiful dresses.

We had eight-week terms, and three times a year I traveled back to Yorkshire. At home I could lay out the fabrics on the floor and crawl around and make a huge mess. During the second summer I took a paid job in a B and B in the Suffolk countryside. My parents thought it déclassé and wanted me to stay at home, but I insisted. I wanted to work because most of my contemporaries were. I was put to cleaning the guest rooms, and the job gave me a lifelong respect for a trained housekeeper.

On the whole I was slow about dating. I went out with one or two people and one year was invited by one of my fellow economists to the great celebratory May Ball at the end of the academic year. I wore a shimmery gold strapless dress with a huge, great puffed skirt and my date tried to lure me onto one of the sofas in his rooms, but I hitched up my petticoats and made my way out of there because I wasn't in love. I didn't fall in love until the very end of my years at Cambridge. Then I fell head over heels with a man called Brian Fagan, an archaeologist who was going to Africa after graduation to work with the famous Louis Leakey.

At the end of the three years, worried about my exams—my answers had been a bit touch and go—I traveled home before results were posted. I was at my aunt's house when the phone rang, and I heard Brian's voice saying, "It's okay, Anne; you've passed. You've got a third." Though this was the lowest class of degree, I was greatly relieved. But what I would do next was a puzzle. Before leaving University I had spoken with a career advisor who said firmly, "Well, with a third-class degree you would not be qualified to teach." I'd never even thought about teaching, but she went on. "With a degree in economics, I think you'd better take a secretarial course, dear."

I said nothing to her, but to myself I said I'd be damned if I was going to take a secretarial course. That's what all those girls at Winkfield were doing, and damn it, I knew I could do better than that. The question was what. Back in Northallerton, a fussy friend of my parents came to visit and said, "Well, I can probably get you a job as a filing clerk in the Foreign Office," and again I was furious. I knew that the Foreign Office was a kind of marriage market for nice girls to meet budding diplomats. I restrained myself from being rude, but I did tell my parents very clearly that I would not take their friend's advice.

"She's only trying to be helpful," my father said. In those days, in 1959 when I was twenty-one, sensible young women were out pecking for a husband, and business careers, even for women graduates of Cambridge or Oxford, were a rarity. Thankfully, someone, possibly it was even me, had a bright idea. Mrs. Dickie had become principal of Winkfield after Constance Spry, and she had taken a shine to me and offered me the opportunity of being her assistant at Winkfield, teaching classes nobody else knew how to teach, such as glove making and lampshade making. In those days girls still wore gloves, and not just with evening gowns; you wore gloves during the day when you went up to London. I didn't know how to make gloves, but I'd always been a quick learner and near my aunt's house there was a wonderful old lady who knew this specific and tricky skill. I'd already mastered beautiful, precise, even stitchery. I learned fast how to make gloves and even made a pair for Mrs. Spry.

At Winkfield, most of the girls were sixteen or seventeen, preparing to be presented at Court, leading into a debutante season in London. A regular stream of visiting young men in their Jaguars would roar up and down the great driveway to the house with a burst of gravel. I recall quite a lot of jokes about how intrusive the gear lever between the seats was. The girls had to learn to curtsey before the Queen following the mantra "Side Two, Three, Bend your knees, Down, Two, Three, Up, Two, Three, Kick the Train," and off you walk. Those who didn't own London town houses would stay with their grandmother or rent a mansion for the season and invite all the top people. If your parents were doing it properly a ball would be given for you, and if not you'd have a dinner party at a place like the Dorchester Hotel. The main thing was if you were on the insiders' list you were invited everywhere and you'd go to Ascot and Henley. Everybody's brother was called in, and the men were always complaining about having to go to yet another formal event. I was never presented at Court so was only a spectator of the scene, and as I later told my mother, I didn't mind.

Most of the cooking teachers at Winkfield were not much older than I, but there was the unforgettable Mrs. Proctor, big and black haired, with an upholstered bosom and a white starched apron. She taught at both Winkfield and the London Cordon Bleu. She was a Tartar, extremely strict, but she turned out outstanding cooks, including Sheryl Julian, my first editorial assistant, who eventually became food editor of *The Boston Globe*. Mrs. Proctor was sharp-eyed and critical, and I recall particularly how annoyed she was the day we had boiled something like sixty eggs for a presentation. If you overcook an egg it gets a black line around the yolk—you'll often see it in a cheap deli—and taste of sulfur. That day this immense pan of eggs was cooked for twenty-five minutes and the whole lot had to be thrown out. Goodness Mrs. Proctor was angry.

I stayed at Winkfield for a year. I was good at what I was doing and I enjoyed the time, but I knew this was a dead end. Besides, we were in the depths of Windsor Forest, not a place I cared to stay. I wonder sometimes now if I didn't perhaps inherit some of my grandfather Todd's traveling spirit, as I seemed even then to be restless. Also, in part thanks to Mrs. Proctor, I wanted to learn more about cooking, so I asked my parents to fund me three months in the advanced course at the Cordon Bleu Cooking School in London.

The original Cordon Bleu opened its doors as a cooking school in Paris in 1895, with the first classes held in January 1896 on Rue du Faubourg Saint-Honoré, named after the saint of pastry chefs. From the beginning, famous chefs came to teach there and its reputation spread when Henri-Paul Pellaprat was the chef; he had been a disciple of Auguste Escoffier. At the same time as teaching at the school, Pellaprat wrote his masterpiece, *L'Art Culinaire Moderne*, hailed as the most up-to-date book on French cooking ever written, and it was translated into five languages. Such tributes echo the importance given to the school, which was setting high standards to an increasing number of graduates from all over the world. Among them was British Dione Lucas, who would become the first well-known female television cook in the United States.

Another early Paris Cordon Bleu student was Rosemary Hume, who in 1933 was given permission to open a Cordon Bleu School in London, the first outside France. It was called l'Ecole du Petit Cordon Bleu and located in the Victoria area of London. After the War the school moved to Marylebone Lane, the location where I was a student. The school's reputation had been confirmed in 1953, twenty years after its opening, when Rosemary Hume prepared the Coronation Luncheon and her Cordon Bleu girls acted as waitresses.

After three months' study at the London Cordon Bleu I was asked to stay on to teach, and it was then that I found my natural home. I started out with the beginners helping another teacher, but after only a few months I was running classes on my own. To do this one has to have a certain natural bossiness, and I would be telling eight women of all ages what to do; although I was only twenty-three, it felt quite natural. Mrs. Proctor would tell me how to do things, and I would go and teach it. I'd always had a strong sense of performance, a strong feeling for occasion, and since that is what cooking class is all about, I felt immediately at home. If I was teaching a dish I didn't know, I would sort of go for it and hope for the best.

Another teacher, Pip Smith, and I had become good friends, and after six months Mrs. Proctor put us to the test when she assigned us to teach the full thirty-six-week Professional Course. Here we had twenty students, far more interesting than in the shorter program's twenty. One memorable afternoon we were put onto making plum jam. Neither Pip nor I had ever made jam, so my can-do approach was under a microscope. We cut up the plums, boiled them, explained about skimming and why the copper pot and why the sterile jars. But neither of us had any experience of telling when the jam was done. The recipe said to look for the "double drip," and eventually I would learn what to look for—you lift the spatula, and if the jam runs off in a steady, thin stream you're only boiling off the steam. After a while it starts to cook and get sticky, and there's a point when the bubbles form around the edge and start bursting more slowly. The sputtering sound changes, and when you lift the spatula it will do a kind of double whammy on the drip. We must have had a thermometer, and perhaps it wasn't working—a lot of our equipment tended to be temperamental.

Anyway, we boiled that jam miles beyond where it should have gone, and it began to smell of caramel. We fudged our way to the next steps, but it was obvious to everyone that something was awry. There was one nice woman in the class who knew all about preserving, but she was kind enough to stand off to the side looking slightly amused. Pip and I said we thought we had gone just a little bit too far. It actually was dreadful, scorched beyond salvation.

What was even further beyond my competence was pastry. Victoria Proctor—we all called her Mrs. Proctor, and I was Miss Willan to my students—had always conducted the three-month course of demonstrations of gâteaux and pâtisserie. Pastry is a whole other world, but Mrs. Proctor decided she was absolutely sick of it and one day said to Rosemary Hume, "You know Anne Willan will try anything; she'll cope with it," and I was launched on an enormously sophisticated and technical program that I had not a clue about.

Pastry is not like cuisine. You cannot adjust and adapt with a bit of parsley or chives. In that class we had to start everything from scratch. We made mountains of fondant and quantities of butter cream. I actually began to be quite good at the technicalities of mirror-smooth coating of fondant and identical, beautiful crisp rosettes of butter cream on top of cakes. But everything happened to me in that class. If you keep chocolate butter cream in the refrigerator overnight, I learned, it sets to a hard, unspreadable lump. If you overwork fondant, at a certain stage it crystallizes. If it's too thin it all runs off, and if it's too thick it sets with nasty bubbles before you've swept across the top with your giant metal spatula. In those days the students were mainly British and very disciplined and always polite, but sometimes in the middle of class if I was doing something difficult as I stopped my running commentary I heard them shift their feet and I would feel the energy in the room beginning to alter.

One such day I was scheduled to make a foot-high confection called a religeuse, a grander version of *croque-en-bouche*, the conical mountain of profiteroles. I had never seen one, but Mrs. Proctor explained the general principle. It is shaped to look like a nun, half coffee, half chocolate, with many éclairs filled with pastry cream and put on a big circle of baked sweet pastry. This took a whole afternoon—twelve of these éclairs adorned with butter cream rosettes, topped with a circle of *choux* pastry and a ball for the head, all stuck together with caramel sugar, which you have to keep at the right temperature—hot so it's melted but not so hot that it keeps cooking. I was in the middle of this and somewhere along the way I got bogged down. There will always be bad days in any kitchen—something gets dropped or burns or isn't delivered on time. And once you're in the weeds, everything's behind. That day I was most certainly in the weeds, and eventually I had to give up and tell everyone to go home.

Our washer upper in that class always put the rolling pins—nice big wooden ones—out on the windowsill to dry, atop the flowerpots. Luckily the demonstration room was only one floor up, because one day one of those rolling pins rolled off its perch and hit a passerby. At the time I was all involved in the demonstration, but I sensed a flurry behind me and I noticed that everyone was sort of looking out the window. The poor lady had to be brought inside and revived with a nice cup of tea. Fortunately, in those days people didn't sue over such things.

My social life was picking up a little. Fiona was married by then. She was the first of anyone I knew from Cambridge to marry, and that was a big thing for me because we were so close and suddenly she had left my world and entered an entirely different one. She started having children straightaway. I would see her now and again, as she and her husband, Charles Clark, lived around the corner from the apartment I shared with Liz, a good friend of Fiona's. Every six months or so, we gave a dinner party. Liz had a young cousin called Newman, a beautiful golden-haired boy on whom she had a crush. But more important, she had a cousin called John Myres. I was still exploring the world of my emotions and retained an affection for Brian Fagan, who periodically came back from digging for prehistoric bones in Rhodesia. But I began to date John, a lieutenant in the Royal Navy, a hydrographer who would go off on six-month voyages to chart the seabed. I seemed to go in for those boyfriends who were often away.

At Cambridge I hadn't needed to worry about birth control since there was no one I wanted to make love with, but when things began to get serious with John I made it my business to find out about one of the volunteer birth control clinics that were still quite controversial in the early 1960s. This one was located in a back street behind the King's Cross railway station and the tired-looking doctor was kind, but she asked me all sorts of personal questions, among them the name of my "fiancé." Still, she delivered the goods, and I emerged with a diaphragm (it would be a few more years before the Pill became widespread). For some reason, I had given my home address as Yorkshire. One afternoon when I was on a visit home, my father called me to the phone and said, "There's a doctor asking for you." He looked at me with curiosity, but I waited until he had turned away, closed the door behind him, and found the lady doctor on the line. She asked how I was doing, if I found using the diaphragm easy, and several other blush-making questions. I could not wait to get her off the line. "If you have any questions, just call this number in your area and our volunteer doctor can help," she said. I was appalled to hear the number was that of my grandfather Todd's second wife (he had died years before); she was a qualified doctor who undertook this kind of volunteer work. I was terrified my parents would find out, but they never did. Looking back, I think it wouldn't have mattered, but at the time the idea was agonizing.

John often invited me to spend weekends at his parents' seventeenth-century stone gentlemen's residence in Kidlington, one of those old villages just outside Oxford, marred only by the express train that whistled past the garden where we played croquet. His father, known to his two sons as Mr. Pudd, sported a long Saint Nicholas–style beard and was chief librarian of Oxford's Bodleian Library, the oldest library in England, founded in the fourteenth century. John's mother, known as Auntie Mudd, had been an Olympic diver and was almost totally deaf as a result, but she spent a great deal of time in the kitchen; preserves were her specialty so I had a much-needed lesson. During the War she had taken her garden fruit to the Women's Institute in the village, where a special allowance of sugar was weighed out to make jam. The village women, she told me, were experts who could judge at a glance whether or not the jam was jelled (so unlike me). Since then she had always grated her sugar from great cone-shaped solid blocks; though she had quite a lot of trouble finding them, she said it made better, purer jam.

John's parents were enthralling—besides her Olympic career, Auntie Mudd had also graduated with a first-class degree from Oxford. Indeed, I liked them rather more than I liked their son, who was reliable but also a little dull. His father once took me around the library and was enormously proud because they'd been doing renovations and had sculpted him as a gargoyle. John would have been the ideal son-in-law for my parents, and when I eventually turned down his marriage proposal they were dashed. I had thought all along I would marry and move back to Yorkshire. I still believed that while I was at the Cordon Bleu. But Fiona's marriage had made me realize that the closeness of her partnership with Charles was a different world. Still, I was looking around for someone I might want to marry. Brian remained at the top of my list, but my parents called him Bloody Brian because they thought he kept me dangling on a string.

Also, I was beginning to think cooking might possibly be a career, and I was becoming interested in traveling. Liz, Newman, and I traveled to France for one holiday. Before we departed, my very sensible father gave me one of those white five-pound notes with black copperplate engraving that were, in the early 1960s, the official five-pound currency and the highest banknote. "Get yourself a good meal," he said. He had his priorities straight. When we reached the village of Les Baux in the mountains of Provence, famous for the Wolves of Orange who lived in caves in those mountains, we took my father up on his offer and ate at L'Oustau de Baumanière, a wonderful three-star restaurant. Afterward we thought we would find some cheap lodging in the village, but there was nothing—it was just a remote Provençal village with a famous restaurant. And so that night we slept in the caves—the first time I had ever slept out. We watched the sun come up over Provence. I was awed by the sight of the way in just a few moments the world around us transformed from shades of gray to vivid color.

During this time, I also received my M.A. At Cambridge and Oxford, B.A. graduates with honors degrees can wait two years and pay a fee to get an M.A. without taking further exams. My mother returned to Cambridge with me for the ceremony, and I felt so proud in my long gown walking up the aisle of the great school's hall dating back to the fifteenth century. We walked in groups of five toward the chancellor, who held out a hand, and each of us took one finger. As we did, he pronounced us, in Latin, M.A.'s in our disciplines. Afterward I took my mother across the road to Caius College to meet Peter Bauer, who welcomed us with a glass of sherry. My mother, as always beautifully dressed, thought Peter Bauer was the cat's meow. Peter (we were now on first-name terms), more than equal to the occasion, said, "Ah, Anne, I see you get a great deal from your mother." He also said something like, "Oh, yes, Anne and I have met for lunch a couple of times in London," and I'm certain my mother guessed about his earlier proposition, though she never said so.

After eighteen months at the Cordon Bleu, I fell ill and was off work for a month or two. During those months I stayed in London and someone told me I ought to collect unemployment benefits. For six weeks or so, I went to the local office and signed up—to my parents' horror; they felt it was a disgrace. Each week I stood in line with the other regulars, among them twins who were stage performers. A few times I was interviewed for teaching jobs, but when they asked, "Would you teach English?" I tried to explain I wasn't suitable. "I'm a cook," I'd say. "I can teach cooking." I was quickly realizing I wanted to move on.

The Cordon Bleu had done wonders for the standard of cooking in England, but French cooking outside of France was still a shadow of the real thing and I wanted to learn more. At that stage in the game, absolutely nobody in France or anywhere else took women into a restaurant kitchen—it would be many years before they did. Women were not only physically weaker, they complicated matters in the small, hot, sweaty environment of a restaurant kitchen. I felt strongly about admitting women to a kitchen—I don't remember being militant about it, but there was no question to me that women could do the work required. For a short time then I thought about going into catering in England, but I wanted to learn more about the finest food in the world at its roots. That meant going to France, to the Cordon Bleu in Paris.

I began to exchange letters with them, and I also saw that if I was truly going to learn on the spot I must know more French. I had taken middle-level exams in French at school and had good academic French, but I was no good at speaking it. Luckily, as has so often happened in my life, at that moment came a happy chance. During the War my father had been impressed by the efficiency of a guy named Leslie who was running the transport on the airfield where my father was posted, and Daddy had kept in touch. It turned out that Leslie's cousin knew Maisie Quinche, the headmistress of a famous international girls' school near Lausanne. Maisie's husband was Swiss and worked for Nestlé, and she was hopeless in the kitchen. She did, however, know all about teaching young English girls French, and as soon as I stepped off the train on the first of January 1963 I stammered, *"Bonjour, madame, comment allez-vous?"* I wanted to speak French at once. Right away we got along.

So there I was in winter, in Vevey on the shore of Lake Geneva in the very surroundings where Madame de Staël and Voltaire had once lived, looking out over the peaks of the Dents du Midi. It was the coldest winter in memory, so cold that Switzerland, which normally exported electricity, was forced to import it. Twice a week Maisie would take me up the mountains with the school for their ski lessons, and so I learned to ski and met a charming Parisian named Jacques—more help for my French. At Madame Quinche's house I lived in a maid's room in the basement and watched television to learn more of the language. I also took lessons from a nice old lady. Day by day my language skills improved. There were problems, of course. I used to go to the butcher to buy our meat, and one day I asked for oxtail to replicate my mother's recipe. "*S'il vous plaît,*" I said, "*je veux coeur de boeuf.*" Everyone in the shop began to snicker, and I had to go home and tell Maisie I couldn't get it. Eventually she understood the problem—*coeur* means "heart." She sent me back so I could buy *queue de boeuf,* oxtail, with the nuance of pronunciation.

In that winter of 1963 in France, the weather was so cold the canals froze and coal barges got stuck. By the time I reached Paris in April, the Cordon Bleu students were abuzz with stories. One girl told me the only way she had kept warm during those months was to light the oven and open its doors. Electricity was turned off at night, but the authorities couldn't turn off the gas, so everyone slept on the floor with the ovens roaring.

By Easter it was warming up a little. I was just about to leave for Paris when I got a terrible attack of hemorrhoids; I had inherited a tendency from my mother and grandfather to easily get allergic to things, and I had been drinking a lot of lemon juice, which turned out to be my problem. I literally could not sit down. Maisie was away for the holiday, so my mother came out to look after me and get me on my feet for Paris. After a week my mother and I set off on the train for Paris. What we hadn't realized was that in France on public holidays everybody behaves like lemmings—leaving on the dot for Easter, Christmas, and summer. And they return like lemmings all at once on Sunday night. The *grande rentrée,* it is called. When we arrived at Gare de Lyon with my big trunk packed with my things, everyone else was arriving back home from their holidays, too. There wasn't a porter anywhere in sight. We had a huge to-do about that, and so my first immersion into Paris was terrifying.

I had got myself booked into a pension run by a Protestant woman who took in young female students, and after that first night in a hotel my mother and I went around to look at the place. The woman was one of those bossy, commanding types, not unlike Mrs. Lord, the woman who had run my Dame School in Northallerton, and the sight of her took me right back to kindergarten. "Oh," she said when we arrived, "well, actually I've rented the room you were meant to have, but I'll find a place." She led us inside and down into a bleak passageway where everyone hung their coats, and announced this was where I would live. If I had been on my own, I'm sure I would have said okay, since I didn't know where else to go. But my mother spoke quite good French and said emphatically, "Either my daughter has a proper room or we're going elsewhere." We walked out with nowhere to go. My mother quickly came up with the bright idea of going to Air France on the Champs-Élysées, where they had a list of pensions, and we found a little one not run by an intimidating dragon. In fact it turned out to be walking distance from the Cordon Bleu. Although it was a depressing, cold place with terrible food, I settled in and my mother returned to Yorkshire.

And so began my life in Paris. Another adventure.

Florence Van der Kemp needed someone to teach French cooking to Bernadina, who spoke only Spanish. We were a happy team at Château de Versailles.

Chapter Five

. . . .

DUCK'S BLOOD AND ASPIC

If you are lucky enough to have lived in Paris as a young man, then wherever you go for the rest of your life, it stays with you, for Paris is a moveable feast.

—Ernest Hemingway

W e knew one family in Paris. Three or four times each year in Yorkshire my father and my uncle and a half dozen of their circle of friends organized a pheasant shoot. When I was a child I trailed through the fields of turnips behind my father; the icy, dew-laden leaves seemed nearly as tall as me. It was almost always freezing, and Daddy took nips from his hip flask of equal parts of Cognac and port—he had a bad stomach, and when he couldn't eat anything he lived on this sustaining mixture. In the afternoon my mother and aunt joined us in the little schoolhouse in front of a roaring fire and we shared a lovely lunch of hot soup from thermos flasks with Stilton cheese, cold tongue, and ham. My aunt baked the scones and cakes and sometimes a cold grouse pie; the strong dark meat under a buttery crust was a specialty of hers.

One of the people they invited every year was a man called Captain Parlour, who had been one of my grandfather's partners in financial ventures. He was older than my father but not much, and in return for his invitation to the pheasant shoot he invited them to his annual grouse shoot on the moors he owned. Captain Parlour rented off two or three of the guns, and one of those he regularly invited was a prosperous French industrialist called Hubert Charpentier, who owned a confectionery business that made, among other things, a drink resembling Orangina and called Pschitt Citron; it amused me to see Pschitt advertised on all the Paris buses.

One day not long after I arrived in Paris, the Charpentiers invited me to Sunday lunch, and from the moment I met Hubert's wife, Marielle, I was fascinated. She became a strong part of my French experience and I later realized she epitomized the French *haute bourgeoisie*. The family had six children, an unimaginably huge number to me, and in their house in the smart area near the Porte d'Auteuil there was a certain way things were done—the way Marielle did them. At that first Sunday lunch Marielle roasted and served a fresh chicken with tiny potatoes immersed in butter and simmered in a saucepan. They were so good I can still taste them. Haricots verts or whatever vegetable was in season might or might not be added. Everything was simple but the best of the best. A nice country girl worked in the kitchen, but it was Marielle who oversaw all the cooking.

At that first lunch, when the chicken was carved, I was asked which piece I would like. In England the breast, or the white meat, is regarded as best, so thinking to be polite I said, *"La cuisse, s'il vous plaît,"* asking for the dark thigh meat, which, truthfully, I had always preferred. Hubert began to laugh. "Ah, I see you like the best," he said. I was quite embarrassed, but it turned out they were impressed by my taste, and I began to wish I could live with the Charpentiers as an au pair.

In the meantime at the Cordon Bleu I was learning how to clarify consommé, to whip up a soufflé, to prepare a lot of the classic dishes. We had three practical classes each week and five demonstrations, one each afternoon. For the demonstrations Chef Narcès did things like *langouste en bellevue*, but for our hands-on classes the then-owner Madame Brassart never spent money on such delicacies. Her franc-scrounging attitude was in everything we did at the school: We cooked with yesterday's fish and limp vegetables, and we used margarine, even for croissants. Butter scarcely entered the door. Inexperienced and young as I was, having taught at the Cordon Bleu in London, where butter was routine and "margarine" a dirty word, I knew this was totally unacceptable for a professional cooking school, particularly in France.

Chef Narcès was a good cook and a skilled instructor, but he was our only one, and often he was more preoccupied with pinching the knees of the female students than with checking on our pastry-rolling technique. Among the fifteen or so other students in my class were a Nazi–internment camp survivor from Belgium and a heavy-handed English girl who, poor thing, couldn't even boil a proper *oeuf mollet* and thus was barely bothered by the school's shortcomings. One fellow student became my friend. Charles was from California, an older gay man and a bodybuilder, something which was then a total mystery to me. But the main thing was, Charles and I both wanted to learn how to cook things right.

At the time Escoffier-style cooking was the rule and French cuisine was sophisticated, elegant, intellectual, expensive, and dominated by men (as it still is). Paris was its epicenter, and to be even proficient one needed professional training under the apprenticeship system. As soon as he had graduated (girls were in a small minority), a bright young apprentice would be passed from restaurant to restaurant, often starting in the provinces, serving a couple of years under various chefs as he gradually made his way up the hierarchy from *commis* to sous chef. Whether or not he made chef would depend on his talent and lots of hard work. A fourteen-hour day with only one day off a week was not uncommon. Only a tiny elite made it to the very top as chefs of fine restaurants, and they rarely owned the business. Traditionally the chef's wife would run the front of house and the money man would be a silent investor. In 1958 this pattern began to change when Paul Bocuse, considered by many to be one of the founders of nouvelle cuisine (though he credits Henri Gault of the *Gault-Millau Guide*), took over his father's restaurant, L'Auberge du Pont de Collonges, and by 1965 had the three Michelin stars the restaurant has kept ever since.

There has always been great culinary rivalry between Paris and the regional center of Lyon. When I was at the Paris Cordon Bleu we scarcely mentioned Lyon, where a more earthy, simple, and intuitive style prevails. These days this kind of cooking is often called bistro and is right back in style. Two centuries ago, after the French Revolution, many former house cooks for Lyon's once-affluent families began cooking popular meals for the *canuts,* the skilled workers who were weaving the renowned Lyon silk. As these chefs began to create small restaurants, called *bouchons,* they fostered a culture of home-cooked meals. *Bouchon* means "cork," and is used sometimes to mean a traffic jam, but in Lyon it has always referred to these cozy places that specialize in Lyonnais dishes like quenelles and andouillettes, tripe and sweet-breads, usually accompanied by *un pot de Beaujolais.* The Lyonnais were especially proud of the fact that they did not waste a single part of the pig. Women who excelled in such simple, creative cooking became known as the *mères,* the mothers, of Lyon. They fostered an atmosphere of cooking based on fresh foods, so you might not know what you would cook for lunch until you went to the open market in the morning. The mères spirit requires an open mind with the ability to look at your ingredients and cook so that they smell and taste the best they can, with far fewer rules than under classic *grande cuisine.*

But at that time I was on the edge of understanding such things, and only years later, after I began writing about food, did I become more knowledge-able and involved with the theory of cooking. Just a couple of years earlier *Mastering the Art of French Cooking* had appeared in the United States. One day Charles suggested we take a class at l'École des Trois Gourmandes, the school started by Julia Child, Simone Beck, and Louisette Bertholle. It was rather expensive and it was Simca, not Julia, who was giving the class, but of course I was eager to go.

It soon emerged that the class was geared mainly toward American housewives. I was disappointed because I wanted to learn the ultimate professional way of doing things. For instance, one of Julia's recipes, *la bouilla-baisse de poulet,* let me down because, number one, it wasn't a French dish but an American version of a French dish. You could say that *bouillabaisse* means to "boil slowly" and you could conceivably apply that to chicken, but anybody French would look at you as though you were crackers, as they know bouil-labaisse is a fish soup cleverly nicknamed by Alan Davidson "the harlot of Marseilles" because it contains so much trash fish. At the end of class we were invited to taste with teaspoons, which Charles and I thought namby-pamby by contrast with the un-American finger dipping that went on at the Cordon Bleu. This was not the sort of thing I was looking to learn how to do. And the two-hour class showed me that Simca was not an easy woman; she was rather condescending to naïve English-speaking novices. Ten years later she began to consider me as more than one of those tiresome foreigners and was extremely kind to me, but on that day in class she was forbidding.

Charles lived on the Île Saint-Louis with one of the senior diplomats at the American embassy, who had impeccable French and excellent connections. He was eager to entertain a prince and princess of Denmark, and Charles asked if I would like to help him arrange and cook a dinner party for them. Of course I was delighted by the idea, and in preparation for the event he and I went to a dress shop where I ordered a very flossy, stunning dress, a shirtwaist of see-through silk, printed with big crimson flowers, worn over a plain green shift, the latest thing and totally unsuited to the kitchen. I did notice that the saleslady had one of those secret smiles that I didn't understand.

I was still seeing Jacques on and off, the nice guy I had met on the ski slopes in Switzerland and whose parents lived on the Avenue Foch, the wealthiest avenue in Paris. Jacques had been involved with the Algerian War in French intelligence, notorious at the time for torture, and though he never talked about it, reading through the lines I realized he'd had a breakdown and was taking some time off. But he was amusing company, and he was also helping me to navigate the French terrain. I told him about the adventure in the shop and said I thought the saleslady with her smile must have thought Charles was my lover and paying for the dress. Jacques laughed. "No, no," he said, "she thought Charles was your lover and your husband was paying for the dress!" Such a situation was unimaginable in England. Welcome to another world!

Later that spring of 1962 Charles and I visited Saulieu in the quiet corner of Burgundy, where the three-star Hôtel de la Côte-d'Or had become, since its opening in the 1930s, almost a national shrine, a pilgrimage for those wishing to enjoy the glories of *cuisine française*. It was Alexandre Dumaine's belief that you shouldn't diminish the pleasure of your guests by displaying your opulence. The famous dining room, now preserved as a period piece, was small and low-key, very *en famille*, the way three stars used to be before they became fancy and full of Christofle crystal. Charles had ordered ahead for us—*poulet en vessie*, chicken cooked with vegetables in a pig's bladder and served with morel cream sauce, because spring is the season for fresh morels. We drank Vin de Paille, made from grapes from the Jura Mountains in eastern France that are picked late and dried on straw pallets (*paille* means "straw") so that the juice concentrates and you get this extraordinary almost sherry-like golden wine. That was another lesson in the marvels of truly great cooking paired with an outstanding wine.

Charles and I were planning our dinner party for the Danish royals with a rather grand menu of stuffed artichokes and veal Orloff, followed by a hot soufflé Grand Marnier—rather risky when I look back on it now, asking guests dressed in their best to deal with artichoke leaves. There was also the cooking challenge of whisking egg whites at the last minute, then baking a delicate soufflé and getting it to the table at its peak of puffed magnificence.

We wanted more guests, so I invited the Charpentiers, and the dinner party went off beautifully. Even better, Marielle and Hubert invited me to live with them, and I happily accepted their invitation. My three months at the Cordon Bleu were nearly over, and I was planning a visit home. I had recently broken off with Brian, who had returned from his Rhodesian archaeological digging and made it clear he would not marry me. However, just a single day in Paris in kindly John Myres's company made me realize I could not commit to the safety net of marriage he offered. So I became fancy free.

Besides, I had made up my mind I was going to stay in Paris. Realizing I would need to earn some money when I returned from Yorkshire, before leaving I placed a classified ad in the *International Herald Tribune* saying: "Cordon Bleu cook cooks for dinner parties and gives cooking lessons." Back home I told my parents I was going to stay on and take the Grand Diplôme, though I didn't realize then that in those days earning the Diplôme had next to nothing to do with whether or not you could cook but had, rather, to do with paying fees to Madame Brassart. My parents were distressed. They had hoped their only child would settle down to the life they had envisioned for me, in London or, better still, back in Yorkshire. I explained that I would be living with the Charpentiers and would use a nest egg I had inherited from my grandfather, but this did not reassure them. Perhaps they realized more clearly than I did that this was a turning point. Never again would I regard England as home.

I returned to Paris and moved in with the Charpentiers on Rue Boileau on the Right Bank in western Paris. It was with Marielle and Hubert I began to realize the prime importance of simplicity in the kitchen and treating the very best ingredients with love. At the Cordon Bleu I had begun to learn the elegance and edge of fine cuisine, but because Madame Brassart cut corners wherever she could it took Marielle to truly teach me perfectionism. I learned that it was not impolite to take a second helping, that everything in France could be served a second time. In the early days I would eyeball a dish and think, Oh, yes, I'll take two, but that put the whole count off and caused havoc in the kitchen. I learned something new at every meal.

We had bread with everything, and the green vegetable was always the finest of the season, perfectly cooked. We had dessert only on Sunday or birthdays. On all the other days the last course was cheese and fruit, normally only one kind of cheese. Marielle taught me how to cut slivers from a wedge of Brie, something I later would instill in my students. A cheese should always be cut in a way that it retains its integrity. A round cheese, then, should be cut into wedges, like a cake; a square cheese in slices; and a wedge to a pointed triangle—never cutting off the nose. On the soft cheeses especially the nose is the best part, and cutting it this way ensures everybody gets a bit of the best. In later years Mark and the children would tease me by cutting off the nose, and I would get so cross.

At the Charpentiers', we also had great debates at table about such things as whether to discard the rind of cheese. In those days you usually ate only the luscious middle of soft cheeses, but people were beginning to eat the bloomy white outside as well because cheese is so expensive. We always ate cheese with bread, never with salad, which is a recent fad. With pungent cheeses like Beaufort and Comté, we had butter, but if it were Brie or Brillat Savarin wanting butter was very ill-bred. Over time I learned the regional variants, that for instance in Normandy and Brittany butter on the table is the norm, but elsewhere it's only in expensive tourist restaurants that butter is served without asking. I learned from Marielle that vinaigrette dressing calls for only the very best oil and the very best vinegar, mixed proportionally three to one. Even their smallest child, Arnaud, who was four, talked about the food at the table. That was a revelation to me. I learned that in France that's what people did, unlike England, where it was regarded as rather vulgar.

Marielle and Hubert also took me on my first three-star experience in Paris, La Tour d'Argent. Founded in 1582 and mentioned by Marcel Proust in his *In Search of Lost Time,* La Tour d'Argent was another revelation. Hubert had been to school with Claude Terrail, the famous owner, and so we were given the table of honor with a view of the Seine and Notre Dame. That night I learned about Marielle's amazing palate, for La Tour d'Argent had fifteen thousand wines on a four-hundred-page list. She was able to identify a wine and its year just by taking a sip. Hubert was enormously proud of her. We began the meal with the house specialty of *écrevisses à la nage* (crayfish in broth) and for *plat principale* I naturally had to try what they said was only for connoisseurs, pressed duck in a pungent blood sauce. That was difficult to find because for those sauces you must have fresh blood and it has to be carefully cooked so it doesn't curdle; a little demitasse came on the side of enormously concentrated extract from the bones. It was absurdly delicious, and the Charpentiers, who had thought it would be too strong for my taste, were impressed.

Afterward we had vintage brandy; we did a tasting of one of the more recent ones and one of the very old. "Now you tell me which one is the old," Hubert said. I knew right away because I had been brought up on one-hundred-year-old Cognac that my father must have found on our first trip to France. After that every year he would get a half-dozen bottles of Augier Frères, the oldest vintage they had in stock. My mother drank a little glass every night until, sadly, she became allergic to it. After that night Marielle and Hubert knew that I instinctively understood good food and that I was worth teaching. What a joy.

As for my advertisement in the *Herald Tribune,* I received five replies. One was from an American women's group in Fontainebleau who met in Paris and were seeking someone to teach them to cook. Another was from an American women's group in Paris; there was a British embassy councilor who requested help for cocktail parties and one from a gentleman at the swank Georges V Hotel who wanted me to cook an intimate dinner for two. Then there was a letter headed and embossed, written in ungrammatical French and in a messy scrawl: "I have Mexican cooks who know American cooking, and I need them to learn some French cooking as I am going to be doing a great deal of entertaining. I would like to meet you." The return address was Château de Versailles.

I thought it was a hoax to receive a letter from the Château de Versailles, abandoned as a royal residence after the French Revolution. But nothing ventured, nothing won. I replied, and to my surprise the letter turned out to be legitimate. Its author, Florence Van der Kemp, was an American socialite who had recently married Gerald Van der Kemp, the man credited with rescuing the *Mona Lisa* from the Nazis, who had become head curator dedicated to the restoration of Versailles. I drove the two-door MG coupe my parents had bought me for my twenty-first birthday thirty minutes west to the Château. As I slowly drove up the great avenue toward the palace straight ahead with those grandiose gates, I thought, This can't be me making a private visit to the most famous palace in the world. But I was expected and waved through by the guard on duty. I drove in and parked, as instructed, in front of the left-hand Aile Colbert, named for Louis XIV's minister of finance. I rang, the tall main door was flung open, and I was ushered inside.

Florence Van der Kemp was forty to my twenty-five, an outspoken, go-getting, wealthy American, tall and plain, with freckles and a lot of grande dame about her. She was my first encounter with American high society and she was quick to make clear that she had excellent connections. In Washington, D.C., as a young woman she had been the social columnist on *The Washington Star*, and with her first husband, who owned the best independent bookstore in Georgetown, she had a daughter who was nearly my age. Florence had divorced him to marry a German playboy, who took her to Mexico, where she had two more children. Florence had a nice figure and a great sense of style and was almost always dressed in Dior.

I realized as she explained their situation that her French was fluent, but she had a terrible accent. She and her husband—they had just recently married—would be doing a great deal of entertaining as they raised money for the restoration. Florence needed someone to teach French cooking to her cook, Bernadina, who had cooked for Wells Fargo but spoke no English. She introduced me to Bernadina and to the nanny, the daughter of a Mexican general, and to the lady's maid called Ophelia. I also met the chauffeur and a housemaid and I was glad Florence had suggested I pick up a Spanish dictionary, as they all were Mexican. Later I would learn that she had originally come to crack the Paris scene with a woman called Evie Tutino Larson of one of the wealthiest families of South America. I suspect Florence had paid Evie a nice fat sum to take her around to all the smart parties and eventually she happened upon Gerald Van der Kemp, a divorcé on the Paris social scene. People said Gerald had decided it was time he capitalize on his charms and marry money. Their union seemed one of those classic French marriages of convenience and was outstandingly successful.

They became a great celebrity couple, dedicated to returning Versailles after years of neglect to the way it had looked in the seventeenth and eighteenth centuries. President Charles de Gaulle and his culture minister, André Malraux, had encouraged the Van der Kemps to undertake the restoration. Gerald did an extraordinary job, scouring the world for treasures that had gone missing and assembling carvers and plasterers and gilders and silversmiths and seamstresses to revitalize the lost splendor. Above all Florence raised the money, setting up the Versailles Foundation in New York City, fund-raising that brought out the best of many American millionaires. Naturally they needed someone to supervise the kitchen. They wanted to be the couple who gave the most successful parties, the couple no one could give a party without inviting. Thankfully, my skills fitted their needs.

While I continued to study at the Cordon Bleu, I stayed with the Charpentiers and three times a week drove out to Versailles to give Bernadina cooking lessons. I quickly picked up kitchen Spanish. It was understood that after I received my Grand Diplôme I would move to Versailles. So that winter I studied and learned from Marielle. I also goggled at Hubert's Ferrari that he drove at huge speeds along the autoroute. During the Easter holiday of 1964 I drove with the family in their outsized Bentley to their seaside house in Deauville. We stayed, along with forty-eight others, many of them children, in a very large villa and ate pristine local fish. Marielle supervised all the cooking and I recall going with her to buy Pont l'Evêque cheeses, six of them, each one slightly different. Back at the house we had an aperitif. A white-haired gentleman, a member of the family, peeled tiny gray shrimps and set them on a slice of buttered country bread for me to sample.

That was also the spring when Mark Cherniavsky appeared in my life for the first time. Mark and I had a mutual friend in London, Caroline Hanson, whom I had known at Cambridge. When Caroline learned Mark would be living in Paris for a time, she suggested he call on me. And so one day he telephoned and invited me out for dinner. He came to pick me up in a nice little green Mini, very trendy right then. When I first saw him at the door I thought he looked rather English, dressed as he was in a suit and tie. He had come from work and in those days one dressed up in the evening, so I wore one of my better dresses. He took me to a one-star restaurant in Montmartre, near the Sacré Coeur, a nice, authentic bistro, and I was impressed by this. Most Brits I knew thought food was a secondary subject, but Mark's parents had moved to France in the 1940s and Mark had been to a fair number of good restaurants. He knew the gulf between English cooking of the time and the French way with food.

Also, it was a revelation to me that there were men who valued intelligence in a woman. I didn't think of Mark as someone I would fall in love with—he was modest, outgoing, and affectionate, totally different from Brian, who tended to take the lead, like me. But I enjoyed the evening, and in hindsight I see how good it turned out to be to have a partner who is as imaginative and intellectual as Mark. That first night I could see he knew a great deal about literature and music and travel and books, and from the start he was wonderful to talk to, full of stories of his travels, like the one he told of being in Istanbul and seeing Sean Connery filming one of the James Bond movies. I was enormously impressed and amused because I was then a great fan of Ian Fleming's books. But Mark had a girlfriend, and that night we simply enjoyed a lovely, undemanding dinner.

Mark entertained me with stories of his family's fascinating history. He was the only one of his parents' five sons to be born in England in the 1930s, and when Mark was just three his mother and three of the boys sailed from England on one of the last ships out during World War II. They spent the War years in Vancouver, where his mother's family lived. Mark's father, Mischel Cherniavsky, was from Russia, a cellist and the youngest of a trio of musicians. As child prodigies, Mischel and two of his brothers had spent their lives trotting the globe. During the War this did not differ—Mischel played his cello for the troops while Mary and the boys stayed in Vancouver. After the War, Mark's parents moved back to London to their home, one of those lovely Nash houses opposite the zoo.

They sent Mark to prep school at St. George's, the choir school for the Royal Chapel in Windsor Castle, and moved to Guernsey, then the back of beyond that had been occupied by the Germans during the War. Mark was not qualified to sing in the choir, but he was a round-faced, blond child, just right for carrying the cross in the Chapel on Sundays. We talked about shared moments of misery, but on the whole, unlike me, Mark had enjoyed boarding school. I quickly understood that Mark was more worldly than I. After attending Oxford and living briefly in London, he moved to Istanbul as a researcher for the Economist Intelligence Unit. He told me stories of Turkey and the three-month journey he and a friend had taken by rail and bus through Egypt, Persia (now Iran), and Pakistan. In Afghanistan the bus broke down and for three days in the middle of nowhere they were forced to live on dry bread and cans of baby food.

Now the move to Paris and a job with a Norwegian research institute had been easy and after a short time he knew the city well. He was living in a studio on the Left Bank in the Latin Quarter, on Rue de Lanneau, in one of those ancient medieval buildings. Of course I didn't know it that night, but I would come to understand that few people settle into a new place with more ease than does Mark. We both spoke French quite fluently though Mark's written language was much better than mine. We talked about what it was like to settle into a new city, and after dinner we made plans to see each other again.

Within weeks Mark had me visiting museums and monuments and

spending time with his friends, including David Calleo, an American and now professor of European studies at the School of Advanced International Studies in Washington, D.C.—David became a good friend and later sponsored me as an American citizen. Neither Mark nor I had much money to spend on eating out, so on the whole we didn't go to fancy places. In one inexpensive neighborhood restaurant in a splendid stone-vaulted cellar we loved the specialty—the melted cheese called raclette, served over little boiled potatoes. The chef must have been from the French Alps, because once or twice he had *blanquette de veau aux morilles* on the menu, an expensive dish unless he had a secret source for the wild mushrooms.

BLANQUETTE OF VEAL WITH MORELS

A good blanquette is a powerhouse of pure veal flavor, using veal breast with the bones for taste and connective tissue for richness, plus a bit of shoulder for lean meat; get your butcher to cut the rib bones in 3-inch lengths. Above all, nothing should brown during cooking to spoil the blanquette's whiteness and contrast with the blackness of the morel mushrooms (some varieties can be disappointingly beige). Dried porcini can be substituted for dried morels, though there, too, the color contrast is lost. Boiled rice, snowy white, is the traditional accompaniment.

Serve 6 to 8

3 pounds/about 1.4 kg veal breast, including bones, cut in
    3-inch/7.5-cm lengths
1½ pounds /675 g boneless veal shoulder, cut in chunks
2 quarts/2 liters water, plus more if needed
1 onion, halved
1 carrot
2–3 garlic cloves
Bouquet garni of parsley stems, 2 bay leaves, and 2–3 stems thyme
Salt and pepper
½ pound/225 g fresh morels or 1 ounce/30 g dried morels
20–24 baby pearl onions
6 tablespoons/90 g butter
6 tablespoons/45 g flour
¾ cup/175 ml crème fraîche

Trim the veal of any tough tendons and blueish silverskin and most, but not all, of the fat. Put it in a large pot with enough water to cover. Bring slowly to a boil, taking about 15 minutes and skimming often. Add the onion, carrot, garlic, bouquet garni, salt, and pepper. Cover and simmer over a low heat, skimming occasionally, until the veal is almost tender when poked with a two-pronged fork, about 1½ hours.

Meanwhile, if using fresh morels, since they tend to be gritty, brush them thoroughly, splitting the stems, then rinse them in cold water and drain without soaking them. If using dried morels, soak them in warm water to cover for about 20 minutes, then lift them out, reserving the soaking water. Rinse them also in cold water to remove grit. Pour boiling water over the baby onions, let soak 5 minutes, then drain and peel them, trimming the root.

When the veal is nearly tender, add the morels and onions and strain in water from dried morels. Continue simmering 15 to 30 minutes, until the meat, onions, and morels are very tender; the meat should be shrinking from the rib bones. Transfer the meat and vegetables to a bowl and discard the large onion, carrot, and garlic. Cover and keep the meat, morels, and baby onions warm. Strain the cooking liquid.

To make the sauce: Boil the cooking liquid until reduced to 1 quart/1 liter. This may take up to 20 minutes. Do not count the large amount of fat that rises to the surface, but skim with a spoon and discard it. To make kneaded butter, crush the butter on a plate with a fork and work in the flour to form a soft paste. Whisk the paste into the simmering liquid a piece or two at a time—the butter will melt so the flour cooks and thickens the sauce. Add enough paste to thicken the sauce so it coats the back of a spoon; you may not need all of the paste. Whisk in the crème fraîche, bring the sauce back to a boil, and simmer for 1 minute. Taste and adjust the seasoning.

To finish: Stir the veal, onions, and morels into the sauce and check the seasoning once more. Blanquette can be kept in the refrigerator a day or two, and it freezes well. Serve it on a bed of boiled white rice—no decoration is needed.

Mark wasn't exactly a dapper dresser, though he always wore tailored clothes and English shoes. He was famous for extraordinary color combinations like green socks with a pink shirt and a blue sweater. Each item was nice, but when they were put together sometimes his appearance was quite bizarre. After we married, when he was dressing, I would sometimes say, "Darling, do you really want to wear that tie with that shirt?" but he always said, "Will you stop criticizing!" Early on I gave up making suggestions.

In those days most of all we simply enjoyed each other's company, and Mark often drove out to visit me at Versailles, where I moved after I received my Grand Diplôme at the Cordon Bleu. I lived in a tiny maid's room in the servants' quarters in the attic up seventy-two steps from the garage. The bathroom was along the hall for all the servants and me. At Versailles I was responsible for directing the large, well-equipped kitchen with its industrial scale but very old-fashioned ovens (no mystery to me after the Cordon Bleu), plenty of refrigeration, and huge great wooden tables.

Florence's parties were like ballets, and everyone had their part in the theatrical production. Bernadina was experienced in preparing dinner for up to thirty seated guests, with three helpers and four maître d'hôtels in their white ties, tails, and gloves. At any seated formal function you can assume there are the same number of people in the back as there are out front, since there is so much work in the kitchen—vegetable prep, trimming and storage and washing things and God help you before you even start to cook. I was the conductor, linking Madame Van der Kemp, the maître d's, and Bernadina in three different languages—English, French, and Spanish. My job was to work out and time the whole thing so that everything went out to the dining room at the peak moment when it was wanted.

It was I who had found Serge, the primary maître d'hôtel, at an embassy party I had catered. He was young and good-looking, very flexible, and very good. Florence knew all about how to give an elegant party, though she didn't know the first thing about either how to cook or present French food or the French protocol for setting and serving at table. She would have been the first to admit that. But she was not your usual hostess, and it wasn't everybody who could deal with her outspoken nature. Serge was perfect. We spoke French with each other, and for each meal he supervised the dining room just as I supervised the kitchen.

Occasionally we did smaller lunch parties. Although I've forgotten many of the Escoffier rules since then, I do know certain dishes were dinner dishes and others were for lunch. The lunch table would be set with embroidered place mats while at dinner huge white damask tablecloths were de rigueur. Soup was served in the evenings only; hors d'oeuvre meant lunch. The big formal platters would be for dinner, but *boeuf à la mode* must have been a lunch dish, because it was cold. For dinner you were permitted cold desserts—fancy gâteaux, towering soufflés, and mousses set with gelatin—but never a cold main dish in the evening. And everything was plattered. Plating came in the 1970s, but back then it was regarded as a cop-out because any fool can place a plate and take it away. Serving a platter is far more of a challenge for the chef, tricky and creative, because the visual aspect has to work and at the same time the food must be kept at the right temperature. It is also a challenge for the server to insert a large platter of hot food (always to the left of the diner concerned) between two closely seated guests. You have to have the right number of portions, and plate presentation must hint how many slices of meat or bouquets of vegetables a guest is supposed to take.

At Château de Versailles we followed Escoffier rules to the letter. I still have the big box with recipes of the dishes I had learned to cook at the Paris Cordon Bleu, and the food we presented at Versailles—dishes like *langouste à la Mozart,* which involves mayonnaise set with aspic—were the kind of thing we were doing all the time. We never served pork—it was regarded as a cheap, unacceptable meat (though I happen to think that pork is better than inferior veal). We had the choice of veal, lamb, beef, or chicken, though at that time there really were no broiler chickens, so chicken was a luxury, and very popular—*chaud-froid de poulet,* decorated with truffle slices cut out in diamonds, hearts, spades, and clubs, was one of our signature dishes, as were *kromeskies* of chopped cooked chicken in a white sauce dipped in bread crumbs, originally a Russian dish. *Pommes dauphine* (in tribute to a royal princess married to the dauphin or heir to the French throne) consisted of equal quantities of *choux* pastry and potato purée deep-fried—so good! *Bouchées à la reine* (the queen's chicken in small puff pastries) was standard fare, as was *abricots Condé* (named after a royal prince), cold rice pudding in a mold topped with poached apricots, and charlotte russe, of course. We often served my ribboned Bavarian cream—three stripes, vanilla, chocolate, and coffee. This was a tour de force of mine. I had a special peaked mold that I liked to use so the pinnacles would be snow-colored vanilla, followed by crags of coffee and finally a foundation of chocolate.

RIBBONED BAVARIAN CREAM

A metal bowl will do very well for this cream instead of a peaked mold, though the bowl must be deep so the ribbon stripes of the creamy mixture show clearly. No decoration is needed; the shining, peaked cream, shivering slightly on the plate, is a decoration in itself. A bundt pan is an alternative to a Kugelhopf mold.

Serves 8 to 10

3 tablespoons/30 g powdered gelatin
¾ cup/175 ml water
1 tablespoon instant coffee, dissolved in 2 tablespoons hot water
2 ounces/60 g dark chocolate, chopped
1½ cups/375 ml heavy cream

For the vanilla custard
6 cups/1.5 liters milk
1 vanilla bean, split
12 egg yolks
¾ cup/150 g sugar

2½-quart/2.5-liter Kugelhopf or peaked ring mold

Before you begin, prepare a roasting pan of ice and water for chilling the custards. Rinse the mold with cold water. To soften the gelatin, pour the measured water into a bowl, sprinkle the gelatin over it, and leave until spongy, about 5 minutes.

Meanwhile, make the custard: Bring the milk to a boil with the vanilla bean. Take off the heat and leave in a warm place to infuse, 10 to 15 minutes. In a separate bowl, using a whisk, beat the egg yolks with the sugar until thick and light, 3 to 4 minutes. Stir in half the hot milk and stir this mixture back into the remaining milk. Heat the pan over medium heat, stirring with a wooden spoon until the custard thickens lightly, 2 to 3 minutes; if you draw a finger across the back of the spoon, it should leave a clear trail. Do not overcook the custard or it will curdle.

Take the pan from the heat as soon as the custard has thickened and stir in the spongy gelatin until melted by the hot custard. Strain it into a bowl—the vanilla bean can be rinsed, dried, and used again. Pour a third of the custard into a smaller bowl (preferably of metal as it will cool more quickly). Pour half the remaining custard into another bowl and stir in the dissolved coffee. Add the chopped chocolate to the remaining custard in the bowl and stir until the chocolate is melted. (If necessary reheat it over a bowl of warm water.) Let the custards cool at room temperature 10 to 15 minutes, stirring occasionally. Meanwhile whisk the cream until it holds a soft peak.

Put the bowl of vanilla custard into the pan of ice water and chill, stirring, until the custard is cool and starts to thicken slightly. At once take the bowl off the ice and fold in about a third of the whipped cream. Pour the vanilla custard into the mold, set the mold in the pan of ice water, and let cool until the custard is just set, 15 to 20 minutes. Cool the coffee custard in the same way, fold in the cream, and pour it into the mold on top of the layer of coffee custard. Repeat with the final layer of chocolate custard. Cover the mold and chill in the refrigerator at least 6 hours, or overnight.

To finish: If the mold has been chilled more than 6 hours, let it stand at room temperature for a half hour to soften slightly. Turn out the custard cream just before serving: Tip the mold slightly sideways with one hand and with the fingers of the other pull the cream away from the sides of the mold, rotating it to loosen the cream and break the air lock. Set a flat platter on top of the mold and, holding it firmly on the plate with both hands, invert the cream onto the plate. When serving the cream, cut it into slices with a knife dipped in hot water.

At Château de Versailles I was in the position of "the governess," who, when there were any important guests around, was occasionally seen but never heard. Every morning I would come into Florence's bedroom (she was a late riser; those grand parties ran long) with my little notebook, ready to hear what she needed that day. She also had me making phone calls and sending out invitations and driving her places and of course ensuring her parties were perfect. I learned much more Spanish, absorbing the contents of the Almanach de Gotha, the directory of Europe's royalty and nobility, and I quickly became familiar with the protocol. Custom required that once the dinner was over all of us in the kitchen were offered a glass of Champagne;

even in those Gaullist days, life on the wrong side of the baize door was a polyglot world of Spanish, Portuguese, and North African tongues into which I was accepted by everyone without question.

Florence had a son and daughter by her second husband. Barbara, a good-looking girl, was twelve or thirteen, and Henrik, or Henriquito as he was called, was perhaps ten. Occasionally the nanny had time off and I babysat for the children, who had learned when they were quite young to make small talk with Rockefellers and Rothschilds, the Duke and Duchess of Windsor, Pablo Picasso and General de Gaulle, friends and visitors to Versailles. Years later Florence told me that when Henriquito was seventeen one day Gerald said to her, "Ah, we've got to find a woman to show Henriquito the ropes." Gerald lined up a good friend of about forty, and Henriquito was taken in hand and taken to bed. That was life at Versailles.

When I first went to work for Florence she said, "Well, dear, I'll ask you to one or two lunches when it's nothing too formal, but you'll need to be so-cially acceptable, so I'll say I went to school with your mother." I was amused, but this infuriated my mother. She regarded Florence as an ill-bred Ameri-can, for in our home there was always a feeling that everyone should be treated equally. My parents would come out to stay in Paris sometimes. Once or twice I took them for coffee or tea with Florence. My mother, who disliked social occasions, treated Florence with distant but scrupulous politeness.

On the whole I did my job well. I had learned a bit about gadgets at the Cordon Bleu, though equipment was sparse, and I'd taken myself a dozen times to Dehillerin, the Paris equipment shop near Les Halles, the wholesale food market that in those days was in full swing in the center of the city. Marielle had been very frugal, but in contrast Florence was totally American about that sort of thing and sent me to purchase every imaginable pot, pan, and utensil. How I enjoyed finding her just the right mold for eggs in aspic (fashionable at the time) or a razor-sharp mandolin for cutting perfectly sliced vegetables.

Naturally there were mishaps sometimes. One day Florence decided to offer her guests a real American rib roast of beef. The butcher was mystified by such a crude, expensive cut, which made no demands on his skills in bon-ing and tying, but after I gave instructions two massive seven-rib roasts fi-nally arrived. I had never cooked anything larger than a fillet and decided that an hour in a hot oven would suffice—cooked at the last minute, of course, for finest flavor. My timing had left no room for error. When I opened the oven and saw the purple meat, still stone cold at its center, I was struck with terror. Forty guests awaited their main course beyond that paneled door emblazoned with the arms of Colbert, and my job was on the line. Bernadina saved the day and my reputation by slicing the raw meat, boosting the oven heat, setting the meat on trays, and baking it. Not even the waiters were ever the wiser.

On another occasion Florence was giving a multi-national ladies' luncheon and the guest of honor was Comtesse Mapie de Toulouse-Lautrec, grande dame and directrice of Maxim's finishing school, famous for her exuberant hats. She had just published her cookbook, and people queued up to devour the Comtesse's recipes, which were illustrated with well-known paintings by Henri de Toulouse-Lautrec, her nephew by marriage. Florence had asked me to prepare something really grand, so I decided on *boeuf à la mode en gelée,* a recipe we had learned at the Cordon Bleu. The beef is cooked in lots of liquid with vegetables, and there's this wonderful, rich juice that you clarify; then you slice the beef that is marbled with fat, cook lots more baby vegetables, and layer the whole lot. The dish can be done either in a mold or coated with aspic on a platter, and either way it's a big deal and even for a professional a bit of a challenge. The real thing is served on a huge silver platter with layers of aspic extracted from bones—really good consommé is made only from bones, and Marielle had always been absolutely insistent upon it. At the Cordon Bleu the chef had added quantities of commercial gelatin. That day at Versailles I decided to play it safe and add a bit of gelatin; I feared that otherwise in the warmth of the dining room the dish might develop cracks and gently collapse. As it went out to the table in all its glory, I felt pleased.

It was Serge who later told me that when the dish was served Mapie de Toulouse-Lautrec raised her lorgnette and inspected it. "*Oui, c'est bien jolie. . . .* Pretty . . . ," she said, "but I suspect the presence of artificial gelatin." That was her judgment from-on-high, and she was dead right. I felt bad about it, but the lesson I learned did not change my conviction of better safe than sorry, and I still add a sheet or two of gelatin (the French stuff comes in sheets) to my aspic as well as using lots of calfs' or pigs' feet for their natural gelatin.

Very rarely was I asked to sit down at Florence's table. One occasion was Thanksgiving, to which she asked a multi-national crowd for whom she was determined to offer the full-on American experience. I had been in on the preparations that were supervised by Bernadina. First off the turkeys had caused trouble. The French poulterer was puzzled by his best customer not only demanding the birds in November, a month before the French holidays, but also wanting them to be outsized and thus despised by any knowledgeable

Frenchman. After another little hurdle, I was sent on the morning of the feast to collect a hundred shucked oysters for the stuffing. These, too, appalled the fish man—how could a connoisseur not require them served in splendor on the half shell? Most ominous of all, I had collected from Fauchon, the top grocery on the Place de la Madeleine, a beverage that was new to me—something called sparkling Burgundy, from America.

At the table, we were surrounded by little dishes, spiced pecans, smoked almonds, and raisins to nibble before the food was even served, but no bread, unthinkable in France. Borscht soup was the first course, not my favorite. Then came the heralded main-course turkeys, carved and reshaped on the bone for easy serving, surrounded by a pile of oyster stuffing, another first for me and, it emerged, for several other guests as well. Serving was family-style. As laden plates were set in front of us, bowls of red cabbage with apples, mashed potatoes, and a curious white-topped gratin, which turned out to be mashed pumpkin with marshmallow topping, were passed around. Marshmallows? With turkey? How very strange. The gravy was too thick for French taste but looked savory. It was the strong whiff of stewed oysters that took me aback.

We all tucked into the turkey. The vegetables were acceptable, but the stuffing stopped us in our tracks. Florence and Bernadina had not realized how strongly French oysters taste of the sea, quite unlike fatty, plump American oysters. We pushed the mixture around our plates, trying not to contaminate the turkey. When, thankfully, the smelly plates were removed, we turned with relief to the predictable run of pies—mincemeat, apple, pumpkin, sweet potato, and pecan. The sweet sparkling wine tasting like Cold Duck was no help in clearing the palate. After three hours at table, we emerged into the dusk and I climbed gratefully into my chilly car. I was overwhelmed—so many strange combinations and so much sugar: sugar, sugar everywhere. Florence was so proud of her Thanksgiving initiative, but for me, it was the worst meal so far I'd had a hand in helping to prepare. I did pick out one dish in the chorus of desserts that has survived in my memory and on my table—pecan pie. Mark and I have served it at almost every Christmas dinner since we married.

Gerald was a big, attractive guy, and occasionally in the mornings, when Florence was away, I would see him because I had to get up early to take the children to school. Gerald would be sitting at breakfast wearing his hairnet. Once Florence departed for two weeks for a facial peel and I was left behind. One morning I joined Gerald at breakfast with my wet hair in curlers. When Florence returned she told me, "I have to be totally straightforward with you. When I'm away someone always gets on Gerald's wick and irritates him, and this time it was you." I told her I was sorry. Privately I realized that the problem was that I probably wasn't deferential enough to Gerald's dignity, but Florence brushed the curler incident aside, saying, "Oh well, nothing to be done about it. Let's move on." And so we did. One of the many good lessons I learned from her.

But there was something important Gerald said to me one day that has stuck all these years, something that leads me to believe that it was at Versailles that my dreams truly began to blossom. Until I attended the Cordon Bleu, no one outside the family had ever thought of me as anything out of the ordinary. At school I was bad at sports, did not try to make friends, was a bit of an outsider, and never made it to prefect. Even at Cambridge I pursued my own way and acting was my only outlet in a rather solitary life. On vacation I was isolated in Yorkshire. At the Cordon Bleu outsiders began to see that I had potential beyond the average middle-class, well-educated young woman, but even then I wasn't sure of my potential. But one day Gerald Van der Kemp said, "*Je suis convaincu que vous avez un bel avenir* [I am convinced you have a bright future]." Although at the time it didn't seem important, I still remember.

Florence and I got on well together, though some things about me were trials to her. One of these was my erratic dress sense. One day as I was driving her briskly down the Champs-Élysées, she looked over at the frilly shirt I was wearing that wasn't really my style. After she had looked sideways at it for a while, she sighed and said, "Let's face it, dear; we are none of us as young as we were." Another day, just before I was leaving, Florence decided she wanted to take me to Maxim's for lunch and decided to bring Bernadina. Florence dressed Bernadina in her own second-best mink coat, and we went off in the chauffeur-driven car. At lunch Florence introduced Bernadina as the daughter of a general. Apart from the delicious food, it was an excellent lesson in uniting disparate tablemates with polite conversation. I loved being at Versailles and wasn't overwhelmed, perhaps because I was always so busy.

On occasion I did have free time. Once when Florence was away, I was staying downstairs in her bed because she wanted me near the children. Mark came to visit me, and we made love for the first time in this great, huge baldachin bed done up to the nines. Years later, when that bed appeared in *Vogue* magazine, I showed the picture to our then-grown children and told them the story. "Mum," they said, seemingly mortified, "how can you tell us that?"

Ah, but that was just one of the earliest of so many wonderful times I spent with the man I was just beginning to imagine I might love.

Holding hands after our runaway wedding

Chapter Six

....

THE CALL TO PRAYER

When love and skill work together expect a masterpiece.
—John Ruskin

I had spent New Year's Day of 1963 crossing the English Channel. The following year, 1964, just before my twenty-sixth birthday and after a Christmastime visit to my parents, I was traveling with Mark on the Mediterranean, fourth class on a Turkish cargo boat to Oran, Algeria. On that trip for once in my life I was unable to think about food. Mark and I drove my car through the snowy Paris streets and out onto the autoroute, down to Marseilles. It was Mark who insisted we travel the cheapest way since neither of us was earning a lot of money. "I've been on a Turkish boat to Israel; this Algerian ferry will be fine," he promised. "We'll save money in fourth class." He went on about just how fine it would be.

Before we boarded, two or three Algerians asked me to fill in their papers, and when they did I realized they couldn't read or write. On board ship came another realization: I was the only woman in fourth class. But that didn't matter—I was excited by the adventure. I stayed on deck as we pulled out of the harbor. I love that sensation of leaving land behind, and I was moved by the sight of the statue of Notre-Dame de la Garde, patron of sailors, overlooking the port of Marseilles.

But even while we still were in harbor the sea began to feel choppy. Mark moved downstairs to the cabin, and as soon as we were out at sea I joined him. He was feeling uneasy and had lain down in the lower bunk, so I took the upper. For the next thirty-six hours—we were twelve hours late reaching Oran—that ship gyrated. I could more or less deal with the up and down, but when we began to corkscrew it was torture. I lay as still as I could on my bunk and watched the cockroaches running to and fro above my head. I couldn't have cared less. At one stage the sea became a little calmer, and I scrambled down to take a pee. Poor Mark, he was too ill even to lift his head. Taking care not to disturb him, I walked outside, but when I saw the sordid trash cans where the rest of the passengers were getting sick I quickly returned and peed in the cabin washbasin.

When we did finally touch shore, Mark quickly recovered his land legs and we climbed into our car and drove off. Mark is a tremendous traveler, the kind who is always ready to explore and always able to find a good hotel, even in the middle of nowhere. That night we stopped in Tlemcen. He had read about this crossroads between the Mediterranean coast and the Sahara that had flourished as the capital of a Muslim Berber dynasty in the thirteenth to fifteenth centuries and still retained the atmosphere of medieval Muslim life. Mark wanted to see a mosque noted in the old travel books. Tlemcen felt like a long-lost world, and of course we had the usual trouble about a woman going into a Muslim place of prayer. In his efficient way, Mark found a nice, deserted hotel for us. Exhausted from our journey, we lay down and fell dead asleep. Only a few hours later, at 5:00 a.m., we were awakened by the sound of the muezzin echoing through those empty streets. As the sun rose, Mark and I made love. Forever after that, we called our lovemaking The Call to Prayer.

The next day we drove the empty double carriageways where once again Mark proved his comprehension of the Muslim world, which had begun in Turkey. "The results of the Algerian War," he explained as we drove past empty shops with windows still full of displays but thick with dust and spiders. He navigated the traffic islands, installed under French colonial rule to guide the now-non-existent cars. Soon we decided against going to Algiers and instead to drive on to Morocco. Even at the border we could see the road in front of us was more prosperous. Once we had crossed, right away everything looked up, including the cooking. We stopped for a lunch of *mezze* of hummus, eggplant caviar, tabbouleh with black olives, and *harissa*, the fiery red chili sauce that I have never been able to stomach. The meal came with lots of spongy Moroccan bread and was washed down with orange juice—oranges are in season in January. Then we traveled out into the desert and drove south for what seemed forever under a gray, snow-laden sky. It was bitter cold. Somewhere we stopped for my first ever glass of vigorous wild-mint tea.

Marrakech was the first Arab city I'd ever visited, and I found it mysterious, igniting my imagination. In one of the local restaurants we sat on cushions and ate another first, that remarkable pigeon dish *pastilla*, with its leafy pastry sprinkled with cinnamon sugar, washing everything down with more delicious mint tea. Afterward we explored the souk and bought small handicrafts—carved boxes and pretty bowls patterned in arabesque patterns—plus a handsome desk set in red Moroccan leather for my birthday later in the month. Later bringing home such souvenirs became a tradition. I know it's a tacky habit, but I can look around any room in our house and recall happy memories of when and where we bought the globe-shaped wooden box where we keep the keys (Marrakech), and the marbleized paper penholder (Venice), and the carpet (Delhi).

We couldn't afford to stay in the swank hotel La Mamounia, built in 1922 on the site of a garden given to Prince Moulay Mamoun by his father as a wedding gift, but Mark explained one of his travel rules: "Always go for a drink at the best hotel." I had to agree with him as we sat and enjoyed the local brandy sparked with lemon juice beside Mamounia's lovely Arab-style citrus garden, a place Winston Churchill, who was a frequent guest, called the most lovely spot in the world. In Marrakech Mark and I began what would become another naïve custom—we collected the Mamounia hotel labels and stuck them on our bags to show where we had been. At one time this was quite a cult, but then the airplane made travel all too easy. Marrakech with its timelessness and strong sense of identity was beautiful, and best of all, in Morocco we found the spirit of France, an appreciation of artisan workmanship, particularly carpets, and of course of good food. Even simple restaurants cooked and seasoned well, and at mealtimes we tried half a dozen tagines, the conical earthenware containers in which all manner of ingredients would bake together over a primitive charcoal stove. Nearly everyone spoke French, so we communicated easily.

Mark and I were having a wonderful time. We already shared the same taste in architecture, in theater, in music, in food, and, most important, we began to discover we often had the same opinions about other people. But even as I enjoyed our journey, I tried not to think too much about Mark. He liked the company of women and was very sympathetic to them, and he attracted a lot of girlfriends. Conversation with Mark was never anything like "what a pretty dress you have on today." Rather, he was always interested in what women had to say. He was opening up to me not only a new geographic world but also a totally different intellectual world. But he told me he would never marry me. He felt that our backgrounds were far too different.

By then I was in love with him and kept hoping he would change his mind. But I also knew I wouldn't let my life revolve around a man who wasn't certain about me. Then one night in a hotel on our way to Fez, I had a dream. In the dream I was hanging from a rope on a ship, swinging to and fro until at last I couldn't hang on any longer and I fell into the water. To my amazement, the water was much warmer than I had thought it would be. When I woke I realized the dream meant that I was sure I wanted to marry him. I certainly didn't tell Mark because I also knew if I had he would have been alarmed.

When we returned we drove north through the desert in the rain on that straight road that runs parallel to the railroad, the two going on and on, and we watched the red land of Marrakech and southern Morocco turning to the white-washed walls of the Mediterranean. We crossed the Strait of Gibraltar on the ferry to Algeciras, in Spain, and took a side trip to Jerez, where we picked up some bottles of bone-dry sherry. In Andalusia, we stopped in those cities that retained the Arab influence—Seville and Córdoba, Granada. In Seville I was enchanted to find the streets of the old town lined with orange trees in full fruit—the ancient, bitter variety that's the secret of the best English orange marmalade. The cathedral in Córdoba is unforgettable for its 856 columns of jasper, onyx, marble, and granite that stretch into the distance like a forest of trees and for the alternating red and white voussoirs of the arches inspired by the Dome of the Rock.

From Valencia we still had a long drive ahead of us to reach Paris in time for Mark's job interview with the World Bank in three days' time. That night he got sick with flu, but the World Bank job was one he was hoping to get. The next day he could barely lift his head from the pillow, and together we made a decision. I would leave him to fly back to Paris—he really was too ill to drive—and I would drive home alone. I didn't think more than once about it, though on that trip I did get lost in Barcelona and the policeman who offered help was stunned to see a girl alone in a foreign car. Luckily, by then my Spanish was serviceable. It's only in looking back that I see how independent I was for those times.

In those days my view of myself and of my future was rapidly changing. I had begun to find myself when I first got to France. I had never felt more at ease than in this country where women with a trained intellect were treated with far more respect than I'd grown accustomed to in England. In France women were doing things like running restaurants. And ambition was encouraged. I was also beginning to develop an entirely different notion of who I could be. On that three-day drive back to Paris, although I was preparing to move on, I had a very clear sense that I was on the right path.

I had applied the previous year for a green card to work in the United States, and once we returned to Paris I began to make serious plans to go to New York. Florence had offered me, free of charge, the maid's quarters in her daughter Roberta's apartment in Manhattan on East Seventy-fifth Street, near Lexington Avenue, and Florence gave me the names of some contacts for work. It had been obvious for a while that my job at Versailles was coming to an end—I had that sense that you don't want to be someone's personal assistant for more than a year, and I had grown tired of whisking béchamel sauce even for Princess Grace of Monaco and the Duke and Duchess of Windsor. (Another lesson I had learned: The Monacos and the Windsors could not be invited to the same party.) True, the prestige was abundant, but the financial rewards were thin. There was also the fact that the World Bank had offered Mark a job and in June he would be moving to Washington, D.C. A lot of our generation at Cambridge and Oxford had gone to visit the States when they graduated. Of course my parents didn't really want me to leave Europe, but it was clear to me that it was time.

Just before my departure for New York, I was all packed up and Mark and I were getting ready to go out for a last good meal. I put on a coat I hadn't worn for a while and in the pocket found some francs, just enough for a dinner at La Tour d'Argent. We had both, from the start, always enjoyed fine dining together, and this meal was as wonderful as any I remember. King Hussein of Jordan was there, but even better, I was with the man I loved.

In April Mark drove me to Le Havre, where I was to board the liner *Le France*. As usual I had my great big black trunk with my initials, EAW, that Daddy and I had stenciled in white on top—the same trunk I had traveled with since I was a little girl going off to boarding school. On the way we stopped at Mark's parents' place near Dieppe in Normandy. By that time Mischel and Mary lived in a picture-postcard thatched house, Ferme des Moines (the monk's house), so garlanded with flowers that it did actually feature on one of the standard black-and-white postcards for sale in the area. It had been built in the sixteenth century at the same time as the fine parish church just opposite.

Mischel and Mary had first come from England in 1951. For many years they lived in Vence on the Riviera, in a villa terraced with citrus trees, with the Mediterranean visible on the horizon. Notables like conductor Sir Thomas Beecham and stage designer Gordon Craig were frequent family visitors, and Marc Chagall was a neighbor and friend. Mark thought that his parents' decision to swap the Riviera for a home in Normandy had been a mistake, but they didn't seem to mind their new, less lively lifestyle. Some days Mischel would go to the casino in Dieppe and gamble away what was left of his pocket money. His cello stayed in the barn. As I learned on that visit, he had not played since the early 1950s—indeed, he seemed to have abandoned the world of music he had entered at the age of seven. Although I got to know them a little better on that visit, neither of the Cherniavskys showed much interest in me. They were a generation older than my own parents, and having had five sons, I supposed they had seen too many girls pass through the house to be curious.

Mark's parents were blessed with a real gem of a housekeeper. Françoise lived in the village and had started work for them when she was only twelve; she stayed with them until their deaths. Although Mark's mother was not interested in food—she ate plain English stuff, roast meats, slightly overcooked vegetables, poached fruit—Françoise was a born cook. She knew instinctively how to season a dish and when it was done just right, and her cooking was always an inspiration. After Mary died, I cooked once or twice in her kitchen and was amazed at how little equipment Françoise had had to turn out her superb *coquilles St. Jacques,* or golden, butter-roast chicken.

Françoise liked to roast her chicken with baby onions, chunks of potato, and lardons of bacon in the roasting pan for a one-pot meal. I'm sure she never realized that the same combination, with a sausage meat stuffing, adds up to a classic from Escoffier. She would have laughed to think she was cooking like the most famous chef in the world!

POT ROAST CHICKEN WITH POTATOES, BACON, AND ONIONS

The French, Françoise included, call this recipe Poulet Grand-mère, perfect name for a quintessentially homey dish.

Serves 4 to 6

10–12 baby pearl onions
3 large russet potatoes (about 2 pound/900 g)
One 4–5 pound/about 2.25 kg chicken
2 tablespoons/30 g butter
3–4 thick slices of bacon, diced

For the stuffing
3 slices whole-wheat bread
1 tablespoon butter
½ medium onion, finely chopped
2–3 breakfast link sausages (about 6 ounces/170 g)
2 chicken livers, chopped
1 tablespoon chopped fresh parsley
Salt and pepper

String for trussing; flameproof casserole

For the stuffing: Dice the bread slices and freeze them until firm. Heat the butter in a frying pan and sauté the onion until lightly browned. Skin the sausages, pull apart the ground meat, and add it to the onion with the chopped chicken livers. Sauté the stuffing, stirring, until the sausage meat and livers are brown, 8 to 10 minutes. Stir in the parsley with a little salt and pepper and let cool. Work the firm bread in the food processor to form crumbs. Stir the crumbs into the stuffing, taste, adjust the seasoning, and let it cool.

Heat the oven to 350°F/180°C. Pour boiling water over the baby onions, let soak 5 minutes, then drain and peel them, trimming the root. Peel the potatoes and cut them in ¾-inch/2-cm cubes. When the stuffing is cool, spoon it into the chicken and tie the bird with string.

Melt the butter in the casserole, add the bacon and onions, and brown them, stirring often, 5 to 7 minutes. Lift them out with a draining spoon, add the potato cubes, and brown them also, 5 to 7 minutes longer. They will absorb most of the fat. Add them to the bacon and onions. Put the chicken in the pot and brown it thoroughly on all sides, taking 10 to 15 minutes. Cover the casserole, transfer it to the oven, and cook for an hour.

Add the bacon, onions, and potato to the pot, lifting the chicken so they fall to the bottom. Cover and continue cooking until the vegetables are very hot and the chicken is tender, 15 to 25 minutes longer. The juices should run clear, not pink, when you prick the thigh with a fork.

To serve the chicken, transfer it to a platter and discard the string. Discard any excess fat from the pan and spoon the vegetables and bacon around the bird. Carve the chicken at the table, scooping out the stuffing.

My five-day trip across the Atlantic on my way to New York was uneventful. I was of course sad to have said good-bye to Mark, but he would soon be moving to Washington, D.C., for a job at the World Bank and we planned to see each other in the States. And then, on April 14, 1965, I walked up on deck at dawn to see Manhattan before me, the mist lifting off the water, the sun rising. I was excited to step foot on land and was up on deck again to watch our arrival into port. After we had docked, I walked down the gangplank to queue up to go through Immigration. There I was amazed to see two people waiting to greet me where I had expected none. Charles was there, and to my complete surprise so was another character from my days at the Cordon Bleu in Paris, Clay Johnson, a kind young man with a pronounced limp from what I suspect was polio. He was from New York and worked as a personal assistant to Gian Carlo Menotti, the famous composer who had just a few years earlier founded the Spoleto Festival.

When I saw both Charles and Clay awaiting me, I felt almost immediately at home in this strange new place. Charles, the bodybuilder, had come all the

way from Los Angeles, a gesture of immense kindness. He seemed a bit upset that Clay was there to meet me, too, and over the next few days it became
clear that Charles and I had grown apart. Still, it was lovely for me to feel so
welcomed. I enjoyed America from the moment I arrived. I fitted into the
pace of life, and I loved the fact that in New York I was taken for what I was,
not for where I came from or who I knew. Right away I knew this was a place
that would come to feel like home—or at least one of my homes—if only I
could manage to support myself financially.

I had brought just five hundred pounds, since British exchange controls
decreed you could take no more than that, and when it was gone my time in
the States would be over. So I had to be very careful. I had a place to live, but
I had no job, nothing beyond a few phone numbers Florence had given me.
That very day I moved into a tiny maid's room in Roberta's basement where
she was kind enough to let me use the upstairs bath. But the poor girl was
always trying to get thinner—she didn't have my love of good food. In the
first months there was one nasty incident when Roberta mislaid some valuable jewelry and naturally suspicion fell on me, the unknown stranger. A few
days were tense, then eventually she found her misplaced treasures. When
the heat came very quickly that spring, the maid's room was brutally stifling,
and thankfully Roberta invited me to live in the apartment.

As I had in Paris, I put an advertisement in the *New York Herald Tribune*
offering my cooking services, and very quickly one or two of Mark's friends
offered to hire me for little parties they were giving. One of these friends was
John Guinness, who was attached to the United Nations and liked to explain
that he was from the banking Guinnesses, not the ones who brewed beer.
John would eventually wind up as energy tsar to the British government as
well as an advisor to the Queen on her royal portrait collection. John and I
were contemporaries at Cambridge and in New York. I would cook for him
when he had a few friends round to dinner, but he never asked for anything
too grand. For those small parties I did dishes like *canard à l'orange* and *soufflé aux framboises*. The concept of a grand party dish was far more elaborate
then. One of my specialties was a galette of hazelnut pastry filled with strawberries and whipped cream in three layers. There was no way I could load two
of them onto a bus, so I walked down Madison Avenue with the two galettes
dangling one from each hand like the buckets of a milkmaid. It was warm, so
I had to walk very fast.

HAZELNUT AND STRAWBERRY GALETTE

The cookie-like dough of this galette is baked in three rounds and sand-wiched with strawberries and whipped cream. The top round, cut in wedges, is arranged like a pinwheel on the whipped cream. If you can find peeled hazelnuts, snap them up, as the skins are the devil to peel!

Serves 8

1 pound/450g strawberries

For the hazelnut pastry
2 cups/250g hazelnuts
1⅔ cups/200g flour
8 tablespoons/120g unsalted butter
⅔ cup/140g sugar
1 egg yolk
½ teaspoon salt
2 tablespoons/30ml water, plus more if needed

For the Chantilly cream
1½ cups/375ml heavy cream
1–2 tablespoons confectioners' sugar
2 tablespoons/30ml Cognac or 1 teaspoon vanilla

Pastry bag and medium star tube

To toast and grind the hazelnuts: Heat the oven to 350°F/180°C and set the shelf in the center. Spread the hazelnuts on a sheet pan and roast in the oven until golden brown, 12 to 15 minutes. If the nuts are not peeled, it will take a few minutes longer so their skins are really loose, but take care, as hazelnuts scorch easily. Let them cool slightly, then rub them with a cloth if necessary to remove skins. Let them cool completely, then in a food processor grind the nuts with the flour in two batches. The flour prevents them getting sticky.

For the pastry dough: Spread the ground nuts on a work surface and sweep a wide well in the center with the back of your fingers. Add the butter, sugar, egg yolk, salt, and water to the well and work with your fingertips to a paste. Using a pastry scraper, draw in the nut mixture, cutting with the scraper and working with your fingers to a crumbly dough; if it seems dry, work in a tablespoon or two more water. With the heel of your hand, knead the dough until smooth, pushing it away and gathering it up as if kneading bread. It should peel easily in one piece from the work surface.

Divide the dough into thirds and pat each piece out on a baking sheet with the heel of your hand to 9-inch/23-cm rounds. Chill until very firm, at least 20 minutes. Heat the oven to 375°F/190°C. Bake the rounds one by one in the oven until the pastry is firm and the edges are darker, 15 to 20 minutes. It will scorch easily. Remove from the oven and, while still warm on the baking sheet, trim the rounds neatly using an 8-inch/22-cm pan lid as a guide (the dough shrinks slightly in the oven). Cut one round into 8 wedges. Transfer the rounds and wedges to a rack to cool.

To assemble the galette: Hull the strawberries, reserving 9 attractive small ones with the hull; cut the remaining strawberries in chunks. For the Chantilly cream, whip the cream until it holds a soft peak, add the sugar and Cognac or vanilla and continue whisking until the cream is stiff enough to support a strawberry. Spread a few spoonfuls on one of the pastry rounds—be sure it is cool and does not melt the cream. Top with half the chopped strawberries and cover them with more cream. Fill the rest of the cream into the piping bag fitted with the star tube and pipe small rosettes at the edge of the pastry round. Top with the second round and press it down gently.

Spread the second pastry round with a little more cream from the bag and pipe 8 lines of cream from the center to the edge of the pastry in spoke fashion. Arrange the remaining cut strawberries between the lines of cream. Pipe 8 large cream rosettes at the edge of the pastry on top of the cut strawberries and top each rosette with a whole strawberry. Set the long side of the pastry wedges on the lines of cream, propping them at an angle over the whole strawberries to look like a pinwheel. Pipe a single rosette in the center of the galette and top with the last strawberry. Chill the galette until serving, when it should be cut in wedges like a cake.

This was the only time in my life when I really worried about money. I was not sure if I could afford to buy even a newspaper, and I certainly didn't want to have to go home. My plan was simply to see what I could turn up. Thankfully, my classified ads brought results. One young woman wanted to impress a man she wanted to marry, and I cooked a sticky dessert and a meat dish she could reheat, then slipped out the back door. Another client was an Italian who I assumed was a member of the Mafia when he sent his limo to collect me. A sturdy black man called Al was the driver. That night after dinner, when I mentioned something about never having been to Greenwich Village Al piped up, "Let me take you there." A few days later he turned up outside my apartment in his boss's Cadillac, with a huge bunch of red roses. This time I sat up front with Al and we drove down to the Village, where we had dinner in a nice little place. He was the kindest guy, but I was still hoping Mark might change his mind about marriage.

In late spring a friend of Florence's, a woman named Tatiana McKenna, food editor at *Vogue,* invited me to babysit her daughter and do a bit of cooking in East Hampton for the summer. Alex was sixteen and was going to be on her own except for weekends when Tatiana came out from New York. I spent a rather boring summer with this nice teenager out on the beach, going often to the local country club to which the McKennas belonged. By then Mark had arrived for his job in D.C. and he called me every week. Many weekends we saw each other and for one of them I invited him to visit me in East Hampton. When Tatiana learned that Mark was half-Jewish, she warned me I mustn't mention that fact about him at her club. Her caution and the club's discrimination stunned me. In Europe there was certainly anti-Semitism, but I had never encountered such overt discrimination.

It was at Tatiana's place in Manhattan that I first cooked for Craig Claiborne. I had no idea of his importance until Tatiana explained that he was very famous. I decided to make a soufflé for supper. Ever since the days of my home catering in Paris, soufflés had been my signature dish, and my copper bowl went everywhere with me. At the time soufflés were popular—so French. But there was also this: In making them there was that risk element I've always slightly reveled in. You never know exactly how a soufflé will turn out— whether it will stick to the edge and burst in the middle or scorch on top because the oven has a broiler. I was confident I had mastered the ideal proportions (one cup of filling per four egg whites), and this volume this would produce: a six-cup soufflé for six people. I just hoped my soufflé for this legendary man would rise to a maximum without spilling over the edge.

I knew the key to the whole thing was whisking the egg whites really stiff and folding them gently into the basic flavoring mixture. Unfortunately, as I began I tasted the Parmesan cheese and discovered it was rancid. I had to rush out to buy more, and the dinner began to have a frantic feel. Later that evening I learned that Craig had said he knew dinner was going to be good the moment he heard me in the kitchen whisking the egg whites in a copper bowl. The soufflé turned out to be perfect.

SHRIMP AND CHEESE SOUFFLÉS

These soufflés are memorably light because of thickening with potato starch instead of flour. Once puffed, they cannot wait, so I always ask guests to sit down at the table before I bake the soufflés—they bake in only around 10 minutes. Note that volume measures for grated cheese vary very much with your grater, so it is best to weigh the cheese before grating. Texture is so fluffy the soufflés are best eaten with a teaspoon.

Serves 8

½ pound/225 g raw peeled shrimps
1 tablespoon butter
Salt and pepper

For the soufflés
1½ cups/375 ml heavy cream
1½ tablespoons/22 g butter, plus more for the dishes
1½ tablespoons potato starch
6 eggs, separated
¾ cup/75 g finely grated Parmesan cheese
¾ cup/100 g finely grated Gruyère cheese
3 egg whites

Eight 1-cup/250-ml soufflé dishes

Start with the cheese mixture: Put the cream and butter, cut in dice, in a heavy saucepan and sprinkle with the potato starch. Heat gently, stirring with a whisk, until the butter melts and the sauce thickens, 2 to 3 minutes. Do not let it overheat or it will separate. Take it from the heat, whisk in the egg yolks and both cheeses, and return the pan to the heat, about 30 seconds, whisking so the egg yolks thicken slightly. Take from the heat, taste, and season the mixture highly. If preparing ahead, cover the pan tightly with plastic wrap; it can be set aside for up to a half hour.

Let the egg whites come to room temperature. Coarsely dice the raw shrimps and refrigerate them. A half hour before serving: Heat the oven to 425°F/220°C and set a baking sheet low down. Brush the soufflé dishes with melted butter and set them on a baking sheet. Chill in the freezer until the butter is set, then butter them again. To cook the shrimps, melt the butter in a frying pan, add the diced meat with a little salt and pepper, and sauté until hot, 30 to 60 seconds; set them aside.

To make and bake the soufflés: Stiffly whip the 9 egg whites in an electric mixer fitted with the whisk, adding a pinch of salt to help them hold—do not overbeat them, as they will separate. Heat the cheese mixture, stirring, until it is very warm to the touch. Add about a quarter of the whites and fold them together until well mixed; this cooks the whites slightly and lightens the mixture. Add this mixture to the remaining whites and fold them together as lightly as possible.

To fill and bake the soufflés: Spoon the mixture into the prepared dishes to half-fill them. Sprinkle the warm shrimps over the cheese mixture, fill the dishes to the brim, and run a metal spatula across the rims to level the mixture. Run your finger and thumb around the edge of the dishes to help the mixture to rise evenly. Slide the baking sheet with the soufflés onto the hot baking sheet in the oven. Bake the soufflés until puffed and brown, 10 to 12 minutes.

For serving: Prepare 8 plates lined with a small napkin. Set the cooked soufflés on the napkins and rush them to the table; serve each with a small spoon.

Craig was way ahead of his time in creating what would become a widely imitated system of restaurant criticism, with ratings that were a striking change for newspapers at the time, when many still considered such reviewing a reprehensible adjunct to advertising. I admired Craig tremendously. He was said to give lavish parties on ocean liners and to hold celebrity-studded dinner soirées at his home in East Hampton (though the dinner for him Tatiana gave was in New York). But I had also heard that he did not favor female protégés, so I was stunned when, after dinner, he offered to walk me home. As we covered the twenty blocks uptown, he said, "You should write something about cooking and send it to me and I'll have a look at it." But I hadn't a clue how to write about food and I had no mentor to guide me. I ignored the opportunity. This was precisely the kind of thing that Mark would never have let me pass up if he'd known about it.

Thankfully, despite letting slip Craig's offer, I got an interview with Jane Montant, the executive editor at the magazine *Gourmet*. Montant was also very well known, an outspoken and passionate woman, loyal to the mission of the magazine's subtitle: *The Magazine of Good Living*. When I took the subway down to the spacious *Gourmet* offices on Fiftieth Street with their wide windows looking out on what seemed to be all of Manhattan, Jane took an immediate fancy to me. "We need someone to answer the letters, and I think you would be just the person . . . ," she told me. On the spot I accepted the job, and Jane Montant was terrific. It was she who taught me, among other things, how to write a recipe properly.

Most of the letters to *Gourmet* were complaints about "why doesn't this work?" or "what about using that instead of this?" or "I didn't understand that last recipe you gave," but the magazine had an excellent library that I used often to help me to answer those questions. As I worked, I began to learn how to write. I enjoyed the job, especially letters like the one I received from a monastery that read: "I am a monk and look after the catering for our order. I am in charge of dining, and we're soon having a feast day. I want to make Beef Wellington but need instructions. . . ."

One day early in my tenure a funny complaint came in. *Gourmet* had a column that had been running for years called "YAFI, You Asked For It." Someone wrote in to point out that *Gourmet* had run a recipe that purported to be for Portuguese *broa* bread but was identical to the recipe for white bread in *The Joy of Cooking*. Oh dear, I thought, but luckily I was not responsible, nor was it my fault when the recipe for the resplendent three-tiered *gâteau* adorned with bunches of grapes in butter cream that appeared on the cover of the magazine to celebrate its twenty-fifth year was missing sugar in the cake.

I was often sent out to scout for ingredients or obscure bits of kitchen equipment—like pea-sized melon ball cutters or miniature madeleine pans. For some reason I was one of the few people who got along with Fred Bridge, the renowned and cantankerous proprietor of Bridge Kitchenware, the kitchen store downtown on Thirty-third and Third, the only place in Manhattan where such specialty items could be found. Fred scoured Europe himself for his equipment. He was notorious for throwing anyone he did not like out of his store. I usually visited in late afternoon, and when I did Fred would hitch a bottle of Bourbon from under the counter and share a toot with me while he shooed away other customers.

I was still in my twenties, much the youngest person working at *Gourmet,* and everyone there was far more experienced. But they were very kind to me. There was one other young woman, Ann Semmes, the receptionist, who, poor thing, was stuck in the middle of the building with no windows. When Ann went to lunch, I took over for her, answering phones and letters. One day as I was looking at the stacks and stacks of envelopes that were waiting for a reply, I realized it was an impossible task. Every day the stacks rose higher. When Ann returned from lunch I said, "Look, why don't we simply chuck out any letter more than three months old?" "We can't," Ann said, horrified. But I countered with, "Why not?" and in the end that's what we did. As the stack diminished, John the mailman informed Jane of how we were tackling the problem and she was almost speechless. But most of all she seemed relieved the problem had been handled.

Thankfully, now that I was earning a proper salary I was able to rent my own apartment. I found a roommate, an Englishwoman called Molly Cooper who worked for Time Life, and she and I settled into a bug-ridden apartment with two bedrooms on Madison and Ninety-fifth, the borders of Harlem. We had a nice kitchen and the apartment was perfectly safe, but I missed the little shops and cafés that would have lined a similar neighborhood in Paris. Molly and I did quite a lot together—including traveling up to 125th Street in Harlem to attend a Revivalist church service. There we were welcomed warmly amidst the congregation holding hands and praising the Lord, and like nearly everything I was experiencing in America, I enjoyed the energy and spirit.

Here and there Molly and I went out with men, and we had a happy year. I was relatively well paid at *Gourmet* and also did some catering for fascinating people, among them a woman called Ilka Mae Chase whose mother had been the editor of *Vogue.* In wintertime Molly and I joined some friends in New England for a ski holiday, the first time I'd skied since my time in Switzerland, and although I generally loathe sports, I enjoy skiing and was rather good at it. In November of that year, 1965, the big New York blackout struck and Molly got stuck in the Time Life building and had to walk down thirty flights. I had taken a bus downtown and began to walk back home, at least fifty blocks. But we were young. I was certain the blackout would last only an hour—after all, in Europe we were used to them. As I tramped back home, I rejoiced in the collegial atmosphere the crisis had created. New York felt totally different—usually nobody in our building even said hello, but that day everyone was friendly. Later I learned that that night New York had its lowest crime rate in the city's recorded history. Nine months later the birthrate skyrocketed.

By this time it was absolutely clear to me that I was never going to move back to Yorkshire. London remained a possibility, but I was certain I couldn't make a decent living in Paris. And yet, as always throughout my life, I had no real future plans beyond the dim hope that Mark might ask me to marry him. He was enjoying his job at the World Bank, especially the travel. In early 1966 he took one of his many trips that brought him, on his return to Washington, to a stop off in London. There he saw the girl he had once adored, and though he doesn't recall this, I remember he wrote to tell me that he was sorry, but he thought he ought to let me know he would never ask me to marry him. I was devastated, but looking back on it, I see that Mark has always been totally honest.

I thought there was no sense even thinking about him any longer. I had to put this behind me and enjoy the fact that Jane Montant had just named me assistant editor—my name was going to appear on the masthead. Also at *Gourmet* I had begun to write my own recipes and was enjoying the job immensely. And I was meeting people I liked. I found that if the people I came across were interested in food I was more interested in them. For instance, in June my good friend Hugh Johnson, who had already become editor of *Wine & Food* magazine, invited me to join his family at his sister-in-law's house in Connecticut. Hugh and I had known each other at Cambridge, where he was a member of the Cambridge Wine and Food Society at King's College. Along with Hugh and his wife, Judy, there was his brother, Brian, and Brian's then wife, Pamela (whose aunt had written *The Guns of August*). It was a fun group, and despite my heartbreak, I was making the best of the summer.

Mark remembers all this differently. He says he simply couldn't imagine marrying a Yorkshire girl from a farming family—it was incredible to him that he might even consider it. But he was busy and unaware of how strongly I felt. He had entered the World Bank on an elite program called the Junior Professional Program that recruited talented young people from all over the world. As a junior professional he would spend two years rotating in different departments, and he had started in the secretary's office, where they made use of his ability to write well. But now he was working in the transportation department and had just been sent to Guatemala. There he began to think about the fact that despite our differences, he and I shared so many interests—books and concerts and food. Each of us was always aware of our individual strengths and weaknesses. And, Mark told me only later, he had never known anyone who paid so much attention to him and loved him as much as I did.

But I didn't know that was what he was thinking when on June 28, on a scorching morning, I walked into my office and found a telegram from Mark down in Central America:

> Sweetie, would you like to marry me. If the answer is oui, oui, please join me here soonest for marriage July nine, San Jose, Costa Rica.

I was overwhelmed with surprise. After I'd taken an hour to recover and looked up on a map where San José was, Mark telephoned to ask for my answer. "*Oui, oui,*" I said, giddy with joy, and I listened carefully as Mark, farsighted as always, explained that I would need to secure our birth certificates in order for us to marry in San José in two weeks' time. That was his next stop on his World Bank mission.

By then my mother had met Mark twice and had said, very perceptively, that she found him to be both intelligent and kind, a rare combination. When I called transatlantic (the first such call I had ever made) to tell my parents the news, to their eternal credit they were calm. "Mark's asked me to marry him in Costa Rica next week, and, Daddy, I need my birth certificate." My canny father knew precisely where my birth certificate was and sent it the next day by rapid post. My parents were wise enough not to ask if they could come to the wedding. They said, simply, "We're very happy. That's good news," and just before I rang off my father asked, "What's Mark's family name?" Daddy had never met him.

A few days later Pamela Johnson took me to Bergdorf Goodman to buy a wedding dress. I didn't want the traditional white—that was too unlike me. I chose a lovely cream-colored dress and matching coat, and as I tried it on the saleslady, who was very French, said, "Ah, yes, *c'est un type bel animal.*" Of course she didn't know I spoke French and understood that she was describing me as someone who is not beautiful but is a fine animal, full of life. I'd never before heard the expression, but it stuck with me.

A week later, I took the shuttle from LaGuardia down to Washington to get Mark's birth certificate. His neighbor and friend, Stephen Breyer, who in later years would become a Supreme Court Justice, let me into Mark's apartment, where I secured the papers we needed. Then I flew to Miami. The daily plane for Central America left the United States at dawn and stopped twice before reaching San José—*la lecheria*, the milk run, it was called. I was arriving a couple of days before Mark, so he had given me careful instructions to go to the best hotel, The Royal Dutch. That's where all the World Bank people stayed.

The next day I went to the British consulate, where I learned that they didn't do weddings. We would have to get married at the San José Mayor's Office, in Spanish. My kitchen Spanish was not much help, as I set off to find it, but I stumbled along as I had that day in Switzerland when I tried to order oxtail and didn't know the proper words. And then, at the appointed time, I went to the airport to greet Mark's flight. When the first plane came in, I held my breath as the passengers disembarked. I could feel my heart pounding in my ears, but there was no Mark on that plane. My heart would not settle down. Finally there was Mark on the second flight, disembarking and surrounded by his World Bank colleagues. He looked not exactly embarrassed but slightly awkward. When he saw me, he didn't even kiss me on the cheek. Instead he simply turned to introduce me to his boss, Eric Schaefer, who had agreed to be our witness, and from the airport we went directly to a Costa Rican lawyer. Both Mark and I had to swear before a notary that neither of us was already married.

After that we went to buy a wedding ring, and that evening we attended a concert at the lovely little nineteenth-century opera house just across the square from the hotel. The metal seats were agonizingly uncomfortable, and the young German conductor had to hum to tune the orchestra, which was so very untrained—Toscanini used to do the same; you can hear him humming on early 72 rpm records. This would be only the first of many performances we attended over the years—in Covent Garden, the Met in New York, the Sydney Opera House, La Fenice in Venice, the Paris Opera House, and the Bolshoi Ballet. But because it was a first, it was terribly exciting. Back at the hotel, Mark insisted we have separate bedrooms until we were married—he had to behave while on World Bank business.

The following day we sent a telegram to my parents: "Getting married tomorrow, Love, Anne and Mark." Shortly we received one back from my father saying: "Please advise after the ceremony, not before. . . ." My poor father. I later learned that that very day his greatest friend had telephoned and asked how I was doing. My father couldn't tell him because—like other skeptical fathers—he suspected Mark was going to run. In fact, Mark did later confess that he was afraid if he'd gone back to Washington he might change his mind and that is why he felt we must marry in Costa Rica. Eric very kindly said, "Mark, you'd be crazy not to marry this woman," and Mark agreed. But at the time he felt ours was a *mariage de raison*—a French term that doesn't translate precisely but loosely means not a marriage of convenience but a marriage that makes perfect sense.

And he didn't run. The next morning in the registry office in San José, Costa Rica, we were married in Spanish, with Eric Schaefer translating the ceremony. Mostly it was like any other civil marriage, the only difference being Mark and I had to swear in front of the nation instead of before God. Afterward, the British consulate sprang to life with diplomatic booze. They recorded our union on the ninth certificate issued since the registry had begun in the time of Lord Curzon in the early 1900s.

And then, classic Mark, he decided we had to do something with our afternoon. "We can't just sit about," he said. "Let's go and see the volcano." I changed into casual clothes, and off we went to the same, steaming volcano that would, three years later, erupt and deposit thick layers of ash on the city. As we were coming down, I was stung by a wasp and had to be revived at a roadside café with a banana sandwich. By the end of the day, Mark and I both felt woozy so we ate in the Royal Dutch Hotel dining room. Their specialty was rijsttafel, the Indonesian rice dish that comes with all manner of side dishes of vegetables and condiments. This was my first taste of Indonesian food—ever since I've had a weakness for it.

The next day we flew to Guatemala and spent a weekend in Antigua, the ancient Spanish colonial city with squares and streets all on one level and volcanoes everywhere around, two called Agua (water) and Fuego (fire). It was the first I'd ever seen of such a place. I loved it, and perhaps the travel bug truly hit then. I was very glad we were married. Mark, though, continued to worry and as we flew back to the States he kept asking, "What have I done?" His comment only emphasized how apprehensive I myself was about the unknown future. I realized on that plane ride home that we had never even discussed our future together beyond our knowing that he was returning to work and that I would spend my last few weeks at *Gourmet* before moving on to a brand-new life in Washington.

The promotion department at the *Washington Star* did a great job at catching me at my desk soon after I began there as the paper's food editor.

Chapter Seven

....

AROUND THE WORLD

As far as cuisine is concerned, one must read everything, see everything, hear everything, try everything, observe everything, in order to retain, in the end, just a little bit!
—Fernand Point

In late July Mark drove up to New York to collect me and my well-traveled trunk. By then he had rented a nice little Georgetown row house on O Street with a tiny railroad kitchen and a walled garden out back. The heat in Washington that summer was excruciating. I would wash my hair, and after an hour it was wetter than it had been when I stepped out of the shower. At the end of August we traveled to England for the parties my parents had planned in our honor—one in Yorkshire and another at the Savoy Hotel in London.

Mark and I were a little worried about the fact that our upbringings were so different. Mark's parents had seen very little of World War II, while mine seemed utterly marked by those years. And there were the many small things, too. For instance, Mark's parents never wore gumboots while mine were part of what is known in England as the Wellie Brigade, hunting and fishing. Mark, who never knew the difference between hay and straw (and is still uncertain), decided to wear a tweed suit to the cocktail party my parents were giving—he thought that would be just right for country Yorkshire. When my parents' friends arrived and everyone was wearing a dark suit and sober tie, we had to laugh.

My parents also had been worried about Mark's meeting with Auntie Louie, as she was fussy about people. Luckily, from the start they adored each other. Mark fondly remembers one of his earliest initiations into the family as a son-in-law was my father and uncle taking him after dinner at Aunt Louie's (and wearing his tweed suit) into the garden to pee against the wall; after that it was understood he was part of the family. When I look back on it, I realize that Mark was not unlike Auntie's husband, Uncle Tommie, the quiet one but so often the strength behind the scene. Mark would be sitting and observing, spectacles slipping down his nose, listening to people yattering away. Then suddenly he would say something so to the point, often philosophical, and I realized that all the while he had been watching and always thinking. "He's a bugga to think!" said my father, a very Yorkshire expression.

For the party at the Savoy I had one of those beehive hairdos with a hairpiece and my mother had bought me a gorgeous white chiffon dress with a high waist from the couture house Worth. Unfortunately, my parents refused to have a photographer, regarding it as intrusive, so I have no pictures, but rumor ran around that I must be pregnant, accounting for the runaway wedding. About fifty people came—among them our closest friends and more who were farflung, friends like Xavier Guerrand-Hermès, who flew in from Paris especially for the occasion. Unfortunately, one of Mark's closest Oxford friends, Richard Sachs, couldn't make it, but he did send a witty telegram from the Soviet Union, where he was in a ship on the Baltic with his grandfather Lord Chief Justice Goddard, a man so stern he was known as the hanging judge and whom the family didn't dare let travel alone because he was apt to pick a quarrel.

Mark and I had done up an elaborate seating plan, placing ourselves at either end of long tables. When we arrived and saw there were no chairs placed at the ends, we sought out the maître d'hôtel, who looked down his nose at us and said haughtily, "We can't have that—dancers bump into chairs at the end of tables." For the first time I saw Mark's temper flare. "You've made a right royal cock-up, mate!" he admonished. But the problem quickly vanished, and the party was a great success.

Afterward, with family inspections finished, Mark and I returned to Washington, where very quickly my vision of life as a happy housewife turned sour. Within a couple of weeks I was bored and desperate to find a job. One weekend, to escape the heat, we went to a house we had rented with friends at Rehoboth Beach, Delaware. As we were sitting on the beach taking in the cool, fresh air, Mark said casually, "Anne's looking for work. Happen to know of anything?" It turned out Stephen Lloyd knew they were looking for a new food editor at *The Washington Star.*

Mark said, "Anne, you've got to call them first thing Monday." I looked at him as if he were mad. "But I've never edited anything . . . ," I began, but as he would so many times in our lives, he waved away my concerns and called upon another friend at the World Bank. Ron Krieger had worked as a journalist and knew all about the intricacies of news production, so that Sunday he taught me enough so that I could ask and answer questions intelligently when I called *The Star.*

Gwen Dobson was the editor of the Women's Section, as it was called in those days (later it became "The Living Section"). Impressed with my reference from *Gourmet,* she invited me to an interview and then took me to meet the managing editor, and to my surprise I was offered the job. Violet Faulkner, then the food editor, had been there for more than twenty-five years; she was past retirement age but did not want to go. Gwen explained my job wouldn't begin until the New Year, and for six weeks Violet would settle me, giving me time to learn. Violet quickly made it clear she didn't want to help me in the least, and when I saw her desk piled high with press releases from commercial companies I realized that all those years she had simply crossed out the brand name and run the dreary recipes verbatim. To do her justice, unlike today's multi-faceted food departments, this was a one-person section; she had neither a kitchen to test recipes nor a budget for travel.

I soon came to understand that most newspapers organized their food sections that way, and Craig Claiborne had been the pioneer in writing his own stuff. Only a few other papers had real food editors, among them *The*

Washington Post, and there was Betsy Balsley at the *Los Angeles Times*, but the group who commissioned articles and wrote their own pieces was small. I was determined to be part of it. That fall I took some journalism classes at George Washington University to prepare.

As far as the food was concerned, I felt in better shape. We had already developed a habit of motley gatherings on weekends where we drank Bloody Marys or Sangria made with Californian Hearty Burgundy. A one-pot meal was the rule. Whenever I eat paella I'm reminded of those days. We often served it, because it had just enough of the exotic (saffron, chorizo, squid, mussels) to offer a challenge to adventurous eaters and enough of the familiar (chicken and rice) to reassure the more squeamish. Also, we could cook it on the backyard barbecue.

One evening over supper Mark told me his next World Bank mission was to be in Hong Kong and he would be leaving for a few weeks in late September. The Bank had devised a points system that meant that for each night Mark spent away from home he accumulated one point. After he had banked two hundred, I was awarded a free trip on the next mission. By then he had sufficient points, and that night I looked across the table and said, "Can I come with you?" When he smiled, I saw that he was already planning. "Look," he said. "It's halfway around the world from here. If you come, you must go on around the world to see some major sites I've visited." Classic Mark.

In early October we flew to San Francisco, my first West Coast U.S. city, and on to Vancouver to meet Mark's tribe of cousins. Unlike Mark's parents, the cousins in Vancouver wanted to inspect me, curious to see who Mark had picked as his wife. Thanks to my mother, I wore the right clothes and behaved well enough to meet a multitude of aunts, uncles, and cousins, and I think earned their approval. From Vancouver Mark and I flew to Tokyo and then down to Kyoto, where we visited the timeless Nijō Castle with its nightingale floors made from seventeenth-century timbers and designed to make a high squeaking sound as you walk across them, a sort of early alarm system, as no one could enter the palace without being heard. We both wanted very much to make a link with Japanese culture, but already on that trip we found the country and its people mysterious. This was the first of several visits we made to Japan, but however hard we tried over the years, we found the culture almost impenetrable. The food, though, was another matter. Once I got past the strange habit of the wax models of dishes in restaurant windows, I began to appreciate the perfectionist approach to even such simple food as grilled mackerel.

From Japan we flew to Hong Kong, where Mark joined his colleagues, and there he and I spent two or three days together, exploring and buying a few gifts for my parents, among them a jade horse we still have to honor my father's love of racehorses. Too soon came the terrifying moment at the Hong Kong airport when I kissed my husband good-bye and set off on my own to see the parts of the world Mark had selected for me to visit—Bangkok, Delhi, the Taj Mahal, Tehran, Isfahan, Persepolis, Jerusalem, Jordan and Petra, Cairo and Luxor. Only my first stops, in Cambodia at Phnom Penh and Angkor Wat, were places Mark had not been. The plan was that at the end of two and one-half weeks we would meet up in Nice.

Even now the very idea of such a trip is daunting, but back in 1966, when I was just twenty-eight years old and virtually unaware of what I would find, it was astonishing. At the Hong Kong airport I had my first surprise. We were flying on a DC-3, and in those days all passengers were weighed, since many Chinese were emigrating and often carried on their bodies most of their belongings. If you weighed too much, officials searched you for hidden gold and treasures. As I approached the scales, I felt a moment of worry—as a white woman I would surely weigh more than most of the slim Chinese; what would they think? But I passed that first test and took off for Saigon, where we were refused entry into the terminal because of the war in Vietnam. There would be no stopping. Within an hour we flew on to Phnom Penh, in Cambodia.

In Vancouver I'd been given a contact to a man called Chuop Van Deth, who met me and kindly took me around to see the Royal Palace and the Silver Pagoda. The city was charming, a low-key former French colonial capital. On a steamy evening we rode in a rickshaw along the banks of the huge Mekong River. It wasn't until I left Cambodia that I learned that "Chuop" means "prince"—my guide had been a member of the royal family. From Phnom Penh I flew up to Angkor Wat, where I stayed in l'Hôtel Royale. I still have the notepaper with its copper plate heading because I sent Mark a letter in which I described the excellent food I ate there—Cambodia had emerged from French rule scarcely a decade earlier. I went round the grand Khmer temples hacked out of the undergrowth and one evening attended an impressive dance performance with flickering torches and strange music and fluttering hands.

In overpowering afternoon heat, a driver drove me in a jeep from the main complex through dense jungle to more of the famous temples, many of them half-buried in the clutch of tropical creeping plants. On return I was thankful that the Hôtel Royale was air-conditioned. The next morning I was fast asleep when I was suddenly wakened to this huge noise. I leaped out of bed and opened my door only to discover the dawn chorus of hundreds of tropical birds. Later that day I thought I must have exaggerated the racket because of exhaustion, but the next morning the same thing happened. In Cambodia I quickly began to feel overwhelmed by heat, humidity, noise, mosquitoes, and the harsh sunlight so very different from the gentle light I'd always known.

I traveled on to Thailand, where I visited the floating food market on the river and where friends of Mark's invited me to a dinner of spicy Thai food cooked by their houseman on a single charcoal burner in the backyard. He explained to me how the bamboo containers were piled on top of one another to cook by convection over the restricted heat. I listened closely as the dinner guests talked about how terrible it was that Bangkok was getting so built up with roads. "We used to go everywhere by boat," they said, "but now the klongs are all blocked up with sewage." The canal system was being destroyed, they complained, but only a few minutes later I watched as their washing-up water was lifted directly out of the klong.

I flew to India, where I stayed in a modest colonial-style hotel built of concrete and with no air-conditioning. I had one day to see the Delhi sites and was struck particularly at Connaught Circle with the sight of an enormous billboard that showed a handsome Indian woman in a sari with children running around her—a board promoting birth control. Some of the architecture seemed remarkably like Cheltenham Ladies' College, reassuring in a way, since I was alone and on the other side of the world. Alas, the next day I was confronted with Delhi Belly and missed some of the sightseeing. Thankfully, I made it to the Taj Mahal, a place so timeless and universal, I'll never forget it. Day and night crowds swarm the place, yet the architecture is of such perfection I felt only quiet and peace and even my upset tummy did not bother me.

As he would forever after on our many travels, Mark had figured out everything ahead of time, and from India I was on my way to Tehran. When I arrived I found some tranquilizers in a newspaper shop that proved to be helpful, because by then I was quite sick. Even healthy I had felt exhilarated but also tense, and being ill added to the stress—mostly the small things like having to work out how much anything cost in local currency in each country (this is long before the electronic calculator made it easy). In those days nothing was sold in pounds or dollars. I was new to this kind of international travel, but the lessons served me forever after. Mark had booked me all the way in the most convenient hotels in town and insisted that everywhere I should hire a driver and guide, instructing me, "Don't try to be independent. You'll miss so much."

Mark had also introduced me to the books of the travel writer Sacheverell Sitwell, who had written about much of the Middle East with inspiration. Unlike the average guidebook, Sitwell did not bother with boring public monuments; he wrote about what you absolutely could not miss, marvelous if abstruse sights, and we found him always spot on. Where the *Guide Bleu* was exhausting and modern guidebooks fill up with junk about where to buy souvenirs or have a coffee, Sitwell's books were guides to the soul of a place, and Mark was insistent that they would illuminate my journey. So they did.

In Tehran I went to see the Shah's Sun Throne, symbol of the Persian monarchy and a tradition that dated back to the Mogul conquerors of India in the eighteenth century. (Shah Pahlavi was still the ruler at that time.) But beyond that immense gilded throne with its diamonds, sapphires, rubies, emeralds, and pearls I spent most of my time on my first day in Persia recovering. Thankfully, for my next stop, Isfahan, I was booked into the most attractive hotel, a former caravanserai built around an immense square. Each room had a window looking through an arch out on traditional fountains and gardens. I had a good contact there, a well-known scholar, but when I mentioned his name at the desk the clerk said, "Oh, it's not the season; he's not here." By now I was behind in my travel guide reading and had no idea of what awaited me, so I decided to spend a quiet morning writing postcards.

By lunchtime, my strength was returning, so while the whole city seemed to be taking a siesta I took a taxi to see the sights. I was totally unprepared when we bounded into the most famous square in the world, Naqsh-e-Jahan, then called Shah Square and now Imam Square. The sun was beating down on the magnificent mosque that dominates one end, and I was dazzled by the turquoise and deep blue tiles of the seventeenth-century façade (there are almost five hundred thousand of them!) topped by the 160-foot dome. It was the most wonderful building, and so utterly different from the Taj Mahal. To the west was Ali Quapu Palace, the residence of Shāh 'Abbās the Great, who moved the Persian capital to Isfahan in 1598 and commissioned the building of the square. To the east was Sheikh Lotf Allah Mosque, which was built as a private mosque for the royal court, no expenses spared. It also led to the Shah's harem. The fourth side of the square opened to the Isfahan Grand Bazaar, an immense tangle of narrow alleys that closed around me when I stepped inside. It felt like the center of the universe.

Standing there in bewilderment, I began to truly understand the gift

Mark had given me—he had launched me into worldliness, and I felt immensely grateful, not only for the opportunity of seeing such wonders but for all the wonders of the food world, too. I had enjoyed a typical lunch of falafel, fresh white paneer cheese, and pickled vegetables accompanied by lots of chopped fresh herbs and flat naan bread. That evening, feeling better, I decided to celebrate by going to a good Isfahan restaurant and asked the hotel desk for a recommendation.

"Oh, you can't go on your own," the clerk told me, and so the hotel sent for one of their junior managers, who accompanied me to a nice little place where we sat on silk cushions in a tent and ate spicy kebabs. I quietly hoped the manager would not offer other services as well, and thankfully he did not. Indeed, so far on my journey I had never been bothered by anyone except, oddly enough, a Yale professor whom I had encountered one evening in Phnom Penh. Touring around Persia, I quickly got hooked on not only all the beautiful sights but on traditional Persian sweetmeats, such as this apricot and pistachio brittle, too.

APRICOT AND PISTACHIO BRITTLE

Brittle can be kept up to a week in an airtight container but will soften quite quickly in the open air. The green of pistachios contrasts wonderfully with the golden apricots, though I've also made this recipe with unsalted peanuts.

Makes a generous 1-pound/450-g brittle

Butter, for the baking sheet
½ cup/75 g dried apricots
1 cup/200 g sugar
½ cup/125 ml corn syrup
Pinch of salt
½ cup/125 ml water
1 cup/150 g shelled pistachios

Sugar thermometer

Generously butter a baking sheet. Finely chop the apricots with a large knife and spread them on the baking sheet.

Put the sugar, corn syrup, salt, and water in a heavy saucepan and heat gently, stirring occasionally, until the sugar is dissolved. Bring the syrup to a boil and boil over medium-high heat without stirring until the temperature measures 275°F/140°C on the thermometer, 7 to 10 minutes. Stir in the pistachios and continue cooking without stirring until the syrup starts to turn light gold around the edges, 300°F/150°C, 2 to 3 minutes. Take care, as this caramel is very hot.

Remove the pan from the heat, quickly stir in the pistachios, and pour the mixture onto the baking sheet, over the chopped apricots. With 2 forks, lift and pull the mixture into a roughly 12-inch/30-cm round—work fast, as the brittle sets quickly. Leave to cool—it will set quite quickly to be crisp. Snap the brittle into pieces and store in an airtight container.

———————

After returning to Tehran and taking a side trip to Persepolis (chariots and horses in high relief panels, lost in the sands of the desert), I traveled on to Amman, Jordan, where I got into a taxi that had no meter. This was one of the constant problems I encountered, particularly in Arab countries. "How much to the hotel?" I asked. As always the driver said, "Don't worry; it's okay. . . ." At the hotel, I asked the porter how much a taxi from the airport ought to cost; he looked at me strangely, as if to say I shouldn't ask, but he gave me a number, and when I conveyed this sum to the taxi driver he was annoyed. But I was proud of myself for learning the way to do things.

Traveling in Arab countries gave me another lesson. Men began following me and trying to overcharge me or treating me in the classic "tourists are to be exploited" way that I hadn't experienced in Asia. There wasn't much to see in Amman, but at the end of the day the driver did offer to take me to supper with his family. I was touched and very much enjoyed our visit, but that night he tried to follow me to my room and was quite a nuisance to get rid of. Still, the next day he drove me to Petra, the "red-rose city half as old as time" and named by the BBC as one of the forty places everyone must visit before they die. As the driver and I passed the Dead Sea, he began to tease me. "You wouldn't dare to be doing this trip without me." He laughed.

"Why not?" I asked.

"You could not do this drive," he said flatly.

I wanted to shut him up, so I said, "Let me try," and I took over the wheel and drove with ease for a few miles. Alas, even this didn't silence him, but seeing Petra made all the troubles worthwhile.

On the Jordanian side of Jerusalem (which soon after my visit was to be reclaimed by Israel in the Six-Day War of 1967), the tradition of the Wailing Wall mystified me. But I was instantly in tune with the golden, glowing Dome of the Rock that dates back to forever and is a sacred site for both Jews and Muslims. This was the way I had always seen the world. I'd long had a strong sense of history, which was very evident in England with its Gothic cathedrals and in Yorkshire with its Roman walls. But here I was being exposed to civilizations and beliefs far more ancient than any I'd known.

My perspective only expanded as I flew on to Beirut and then Cairo, where, following Mark's direction, I enjoyed the old quarter that tourists rarely visited with the evocative Al-Azhar Mosque, a millennium-old building that houses the Muslim world's most prestigious university. Women tourists were allowed only to peep through the main gate at the vast courtyard. In Cairo I stayed at Shepheard Hotel, went out to the pyramids, sat on a camel, and bought an amber necklace in an antique shop and a couple of bits of pottery for Mark. But it was also at the pyramids in Cairo where I was very badly bitten by mosquitoes, and the following night I staggered onto the plane bound for Nice and Mark, who was coming from Hong Kong, where he had finished his mission.

I was feeling dreadful, feverish and nauseous, and didn't know why. It turned out this was the first time—though hardly the last—that I had an allergic reaction to mosquito bites. Years later I found out that the only thing that does any good is a stiff Cognac. While we were in the air, we also learned that there was a freak hailstorm in Nice, and although Mark's plane had landed, he had no way to let me know as we flew on to Barcelona. The plane bounced up and down with the stewardesses refusing to allow me to go to the restroom. I was sure we would never land, but at long last we did, and those of us traveling back to Nice were parked in a little hut on the runway where we were given a most delicious glass of extra-dry Tio Pepe sherry. I felt much better at once.

When I did finally meet up with Mark in Nice, we had a grand reunion, though for the next three days I lived on rice while my stomach settled. Mark's parents weren't the least fazed by my illness, nor were they much interested in hearing the stories of where I had been. They had, after all, already been everywhere. We visited Mark's father's friend Marc Chagall at his new home in St. Paul de Vence, and as a newly married couple Mark and

I were toasted with Champagne. When Mark offered Chagall a glass, he declined, explaining, *"Vous savez, ça me fait,"* adding a rude farting sound with his lips.

Even before that trip—the first of many we took in our early married years—Mark and I had begun giving dinner parties in Washington. When he was single Mark had been active on the social scene, and he had many friends he was eager to invite to our parties. We had become friendly with our neighbor Stephen Breyer, who had been a researcher on the Warren Commission and was at the time a clerk at the Supreme Court. Stephen loved to cook, and we often exchanged suppers. I admired his soufflé dish with fresh strawberries and a thick layer of whipped cream on top, sprinkled with brown sugar broiled to caramel—just three ingredients and delicious.

STEPHEN'S STRAWBERRY BRÛLÉE

If you have a kitchen blowtorch this recipe is easy, but if not you can use the broiler, heating it well in advance. Serve the brûlée as soon as it is caramelized.

Serves 4

    1 pound/450 g strawberries
    1 cup/250 ml heavy cream
    ¾ cup/150 g dark brown sugar

Heat the broiler and set the shelf within 3 to 4 inches/7.5 to 10 cm below. Hull the strawberries and cut large ones in half. Spread them in an ovenproof dish to form a shallow layer. Stiffly whip the cream and spread it on the strawberries; the layer should be flat, about 2 inches/5 cm thick, and touch the edges of the dish. Using your fingers, sprinkle the sugar thickly over the cream. Put the dish on a baking sheet and broil until the sugar caramelizes, 1 to 2 minutes; watch carefully so it does not scorch. The cream will start to melt, but this is the intention. Serve at once.

I kept a little red book with a list of the guests and menus for all those Washington dinner parties, and that proved to be an inspiration for the first book I wrote, called *Entertaining Menus*. It's thanks to that book that I know our first dinner party included Stanley Johnson, a colleague of Mark's at the World Bank, and his wife, Charlotte; their little boy, Alexander, would eventually become mayor of London under his middle name, Boris. Charlotte was a gifted painter, and her intuitive portrait of Mark dressed in a resplendent black silk dressing gown, his eyes focused and intent, still tells everything about his personality—the intensity and intelligence and humor. Stanley was an outrageous character, forever uttering awful puns like "Tant You, U Thant." Also at that party was Joanna Hare, from a well-known British family in politics and public service who eventually married Stephen Breyer. Another guest that evening, Benedicta Valentina, had lived all over the world because her father, a Danish admiral, was a diplomat, so she was accustomed to our kind of more formal entertaining. When Benedicta later became the director of Blair House, then the White House annex for official hospitality, she regaled us with amazing tales, such as the night Boris Yeltsin ran out of alcohol and was found in his underpants on the stairs trying to find more. Then there was the day a chandelier fell from the ceiling onto the bed where the King of Morocco was staying; luckily he was not in it at the time.

Over the years Mark and I dined with many of the world's lights. My strategy for inviting top-level guests was, as Sheryl Julian would later describe it, "so Washington." For instance, I might call up David Brinkley and his wife and say, "Do hope you can come to dinner on so-and-so; I've invited Julia Child and Jim Beard." Then I would tell Julia and Jim, "Oh, I do hope you'll be free on so-and-so, I've invited the Brinkleys." Mark's good friend Carter Brown, director of the National Gallery, and his brother Nick Brown, who would become a vital player in the creation of La Varenne Cooking School, were frequent guests. I recall the sight of Nick, a great gourmet and wine connoisseur, tucking happily into the crispy browned cheese that accumulated on the base of the fondue pot.

Mark says everyone came because the food and wine were so good—people expected as much from the new food editor of *The Washington Star*—and early on we worked out a system we have kept all our lives. Together we prepared a guest list and issued invitations. Mark supplied drinks; I was in charge of shopping, cooking, and table-setting arrangements. He took care of meeting and greeting. I go a total blank whenever I try to remember names, but Mark was always terrific at creating a party atmosphere. We also got return invitations to many dinners, usually in Georgetown. Although our parties were probably more formal than some, engraved, printed invitations were not uncommon. We would perch them English-style on the mantelpiece. Our rented house was small, but my parents had sent us some antique furniture and we had silver on the table and matching china and some lovely Persian rugs from my aunt, a wedding present (they still survive unscathed on our floor).

At the end of 1966, shortly before I started work at *The Star*, our friend John Guinness was planning his return to London and Mark and I held a farewell party for him. The menu looks distinctly odd by today's standards, but I was aiming for dishes that could be prepared ahead and would do well in combination on a buffet: *terrine de jambon*, *pâté de foie de poulet*, *crêpes farcies au poulet*, haricots verts, *salade verte*, and a seasonal dessert of *sorbet aux mandarines* and hot mince pies. When I look at it now, all that French seems pretentious for a young woman not yet thirty and living in America, but that menu book serves as a memento, even though originally I kept it so as to avoid the future overlapping of guests and menus. I was quite a good cook and usually the meals tasted good. The French would have called my style *cuisine de femme*.

Mark has always loved to wander and we often went on weekends to areas around Washington—to old plantations and down to Annapolis and Chesapeake Bay, or in another direction to Pennsylvania Dutch country, where the copious good food and strict traditions caught my curiosity. On each local table I came across rows of pickles and fruits or preserves, in the archaic German tradition of adding "seven sweets and seven sours" to meals to represent a balance in life.

At *The Star* the work environment was so very different from anything I'd ever known. It was a fascinating place full of characters, many of whom worked in one big, active newsroom. I liked the mix of editors and writers with the compositors and printers upstairs in the composing room. I loved sitting in my windowless southeast corner picking up the fag ends of newsroom gossip or stray telephone conversations. Once a week, on Thursdays, I had to get up at 5:00 a.m. to see my section "to bed" in the composing room. The tension was extreme and involved shifting whole trays of metal type (under union rules I could not touch them myself). I loved, and always have, the excitement of working to a deadline.

I had a pretty clear idea of what I thought the food section should be. The paper was family owned and extremely conservative, but they were good newspaper people and had seen what Craig Claiborne had done with *The New York Times*. The space I had usually ran to eight to twelve columns of editorial text, including headlines and illustrations. I named my section "Focus on Food" and always wrote the lead article covering a wide range of subjects. Early on, I was amused one day to read an article by Claudia Baskin describing our section of the Women's Department: "It's beginning to sound like the Duchess of Kent these days . . . because of the infectious inflections of the new food editor." She ended with a pun: ". . . eventually the 'Les Girls' [as she called those of us in the department] Virginia-North Carolina-Texas-Midwest mélange may congeal into the Queen's English, God Willan."

The transition from *Gourmet* to the "earthy realities of daily newspaper," as Baskin called it, was not without its difficulties. After returning from an early assignment, I wrote several pages and Gwen had to explain the rules. In a story I wrote on the Girl Scouts of America, I mistakenly used the British term "Girl Guides"; luckily, the copy editor spotted my error. Far worse was my reference in an article on home baking to "store-bought white bread like cotton wool." Chain supermarkets were a major advertiser for the paper and I had to be rebuked by the managing editor. But my stories took me all over the city—to the beach, to barbecues and picnics and parties. Once I did a series on embassy food. And for one of my favorites I went to the Moroccan embassy, where Mark and I met Olivia de Havilland and her husband, *Paris Match* editor Pierre Galante; she was wearing the most magnificent coral and turquoise jewelry, and we sat on cushions and ate turkey encrusted with honey and almonds, pulling the meat off the bird with our fingers. I looked back nostalgically to that first trip Mark and I took to North Africa.

MOROCCAN SPICED TURKEY

I think of couscous, flavored with saffron and dried fruits, as the ideal accompaniment for this turkey.

Serves 8

1 cup/90 g slivered almonds, very finely chopped
2 tablespoons/15 g sesame seeds
2 tablespoons/30 g ground cinnamon

1 tablespoon/15 g ground cumin
1 tablespoon/15 g ground coriander
2 teaspoons/10 g ground ginger
1 teaspoon/5 g ground cloves
1 teaspoon/7 g salt
1 teaspoon/5 g ground black pepper
One 10-pound/4.5 kg turkey
2 tablespoons/30 g softened butter
1 onion studded with 6 whole cloves

For basting
½ cup/125 ml honey
2 cups/500 ml chicken stock, plus more if needed

String for trussing

Heat the oven to 350°F/180°C and set a shelf low down. Spread the chopped almonds and sesame seeds in a single layer in a shallow pan and toast them in the oven, shaking the pan occasionally, until golden, 8 to 10 minutes. Set aside to cool. Leave the oven on.

In a bowl, mix the ground cinnamon, cumin, coriander, ginger, and cloves with the salt and pepper. Rub both the skin and cavity of the turkey with the spice mixture. Set the bird on its back in a roasting pan and spread the skin with softened butter. Put the whole onion inside the turkey. Truss the turkey in a neat shape with string. Warm the honey and half the stock in a pan and pour this over the bird.

Roast the turkey in the heated oven until it is golden brown all over and the meat starts to shrink from the drumsticks, 2½ to 3 hours. During cooking, turn it on one side, then the other, and finally return it to its back. The turkey is done when you lift it with a two-pronged fork, juices from the cavity run clear, not pink, and when you rotate a drumstick it will feel pliable, not rigid. During roasting, baste the bird often and, when the juices begin to brown, add the remaining stock. Dilute with more stock toward the end of cooking, if needed, as the honey scorches easily.

About 15 minutes before the turkey is done, take it from the roasting pan and strain the pan juices into a saucepan. Skim off the fat and boil the juices to reduce them if necessary—there should be about

1 cup/250 ml of glaze. Stir in the toasted sesame seeds and almonds. Return the turkey to the roasting pan, spread the glaze over the top, and continue roasting, basting very often, until the skin is dark golden brown and crisp, 10 to 15 minutes.

Transfer the turkey to a carving board or platter, cover it loosely with foil, and let stand 10 to 15 minutes. Before serving, discard the strings and onion from the cavity.

I had an opportunity to meet with many of the stars of the food world of the time—Jim Beard, Michael Field, Marcella Hazan, Roy de Groot—and in those interviews I discovered small secrets, some of which I wrote about, many of which I kept to myself. In my first interview with Jim Beard I noticed right away a jar of prunes in Cognac on his kitchen counter and understood he must have had trouble with constipation. I interviewed Michael Field, who was a great rival of Craig Claiborne's. Michael—who had originally been a concert pianist and half of the piano duo known as Appleton and Field—referred to Craig as "just a waiter," and in later conversations I had with Craig he called Michael "a failed pianist." In 1968 when they were competing to become editor of the original Time Life series and Field was selected Craig was deeply upset, and that may be when I first began to notice a kind of back-biting that seemed only to grow more intense into the seventies and eighties as the surge of young and not-so-young chefs became more and more trendy.

Roy de Groot had taken up food writing in the early sixties as his sight began to fail. By then he was writing for *Esquire, Ladies' Home Journal, House Beautiful*. A few years later, in 1973, he would publish to much acclaim *The Auberge of the Flowering Hearth*, the tale of two women who cooked with the seasons that remains a classic. When de Groot was totally blind, I met him at a dinner party at the wine writer Charles Turgeon's house where de Groot intrusively asked if he could touch my face. "Would you mind?" he asked. "It makes all the difference. . . ." I later learned that was a frequent ploy, one he particularly used with young women. Marcella Hazan has long been considered the foremost authority on Italian cooking and credited with introducing Italian food to an American audience—as well as the craze for balsamic vinegar—but at that time she was just becoming a household name. I once visited her Manhattan apartment and remember mostly a room full of smoke with Marcella chain-smoking, not so unusual then but certainly something one wouldn't find today.

Most important, at *The Star* I was realizing the importance of writing for an audience—a wide one—and a news sense was key. I was eager to avoid stereotyping, and I wanted to include the wider Washington scene of families and cooks of all kinds, not just politicians and their families, who were so often covered. I wanted to write about the expats, the journalists, the everyday inhabitants. The publisher himself charged me to do a series of articles that would appeal to weekend cooks who were male, a novel idea at the time. It was still the early days of food reporting; few had done any in-depth stories on what, for instance, the Persians or the Thai or the Chinese were eating. I felt that to understand people it was important to know what was on their table day to day, and the inner spirit of their food. As my world tour had taught me, cooking was a window to the world, one I wanted very much to explore further.

Gwen Dobson was a good editor but never questioned anything in the food section, and I sometimes wondered if she even read it. So I was left to explore on my own, hit or miss. For instance, I knew very little about food photography beyond what I had learned at *Gourmet*. I remembered that the dishes had to hold up without wilting on camera—yet there I was setting up shoots for a whole range of (rather good) newspaper photographers. In those days much of the food you saw in magazines was topped with shaving cream instead of whipped cream and the meat was blowtorched to look charred without shrinking. I began to appreciate all the more that at *Gourmet* we had always cooked real, edible food; I was determined to continue. It is a principle I still insist on. I want things to be real, not imitation. Flowers should be fresh, not plastic; furniture should be antique (or modern) but not fake. People, too—I have no time for anyone who is snobbish or falsely polite, a Yorkshire trait that I get from my father.

One day I interviewed a chef and got his recipe for Sachertorte. This Viennese torte is not easy—any dummy can make the cake; it's the frosting that's special, as it has to be temperature controlled and worked on a marble slab. We had no test kitchen at *The Star,* and I usually could eyeball a recipe and see if something didn't look quite right. The Sachertorte passed my test, so I printed the chef's version. The trouble was, he was used to making dozens all at once and he had divided the ingredients too far down. I ran the recipe on a Thursday before a long weekend, and I took that Friday off. That turned out to be the day when complaints flooded into the paper from people who had tried to make the torte and had miserably failed. After that I never printed a recipe without testing it. Still, despite Gwen Dobson having had to field the complaints, when I eventually left the paper to have a baby she said coolly, "We'll be sorry you're going. There's never been any trouble when you've been here."

The work was exhilarating, but it also was exhausting. Mark and I were having a lot of fun, and outside of work I'd begun doing things like reading *The Economist*, thanks to Mark, and becoming better informed about current affairs than I had ever been. The mechanics of good prose had been instilled into me at school and at Cambridge, and now I was learning how to appeal to readers, how to compose a punchy, five-word lead ("It's always better with butter" was one) and follow through to an amusing or authoritative closing paragraph. Even then Mark edited my stuff, reading my lead article and being moderately ruthless in his corrections; it was he who taught me how to structure articles, since at *Gourmet* I'd written only recipes.

That Christmas on my annual visit back to England to see my parents, Mark discovered the first of the *Cordon Bleu Cookery Course* magazines published by the British Printing Corporation under the helm of its gifted editor, Marie Jacqueline Lancaster, always called MJ. It was Mark who noticed that the recipes were the same as those I had taught at the London Cordon Bleu, and he hit upon the idea that the course could be adapted for an American readership. "You're the perfect person to edit such a project," he insisted. I felt uneasy about it, but he made me call and ask for MJ. "Well," she said, "we'd be interested in meeting you, please come around." And so, wearing my mother's rather silly mink hat, I traveled down to London to visit the BPC offices. MJ was forthright and practical, just my kind of person. "It would be a long way off," she said, "but BPC are in fact thinking of doing a transatlantic edition." We talked for an hour; she told me she would be in touch. After I said good-bye I didn't think twice about it.

My mind was on other things. I had never had any doubts about marrying Mark, though I hadn't really been sure that he was going to hang in there. But now, after nearly two years, I felt more confident, and our travels together had brought us still closer. I was becoming more international. When I was young and growing up I felt that I was English, but once I left I no longer felt home was still back in the British Isles. Mark never had. When we first married I was so proud that through Mark I had another national link—to Russia and to Mark's Jewish heritage and also a sort of sub-link to Western Canada. In those early years one of us traveled to Europe once or twice a year, but we also visited South America, India, and Australia together, in Mark's case by extending a World Bank mission. We also began to think of travel as a glimpse of places we might one day like to live—or not.

Mark's second big assignment in the World Bank was in the Education Projects Department, which financed schools and vocational training in developing countries. He was sent off everywhere, but he was always good at planning, and it was in Brazil that we got sick on oysters before we learned that all the garbage from the favelas went into the oyster beds. On another trip, in Bolivia we ate guinea pig and llama, and a host of mysterious greens and tropical fruits from Amazonas, and we visited astonishing places like Potosí, the mountain of silver in the wilderness, up sixteen thousand feet where there is no water and the miners keep themselves going on cocoa leaves and fermented liquor they call *agua caliente*. When we crossed the city boundary the guardrail was down—the miners were rather rough—but there was no soldier to show our passes to. "We can't go," the driver said, ready to turn back, but Mark hopped out of the car and lifted the rail. "Put your foot down on the gas and go," he said as he leaped back in, and so we did, at full speed. "Put your head down in case a soldier shoots," said Mark. It was the kind of thing he was used to from his years living in Turkey. I felt a rush of adrenaline and never forgot it.

On a separate trip to South America, Mark said I must join him in Buenos Aires in Argentina—one of the great cities of the world. There we took a touristy side trip to a gaucho ranch in the countryside where they put on a family-run barbecue, a *churrasco*. The meat had a gamey, heavy, fleshy smell, totally unlike anything I have ever come across before or since. It had been aged for goodness knows how long—two or three weeks, hanging almost in the open. They cooked it over slow-burning fires, and the flavor was totally unlike European or American beef, not gamey like venison, just tough and earthy, almost primeval.

I had to return home from that first South American trip before Mark was finished with his work in Rio de Janeiro, but he insisted that on my way I stop in Manaus, a thousand miles up the Amazon River. On my own, I took a rickety, twice-weekly airplane flight. It was the rainy season, and the rivers were in full flood. I hired a boatman to take me down to the meeting of the black and yellow waters of a major Amazon tributary, and on the way back upriver on turbulent water we stopped to visit the most primitive tribe of people I have ever seen—they lived in hammocks with no shelter, classic Amazonian inhabitants who today almost certainly no longer exist. "We must be careful," the boatman warned as we set foot on the land. "Don't try to talk to them or threaten them in any way."

I was to catch a plane that evening in Manaus and was jittery about making the flight. As the little boat turned us upriver back to the town the motor died and I had one of my most harrowing moments on any journey. We were drifting rapidly downstream and away from the bank. No one knew where I was or, indeed, of my presence in Manaus. (In those days, international phone connections scarcely existed.) For a few fraught minutes I was terrified, but somehow the boatman finally managed to restart the engine. Back safely in the city, on my way to the airport I stopped at the market, where all sorts of strange fruits and vegetables were on sale. I loaded up, but alas, everything was confiscated by customs in Miami. That became a great lesson. Years later when, for instance, I wanted to bring fresh truffles from Paris to Julia Child in Boston I packed them with camphor mothballs to distract the sniffer dogs.

Mark almost always found themes for our travels, a reason for going to various places. We became more and more intrigued by South America and we traveled to what then were considered faraway places—Ouro Prêto in Brazil, Machu Picchu in Peru, and from there across Lake Titicaca; at 12,500 feet, where only two fish native to the lake remained, we opted to eat rainbow trout, a species introduced in the thirties because Orestias and Trichomycterus were endangered. We traveled on, into Bolivia. We had an overnight cabin on a remarkable old chug-chug English steamship with belle époque furnishings that, in the nineteenth century, had been sailed round Cape Horn, taken apart, carried on mule back up the Andes, and reassembled. A few years later, the ship sank in a freak storm. I still remember a fancy cracked china washbasin. Mark taught me how to be truly adventurous.

In Australia we visited the Blue Mountains just north of Sydney, where the mountains shimmer in the most amazing blue because of the evaporation from the eucalyptus trees. Of course the smells were wonderful. I was on my way to the only professional wine tasting I have ever attended, a two-hundred-glass marathon with a dozen different dishes on the side. We spat out the wines of course, but by the end of the day I had absorbed enough alcohol to feel overwhelmingly sleepy. I certainly could not compete with the seasoned tasters, a tough profession.

India has always been a favorite destination of ours—Mark had first visited in 1963, and from his descriptions I knew I would fall in love with it. And I did. During one trip, we ate a memorable meal at a lakeside palace that belonged to the Maharajah of Dungarpur. In the grand dining room, we ate our kebabs, seasoned just right, with spiced accompaniments and breads freshly baked in the tandoor, surrounded by menacing, magnificent tigers' heads grinning downward—killed and stuffed by the current owner's ancestors.

There's so much still to see, but I guess I'll never get everywhere. We did, in China, have a glimpse of the awe-inspiring terra-cotta soldiers, each one a personality who must have been modeled from life. I would love to catch up on Vietnamese cuisine, and of course I'd like to roam all over China and explore the regional cuisines that rival France in diversity. What about Patagonia? And I've never made it to Damascus. Some places say hello even when I have not been there. I wonder sometimes if I might have visited them in another life.

Hot soufflés were one of my specialties at the dinner parties Mark and I gave in Washington.

Chapter Eight

....

AN ENTERTAINING LIFE

They say Fish should swim thrice . . . first it should swim in the Sea . . . then it should swim in Butter; and at last, Sirrah, it should swim in good Claret.

—Jonathan Swift

Amidst all our adventures and work, Mark and I agreed that one day we very much wanted to have children, and by 1968, when I was thirty, in medical parlance I was already qualified as an "elderly first mother." In those years, there wasn't the kind of talk about how to "do it all," and I suppose I didn't realize I was, like so many women, trying to find a balance of work and family. In the late sixties I was working hard, and during those years I suffered two miscarriages.

There were tensions in our surroundings, too. I'll never forget the Friday in April two days after Martin Luther King was shot and killed. The *Star* building was a fortress of solid concrete walls, like a bunker, set between the Capitol building and what amounted to a ghetto for African Americans. As things outside became tense, management sent those of us who weren't covering live news home early. It was a blazing sunny day, and I drove home past the encampments of the demonstrators. That night Mark and I listened as police cars and ambulances screamed down Florida Avenue, and the next morning from our window we looked east and saw a thick pall of black smoke over the city. Our friend David Calleo was supposed to come for dinner, but in the early evening he called, shaken, and told us he had turned back after attempting to break the curfew. When he had reached the Q Street Bridge just around the corner from our house, he was confronted by an armored tank.

In 1970, pregnant for a third time, I decided I had to change things and work as a freelancer, and I began to go into the newspaper just one or two days a week to receive freelance assignments. A few years earlier, in 1967, my family had sold one of the Yorkshire farms and I inherited some money, so Mark and I could afford to look for a house in the city. One day as we were driving along R Street in the embassy area, we saw a tall English-style row house with four floors on sale. "What a pity," I said as we drove past. "That would be just the sort of place, but we couldn't possibly afford it." Mark insisted we stop to ask, and it turned out they were asking far less than for Georgetown properties, which were just two blocks away across Rock Creek Park. True, the area was somewhat marginal, just opposite was a college dorm called the Nestle Inn that was pretty rough, but the Israeli embassy (not yet in its new, fortified premises) was only half a block away; surely that guaranteed security. But did we really want a house with five bedrooms and five bathrooms? Yes we did. We had fallen in love with it—the first of several slightly crazy property decisions we would make in our lives—and within a week we had made an offer. Although we didn't know it then, within the next two years we would fill up all those rooms.

In the midst of this, more than a year after we met, MJ Lancaster called to offer me the job of transforming the seventy-two-part magazine of the Cordon Bleu School for an American audience. Days later a signed contract negotiated by our lawyer, Bill Kosmas, came for *Grand Diplôme Cooking Course,* a project to be phased over two years, first published weekly in magazine form and later to be repackaged and expanded as a twenty-volume book series. By then I was seven months pregnant, and the doctor insisted I stay in bed, and so we set up an arrangement, with a pile of books on either side of me and a tray on top, with my typewriter upon the tray. Mark was wise enough to know I couldn't do this project without an assistant, whether I was in bed or up and on the go, and the moment he mentioned it I thought of Sheryl Julian. She had been working for our little department at *The Star* as a copy girl answering the phones and was terrific, bright, and capable. When I called to ask her if she was interested, to my delight she said yes.

I had never had an assistant and for the first two or three days I didn't know what to do with Sheryl, but by the end of the week we had it worked out. A typical issue of the magazine featured around fifty recipes and some text. Every week Sheryl typed this up with my corrections on an old Remington typewriter Mark had found in a secondhand store. We had to deliver seventy-two issues, an issue each week, within two years and had little margin for error or vacation, let alone the flu. I've faced many deadlines since then, but they've seemed puny in comparison. We added a few recipes and worked with a photographer called Fred Maroon, who later became famous for his shots of President Nixon during the Watergate scandal. Fred was an early user of natural light and ingredients and equipment had to be lugged up to his studio on the fourth floor of a Georgetown walk-up. Sheryl organized everything, and four years later, when she left us to go out on her own, Sheryl asked if she could please take the ancient Remington.

When the baby was two weeks late and showing no signs of being ready to arrive, I began to wonder how I was ever going to handle this new adventure. In anticipation Mark and I had hired Pamela as nanny/housekeeper, and meanwhile Sheryl and I worked industriously. MJ called once every two weeks from London, full of advice and questions. Converting British weights to American measures caused us a lot of trouble—once, for instance, MJ called to say she didn't believe that grated cheese measured less than the same volume of cheese in a block and Sheryl had to rush downstairs to weigh a cup of solid cheese, grate it, and test its new volume measure.

At last the doctor said I must have a cesarean. On July 21, 1970, I gave birth to a ten-and-one-half-pound, blond, cheerful boy. The moment I saw him, I knew everything was going to be fine. We named him Simon after my paternal grandfather and Leo, his middle name, for an uncle of Mark's. Overwhelmed with love, I held Simon in my arms in the hospital bed, and he managed to get his mouth onto my breast but couldn't find my nipple. "Come on, lazy bones," I said, and immediately he caught on and began to feed like mad. That, I am sure, was the day Simon's pleasure with food began, and it has never ended.

Alas, less than twenty-four hours later I came down with the kind of fever one reads about in Victorian novels—that classic childbed fever, the sort Mrs. Beeton died of. Nurses took the baby away, and doctors filled me with antibiotics. When the infection showed no sign of letting up, everyone grew worried, but all these years later I remember vividly the moment that fever broke. It was the middle of the night, and I was left drenched in sweat, the fever gone as swiftly as it had come on. Mark came to the hospital in our new bright red Alfa Romeo and drove the three of us to our new home. As we pulled up, Pamela leaned out the window and waved and Sheryl flung open the door. Inside I was greeted by the smell of good food, a flurry of activity, and laughter, just as our world would be for decades to come.

I was quite astonished at the turns my life had taken. Here I was married to Mark, mother to a happy, hungry son, and living in Washington. I wrote, Sheryl typed, and Simon bounced in his Baby Bouncer suspended in the doorway. Often in the late afternoon I would prop Simon on the sofa in the front bay window, where he happily watched people walking past our house. When Mark came up the front steps, home from work, Simon squealed with joy.

Mark appeared settled at the World Bank, and it seemed for the time being that our life would be in America. From the moment I had stepped off the boat in New York Harbor five years earlier America had been the land of promise for me. So when Mark suggested I apply for citizenship I quickly agreed. Because Mark was at the World Bank, like all expatriate staff he was not permitted to apply, but I was. I began to study for my test. David Calleo agreed to be one of my sponsors, and Mark's boss, Eric Schaefer, the kind man who translated our wedding ceremony in Costa Rica, was the other. The test turned out to be what we would have called at school Easy Peasy, and in late 1973, along with a dozen others, I pronounced the oath and waved a paper flag and became an American citizen.

As for our social life, most of it revolved around home. Before we were married, Mark had once taken me out to eat at *the* restaurant in Washington, Rive Gauche on M Street in Georgetown. Mark ordered veal, I ordered chicken, and when our meals came I was appalled to find the sauce on both dishes was identical. From then on in Washington for food delights we counted on our own dinner parties and on those in other people's homes. I was pleased to see that, like me, Simon loved food. When I was a child my mother had fed me a healthy concoction of brains cooked in milk, and I fed Simon, and later both children, a weekly mush of kidneys and sweetbreads, full of vitamins.

That Christmas we spent with our friends Marianne and Andrew Beith; their daughter Alex was Simon's age. I noticed when Simon sat beside Alex he looked like a little blown-up Michelin man, and I had to laugh. I didn't think about it again while Mark and Andrew prepared Christmas dinner. They had offered to roast a rather large goose in the Japanese cooker, a tandoori-type oven, and we were enjoying drinks and hors d'oeuvres when Mark suddenly sat up. "The goose must be done!" he said, running to the oven, and when he opened the lid smoke billowed out. We knew our goose was cooked!

After Christmas we flew to visit my parents in Yorkshire, so they could meet the baby, and from Yorkshire we went to London to stay with our friends Rupert and Elisabeth Evans. Perhaps it was here that the idea of opening my own school in France was born. Rupert and Elisabeth often drove through France and thoroughly explored the food they found. I was keen to hear all they had to say. Elisabeth became not just a friend but later also an invaluable help with research and translation of Italian and Spanish food texts. And best of all, that winter she helped me find a proper nanny, the wonderful Yvonne. My memory of Simon sitting beside Alex came back when Yvonne took one look at Simon and said, "He's too fat"; the French term is *dégourdie,* on the heavy side of plump. "We've got to get him walking," Yvonne announced. She promptly did.

By summer of that year, I was pregnant again and Mark was growing restless in the Education Projects Department at the World Bank. Never a combative sort, Mark did not care to climb the bureaucratic tree and instead began to look around for something different. When he learned that the Harvard School of Public Affairs, renamed the John F. Kennedy School of Government in memory of the slain president, was offering a master's degree in public administration, he decided to apply. Within just a few months, the school accepted him, he received a leave of absence from the World Bank, and we rented out our Washington house to a visiting professor from London and were on our way to Boston.

In Cambridge we settled into a draughty clapboard rented house very near the Star Market, where everyone shopped and went to be seen. The best part of the house was the garden, where Simon could play, shaded by a great maple tree. A few blocks away was the fish shop Legal Seafood—not yet a renowned chain. There Mark and I bought fresh lobsters in the cheap summer season and sat on our back porch enjoying those lobsters with melted butter and washing them down with Meursault. We also frequented Mr. Savenor's, the artisan butcher Julia Child had made famous. Mr. Savenor trimmed fat from the fillet for the fat cats and for people like us he kept those tender stringy trimmings that were so rich and delicious; he strung them together and called his affordable creations Honeymoon Roasts. Goodness they were good.

In Cambridge we met a woman who was to become a lifelong friend and important collaborator. Margo Miller was writing for *The Boston Globe* and came from a family that owned a group of small New England newspapers. Her father was one of the country's most respected editors, and her mother had founded Hancock Shaker Village and compiled *The Best of Shaker Cooking*. From the moment we met, Margo and I empathized with each other. She came to be not only a friend but also an editor on a new project in the works.

When we were still in Washington, Mark and I had begun to talk about my writing a cookbook that would focus on the food we served at our dinner parties. We envisioned something with menus for anywhere from two to fifty people, menus for various seasons and meals, from fireside dinners to impromptu picnics, from morning brunch for eight to single-plate suppers for fifty. We were calling it *The Young Gourmet*. In a sense it was a snapshot of the food of the time—paella and lasagna and all those dishes that went out of fashion and have since returned. We had an energetic literary agent called Julie Fallowfield. Coward McCann Geoghegan decided to publish it and changed the title to *Entertaining Menus* and gave me a deadline. A shadowy project had become reality.

BACKYARD PAELLA

Paella pans are quite easy to find nowadays, great circular pans with shallow sides designed for barbecue cooking, and they make quite a difference in the way liquid evaporates. Smoky, salami-type chorizo sausage is important in paella, and the ham should be dry cured; prosciutto is fine and in Spain, where paella originated, the raw smoked ham would come from Bayonne. Paella is a cook's personal dish, a little bit different every time, and by all means vary the fish and add more of your favorite ingredients.

Serves 5 to 6

1 pound/450 g mussels

6 tablespoons/90 ml olive oil

1½ pounds/675 g (1 per person) chicken drumsticks

Salt and pepper

2 onions, chopped

1 small red bell pepper, cored, seeded, and cut in strips

¾ pound/330 g (about 2 cups) Arborio or other round-grain rice

2 cups/500 ml chicken broth

2 large pinches saffron threads, soaked in 3–4 tablespoons hot water
for 20 minutes

2 cups/500 ml water, plus more if needed

1½ teaspoons salt

1 teaspoon ground black pepper

¼ pound/110 g thickly sliced Bayonne or other uncooked smoked
ham, cut in strips

¼ pound/110 g chorizo sausages, thinly sliced on the diagonal

1 pound/450 g tomatoes, peeled, seeded, and chopped

½ pound/225 g whitefish fillets (cod, haddock, or other firm fish), cut
in 1-inch/2.5-cm chunks

½ pound/225 g sliced raw squid

½ pound/225 g large raw shrimps, in the shell

14–16 inch/35–40 cm paella pan

Pick over the mussels, discarding any broken shells or shells that do
not close when tapped on the counter. Heat the paella pan with the oil
over medium heat over a barbecue, or on the stovetop. Sprinkle the
chicken drumsticks with salt and pepper and sauté them until brown
on all sides, taking 12 to 15 minutes so they are partially cooked. Set
them aside. Add the onions and bell pepper and cook until wilted, 2 to
3 minutes. Stir in the rice and cook until the oil is absorbed, 1 to 2
minutes. Replace the chicken; add the chicken broth, saffron, and
water, with the salt and pepper. Simmer the rice 10 minutes, stirring
from time to time. You can pause for a half hour at this point.

Add the remaining ingredients in the following order, pushing them
well down into the rice: smoked ham, chorizo, tomatoes, whitefish,

squid, and shrimps, burying them tails up. Set the mussels on top. Bring the rice to a boil and simmer rapidly, uncovered and without stirring, until all the liquid has been absorbed—this should take 15 to 20 minutes and the rice should be just tender. Add more broth if the pan gets dry before the rice is cooked.

Stop cooking, cover the paella with foil or a sheet pan, and keep it in a warm place for 5 to 10 minutes for the flavors to blend before serving. Serve in the pan, and remove the cover with a burst of steam!

When the cookbook project materialized, I realized I needed help. Mark had always been my first reader and would tell me emphatically, and always correctly, where I'd gone wrong. But Mark was busy and Sheryl was encumbered with the *Grand Diplôme Cookery Course* work, so I asked Margo if she might help with editing. I quickly discovered her extraordinary gift: Margo could edit something of mine and I couldn't tell where she had changed a word. (By trial and error, I later discovered that almost no one else has this talent.) For the next many months, every Friday and Saturday morning she arrived at our house just after I had got the stockpot going on the stove. Besides her gifts as a writer, Margo was also a creative cook. We enjoyed work, lovely meals, and much laughter.

In the midst of all these delights, when I was six months pregnant I was deposed to give evidence at a top Washington law firm. The Paris Cordon Bleu had always been protective of its intellectual property, and they were suing the British Printing Corporation, BPC, for their use of the term "Grand Diplôme" in the title of the book series I was editing. I was being called upon to give evidence as to how the name was chosen. The problem was, I seriously did not know, and besides, if I had once known I likely wouldn't have remembered. Still, I was quite good in deposition—straightforward and articulate. The matter was settled out of court and, thankfully, has been my only direct contact with the law.

The deposition was a diversion. Most days Mark and I focused primarily on simply getting each twenty-four-hour period turned over, with everyone having meals and finishing up work in time to put Simon to bed. Then one day a surprise came in the mail. Julia Child had written to say she enjoyed the work I was doing on the *Grand Diplôme* volumes now being published in book form by Grolier. She liked the serious culinary instruction based on

French techniques, still a rarity in the States. Julia proposed we meet and invited me to come around to a television taping of her next show.

I was terribly flattered. By then Julia was in her fifties, and her reputation as America's television chef was formidable—along with Jim Beard and Craig Claiborne, Gael Greene, in her new role as *New York* magazine's food editor, had recently dubbed Julia one of the country's most important cooks. I had never interviewed Julia while I was at *The Star*, but I knew she liked to be independent, my kind of person. Julia was already outstanding, in a class of her own, and I felt especially honored that she had reached out to me.

On a cold February day, Mark and I drove out to WGBH, the television studio where Julia's show was being taped. It was a modest setup; the budget was clearly small. But Julia was riveting, a born actress. Her presence leapt out to all of us in the audience, and I was enthralled as I watched her go straight through the whole thirty minutes—no budget for editing or time to take a pause. Paul crawled around on the floor holding what they called Idiot Cards, which said things like "Speed It Up," or "Can't See Your Hands," or "Thirty Seconds to Go." At one point Julia was deglazing a pot and when she lifted the lid a great cloud of steam poured out and enveloped her. I laughed when she gaily crowed, "That's what it ought to do!"

After the taping, I walked up to introduce myself. The first words out of her mouth were, "Oh, you must come to dinner." By then I was terribly pregnant, and a few days later, when Mark and I arrived at the Childs' house on Irving Street, I was embarrassed to see another guest offering Julia a resplendent loaf of homemade bread. I hadn't brought anything at all and saw at once that Julia liked her guests to bring things along and share. But I didn't have long to fret. "Anne," she said, "you're from Yorkshire; you're going to make the Yorkshire pudding." "Well, okay," I said, a little shy, "but we'll need a very hot oven." She raised the temperature on her Garland as I set to work in her kitchen (the very one now on display at the Smithsonian). In the center of the room, at the long wooden table, the other guests engaged in animated conversation. We all sipped Paul's famous reverse martinis, more vermouth than gin—those martinis have been, ever since, favorites of mine.

I immediately felt at home. I came to understand that whenever one was asked round to the Childs' house for supper—usually a three-course meal—Julia would ask you to peel the potatoes or grate the cheese or chop the vegetables. She had a talent not only for performance and cooking but also for combining the very best of good things, around the table and on the plate. That night Mark and Paul sort of looked at each other and winked, for they recognized how alike they were—both balding men with spectacles and attached to strong-minded women, both confident enough to deal happily with that strength. Like Mark, Paul had passionate interests. He was a gifted painter and photographer, and Mark regrets that his own talents are not visual, but in the written word.

And Julia and I spoke the same language. She was extraordinarily friendly but never dominated the conversation. Rather, she had interesting views on whatever was the topic of conversation. That night we talked a great deal about France and we both criticized the Cordon Bleu. She was enthusiastic about my pregnancy, full of questions. As Mark and I were leaving, without stopping to think that someone of Julia's stature and more than twenty years my senior might not be so inclined to spend another evening with a young cookbook writer and her graduate student spouse, I invited Julia and Paul to come to dinner. She immediately said yes. Julia was never one to turn down a home-cooked meal.

Then came the hard part. What exactly could I serve to Julia Child? I settled on a classic *pâté de campagne* for cocktail hour, followed by a pair of my trademark Gruyère soufflés, braised lamb with garlic, and *gratin dauphinois*. For dessert I spent hours building a *Doboschtorte*, that towering Austrian layer cake, with ten wafer-thin layers that I sandwiched with raspberry butter cream on the inside and out. I fussed to make sure every layer was as smooth as a skating rink and topped the whole thing with crisp caramel and big rosettes.

Our other guests for the evening were Julia's editor at Knopf, Judith Jones, and her husband, the writer Evan Jones, Margo Miller, Victor McElheny, the science writer from *The Boston Globe*, and Bill Rice, the food editor of *The Washington Star*, another old friend. I had been through the mill when cooking for Florence Van der Kemp's illustrious guests, but this was a meal in my own home for someone I so greatly admired and I was unusually nervous. But then Julia walked through the door, saw the pâté and homemade cracked-wheat bread straightaway, and scarcely before she and Paul had removed their coats said, "My, that looks delicious," and dived in, cutting herself a healthy slice of pâté, so I knew everything would be just fine.

Sheryl, who was joining us for dinner, had always taken Julia's celebrity status with a pinch of salt. She'd told me so. But that night Bill Rice brought along a dish of white purée to serve with the leg of lamb. Sheryl tasted it and couldn't make out what it was. Julia took a taste and said, "Delicious—half parsnip and half root celery." Sheryl's skepticism vanished at once.

We had another round of drinks, and another, and more merriment, and meanwhile what no one but I knew was that in the kitchen my soufflé mixture was in trouble. Since I could barely reach around my belly and the future Emma, I had delegated Bill Rice to whip the egg whites. It turned out he had not quite done the job. I summoned Mark, and between us we whipped up another batch (thankfully, I had enough extra eggs). I raised the oven temperature a notch to 425°F and the two giant soufflés were done by the time everyone had finished drinks. We sat at the table, I dished up one at my end, and Mark spooned out his at the other. When I later told Margo what had happened, we had a great laugh about it, and much later—after we had become good friends—I confessed to Julia.

Our daughter was born in late March in the very Victorian Boston Lying-In Hospital, where the bed was so high off the floor there was a step stool beside it to help one climb in. Again I fell in love at once. We named her Emma Louise, Emma because we liked it and Louise after my beloved aunt. From the start, Julia took a huge interest in Emma. Julia felt she had met the baby even before she was born, she explained, and that winter and spring whenever I went around to visit Julia I took Emma along. I don't remember ever thinking that Julia must have regretted not having children, though much later I began to wonder if that might be true. But it was clear that Julia and Paul had a happy life. They were devoted to each other and their warmth extended to their many close friends. They became very dear friends to us and essential to helping me to fulfill my dream.

That winter, though, the idea of a cooking school in France was only an inkling. In late May, Mark landed his post-graduate degree at Harvard while Sheryl and I finished our work on the *Grand Diplôme Cooking Course.* We returned to Washington, and Sheryl stayed behind to work on *The Boston Phoenix,* where she rose to stardom. With two babies now, I continued work on *Entertaining Menus* (with Margo helping from a distance) and we gave more dinner parties in D.C.—wonderful gatherings with such prominent guests as Ramiro Paz Estenssoro, whose father had been president of Bolivia; Donald McClellan, a curator at the Smithsonian; and Tony Howard, a well-known English journalist. Charles Turgeon, an employee of the CIA who also ran a gourmet group and knew a great deal about wine, mentioned a man in Napa Valley. "There's a winemaker called Robert Mondavi doing amazing things," Charles said. I foolishly dismissed the idea, "Surely he can't be anything but minor in the world of good wine, which is basically

European. He's making that jug stuff." Much later I would get to know Bob Mondavi well, and his wife Margrit Biever.

Our meals were relatively simple. I never roasted meat for a dinner party because it's tricky to get it right, so I braised lamb and beef and often roasted a whole fish. Once when Hugh Johnson was visiting, I served a giant fresh rockfish (a local name for striped bass), and he remarked enthusiastically, "Anne, this is the best fish I've ever had. . . ." I almost always served rice pilaf, so easy to reheat, and I liked to make those lovely French tarts with sweet pie pastry and fresh fruit fillings that look and taste so delicious.

For larger parties I made lasagna or moussaka, and for dessert we often made ice cream in our old-fashioned churn ice-cream maker—this was before the days of Häagen-Dazs. I was always looking for inexpensive dishes that could be made ahead. Now and then I made the complex Russian *coulibiac*, a sour-cream pastry dough filled with layers of poached salmon, hard-boiled eggs, rice pilaf, and duxelles mushrooms, which Mark loved, and I did a rather nice duck pâté where you bone the duck by the glove method, turning it inside out so that all the skin stays whole and forms a bag you fill with delicious ground pork and duck meat spiced with green peppercorns. It is baked in a terrine mold, still in its skin to keep it moist. One of my great things was kedgeree, rice pilaf with smoked haddock, hard-boiled eggs, parsley, butter, and a mix of curry, a Victorian breakfast dish. Mark was in charge of the wine, and because Washington had such a large diplomatic and foreign population he had an abundant and fine selection.

ROAST SALMON WITH SUMMER VEGETABLES

In the days when I was writing *Entertaining Menus,* whole sea bass was to be had for a song and I would set it on a bed of sliced peppers, tomatoes, zucchini, anything that was in season, douse it with olive oil, white wine, and herbs, and then bake it in the oven until brown and just cooked through. Nowadays almost the only large whole fish that can be found at the fish counter is salmon, which is excellent for this recipe. If you are a fisherman, of course use your own catch of any fish, large or small, and adjust the cooking time accordingly.

Allow about a pound of fish on the bone per person. To estimate the cooking time of a whole fish, lay it on its side and measure the diameter at the thickest point with a ruler held vertically. Cooking time will be about 10 minutes per inch/2.5 cm of fish (this useful tip comes from James Beard, a great fish expert).

Serves 6 to 8

7–8 pound/3–3.6 kg whole fish, cleaned with head and tail left on
Bunch of parsley
Bunch of thyme
Bunch of oregano
Salt and pepper
½ cup/125 ml olive oil
6 bell peppers, red, green, and yellow, cored, seeded, and cut in strips
1½ pounds/675 g small zucchini, cut in ⅜ inch/1 cm slices
6 large tomatoes (2 pounds/900 g), cut in thick slices
2–3 lemons, cut in wedges, for serving

Heat the oven to 350°F/180°C and set a shelf low down. Wash the fish, pat dry with paper towel, and trim the fins with scissors. Score the fish deeply 4 or 5 times on each side with a large knife, cutting on the diagonal. Cut most of the stems from the parsley. Insert a sprig of parsley, thyme, and oregano in each slash. Sprinkle the fish on each side with salt and pepper.

Pour half the olive oil into a very large roasting pan. Spread the peppers in the pan, top with the zucchini and finally the tomatoes, sprinkling each layer with seasoning and any leftover herb sprigs. Place the fish, backbone up, in the pan, curving it to fit the pan. Tuck in some of the vegetables around it. Spoon over the remaining oil and sprinkle generously with salt and pepper.

Bake the fish in the oven, allowing 1 to 1¼ hours for a 7-pound fish. The flesh should flake easily when tested with a fork. Transfer the fish to a long platter, cover with foil, and keep it warm. If the vegetables have too much liquid, cook them rapidly over high heat for a few minutes so the liquid evaporates, then spoon them around the fish. Serve with lemon wedges for squeezing.

Among his many other talents, Mark has always had a great nose for old books and one of our first projects together was starting a library based on the cookbooks I referred to at *Gourmet* magazine. Even way back we were exploring old cookbooks. In Paris *cuisine ancienne* was just beginning to be a fad and in 1968, when Alain Senderens opened l'Archestrate, he named his three-star restaurant after a classical Greek poet who loved feasting. One of the specialties was a roast duck with spiced honey nougat that came from the Roman epicure Apicius. My own interest had started with Taillevent, cook to the French king Charles V in the late fourteenth century. A facsimile of Taillevent's *Le Viandier* was one of the first old cookbooks we bought, and it gave detailed instructions for a highly spiced, complex cuisine. When I first tried his recipe for Civé de Veel it was with some misgivings. Taillevent suggested softening toasted bread in wine and beef bouillon, but bread as a liaison made me shudder; I knew it only in that porridge-like English mixture called bread sauce. But to my surprise Taillevent's instructions for thickening sauce with bread were just right and it came out light and smooth. My concern about the heavy spicing and sharp flavoring of vinegar and verjuice was equally misplaced. The result resembled a good Indian curry.

Now that Mark was back at the World Bank, he was finding it had become a very different organization from the one he joined in 1965. This was due to the "McNamara effect." In 1971 Robert McNamara became president of the World Bank. He doubled the complement of staff and the organization had expanded to become a large bureaucracy with McNamara increasing his own span of control. Mark began to dream of returning to Europe. The European World Bank office in Paris was very small and at the time there were no vacancies, but that didn't deter him. Mark had often felt troubled by his older brothers' histories. Only one was seriously employed. Two had been half-embroiled in music and half out of it, and one did nothing at all. Mark feared a similar fate from his own lack of commitment, but he began to focus on returning to Paris. I told him that was fine. But, I said, he would have to find something for me to do.

So when Madame Brassart, the owner of the Paris Cordon Bleu, put it up for sale I pricked up my ears and Mark and I met with her nephew who was in charge of the proposed sale. Monsieur Consigny turned out to be a toffee-nosed *inspecteur des finances,* and he was asking far, far more than we imagined spending. Paradoxically, that inspired our exploration into the possibilities of raising capital. At Julia's suggestion we talked to a woman named Princess Marie-Blanche de Broglie, who gave cooking classes in Normandy, not so far from Mark's parents' house. When I mentioned the plan for the school to her, she was polite and welcoming, but I saw fairly quickly this would not work. Her vision of giving cooking classes to nice, aristocratic ladies wasn't at all what I had in mind, and I saw she was thinking that here was this dumb foreigner who would provide the cash. I decided not to become involved with Marie-Blanche, charming as she was—it ought to have been warning enough that her husband, the prince, came from the Broglies who reveled in imbroglios—a member of the family was mysteriously shot dead on a Paris street in the 1970s.

I wanted to open a school for training professionals. It had to be in Paris because of that city's tradition of gastronomy—dazzling food shops and great chefs. I was determined our students would learn French cooking from French chefs. And just as the concept began to take shape, Mark learned that there was an opportunity in Luxembourg at the European Investment Bank. Luxembourg was only a half day's travel from Paris, and Mark's desire to return to Europe and his belief in the importance of the cooking school led us to move once again.

Mark's parents were growing older and that, too, fueled his inclination to return to Europe. They lived in a picture-book thatched house near Dieppe, and to be near them we bought a solid, cement-laden villa called La Maison Blanche (The White House). The sea was a mile away and the fish were so lively I once had to stun a fresh-caught sole with a mallet. Dieppe to me meant mounds of nutty little gray shrimps, some still wiggling their tails, and scallops in the shell sold by the dozen by weather-beaten market women clad in ancient greatcoats and outsized rubber boots. It was a lovely place to be. We have a couple of Impressionist paintings of Dieppe by Jacques-Émile Blanche and the seafront has scarcely changed in more than a century.

That fall I attended the most ancient of rural festivals, a pig killing in an orchard. I deliberately missed the actual dispatch, and by the time I arrived the carcass was hanging from an apple tree surrounded by sturdy peasant figures in boots and aprons who might have stepped out of a Breughel tableau. Little by little, under the supervision of the local charcutier, the innards were removed and the intestines set aside to be cleaned for the local version of *boudin noir*—blood sausage made with diced fat, fried onions, and the blood collected when the pig was killed. Delicacies like trotters and spare ribs were sent off to the kitchen for supper, with a sharp eye on the back feet known to be plumper and more succulent than the front. The shadows grew longer, swigs of cider more frequent, and the warmth of the fire with its huge cauldron for blanching the sausages became more welcome. Finally the carcass was dismembered and the hams and sides borne away to be salted and smoked. The audience pressed boudin on me for supper, with instructions to eat it with fried apples, Norman-style.

Luxembourg was less than three hundred kilometers away from Bourg Dun, but it was another world. The tiny nation had been incorporated into Germany during the War, and though the official language was French, the locals spoke Luxembourgish, a debased form of German. The food was heavy and unimaginative, with lots of pork, sauerkraut, and little else. Emma was just over a year old; Simon had turned three. Mark and I had envisioned staying for six months, maximum a year, but we were there over two, and they seemed very long.

We lived in a cold, echoing 1930s tile-floored suburban house with a backyard of scrubby grass and no flowers, but safe for the children. We were walking distance from the European Investment Bank—Mark was determined to continue taking his exercise before he got to the office. We had no curtains, just hideous, heavy sliding blinds, all very forbidding. The people were unwelcoming, too. It wasn't a language problem. I could speak perfectly good French, but the only person who talked to us was a chatty Englishwoman with an antique shop who, in a rash moment, had married a Luxembourger. When Julia and Paul came to visit, we took them to the only two-star restaurant, where Julia announced that it made her realize just how good French food was.

But besides the two small children and the cooking, I was writing another cookbook, drafting recipes for the school I envisioned, and, with Mark's help, putting together a business plan. I had no doubt the school would happen, but in the meantime Mark and I evolved a system. The food shops in Luxembourg City were very basic and unimaginative, so every two weeks we drove the few kilometers into Belgium, where there was an excellent supermarket with wonderful wild game in the fall, fish from the North Sea, everything we could possibly want. We went most Friday evenings and loaded the car up to the gills. On the way home we would stop at a nice spot we had found and eat great pots of Belgian mussels. The next day Mark and I would cook up braises and stews for reheating, though actually it was Mark who did the interesting stuff and I would chop the onions. My ideas harkened back to *Grand Diplôme Cooking Course*, simple recipes, common ingredients, and above all easy to reheat.

The nearest French city of gastronomic note was Strasbourg, the capital of Alsace, and that took four hours from Luxembourg in those days before the autoroute. We couldn't go often, but when we did we had a lovely time. It was in Colmar in southern Alsace that we discovered Simon was a gourmet child. Mark and I were taking a nice two-star lunch and the children were officially napping when Simon woke and threatened to wake his sister. We brought him to the table in his stroller, and to keep him quiet we ordered him a three-scoop sorbet—one red, one white, and one yellow. We didn't know what flavors they were going to be, but three-year-old Simon identified each one—red was raspberry; white was pear; yellow was lemon—no easy task at any age.

Mark and I did feel very much in transit, however, and we were both determined to move, though it was taking us longer than we had expected. Mark kept his ear to the ground for jobs in Paris. The World Bank's Paris office had just ten staff at his level and only one could be British, but the deputy director was a good friend of ours. Julian Grenfell (later Lord Grenfell) was an amusing man who married several times—each of his wives was beautiful. One day he told Mark he would be leaving the position as representative of the World Bank in Europe. "You should apply," Julian said. This job would call for Mark to meet with parliamentarians and NGOs and to see that journalists got the right story about World Bank projects. It seemed a perfect fit and Mark applied at once.

In the meantime, there was one good thing about being in Luxembourg. I had time to do all the planning I needed. In those two years I wrote more than five hundred recipes, many inspired by my classes in London and Paris and by *Le Livre de Cuisine de Madame Saint Ange*—she was the French Fannie Farmer who ran both a magazine and a cooking school before World War II. The book, published in 1927, was written as if she were standing right beside you in the kitchen and was a definitive guide for Rosemary Hume and also an enormous influence on Julia in *Mastering the Art of French Cooking*. It proved to me once more that good cooking is timeless.

Mark and I consulted about a Paris school with Julia and Paul, with Jim Beard, Simca Beck, and Nick Brown. I really had no idea about how to run a small business, though Mark had written a masterly business plan. One evening on a visit to France we were invited to Simca's for supper cooked by Richard Olney, her good friend who had a few years earlier begun some of the first high-flying luxury cooking classes in France—a thousand dollars for the week, which at the time seemed a fortune. At supper he told us he always welcomed his guests with Champagne, and although it would be another couple of decades before I launched classes at our château, Mark must have been impressed by the notion, because he insisted we would always serve good wine. Richard was highly strung and sensitive to criticism, but when I tasted his quenelles I could be effusive in praise; they were absolutely delicious, and I came to learn that this cooking was always superlative.

During this indecisive time, I was also hard at work on a new book. *Entertaining Menus* had been fun to write, but *Great Cooks and Their Recipes* was at a different level, requiring a great deal of research, with trips to the Belgian Bibliothèque Nationale and to the British Library. We had a clear vision of what the book would be—portraits of thirteen chefs and cooks over the centuries in four different countries—and the research involved was challenging.

Great Cooks led us to many places, and in Japan we met Shizuo Tsuji, who had created one of the world's largest professional cooking schools, sumptuously equipped with thirty stoves per classroom, one for every pair of students. Shizuo had amassed one of the largest collections of antiquarian cookbooks in the world and had written a massive tome on the subject. He took us to a quiet house in an unassuming street of Osaka. At the front door we undid our shoes and put on slippers, and he showed us to a private room overlooking a walled garden with a fountain. We stepped across tatami mats and sat in special low chairs designed for Europeans uncomfortable with sitting cross-legged. A simple traditional scroll hung in the alcove on one of the walls with a beautiful ceramic piece below it. We smiled and relaxed. Apart from a trickle of water in the fountain, the silence was absolute.

Nouvelle cuisine was just beginning, and Shizuo, a friend of Paul Bocuse, had eaten at all the top French restaurants. "In Japan it is a different experience," he said, as course followed course, at least fifteen, tiny bites arranged to perfection on exquisite antique dishes. The finest French wines were served in our honor, and when we returned to our hotel I noted down everything I could remember—the ideal sequence of flavors, delicate to mild to tart and pungent as the meal progressed and our palates became saturated. Along the way textures and colors were carefully contrasted. I have no doubt each dish brought its own symbolism that was lost on me, but I was rather proud that I understood enough of the menu to know that a dish or two was missing in my notes from the meticulously balanced progression. Even this brief visit opened my palate to Asian flavorings. Decades later when my wonderful assistant Christine Matsuda cooked me miso-glazed cod, I recalled this first introduction.

Meanwhile we were pleased that *Entertaining Menus* had sold about five thousand copies, not bad for a first cookbook. We did find one funny review of the book in galley form in a short-lived magazine, *Scanlan's,* out of New York. The reviewer had picked up on one recipe—*truite au bleu,* or blue trout, for which you begin with live trout. I should have known that for an American audience I'd have to be exhaustive—after reading the review I realized I should have written either "hit the trout on the head" or "immersion in boiling vinegar water kills the trout instantly." Instead I had written only: "Plunge the trout in boiling water," and the reviewer complained: "There are no instructions to kill the trout." Mark and I found this very funny, but my father did not. He was still smarting from something someone else had written about me while I was still at *The Star.* When covering the food in the Johnson White House, I had written about one of the Johnson girls eating cottage cheese with ketchup every day for lunch. When Karen Hess reviewed my piece, she said something nasty like "sounds like an Anne Willan recipe." Mark and I had laughed. My father did not.

Quite early in 1975, Mark learned he had been passed over for the World Bank position. Oh well, we said to ourselves. We'll have to live with it. Then one day when I was preparing to go down to the Gritti Palace hotel in Venice to teach classes with Julia, Julian Grenfell called. The favorite for the World Bank job had been rejected. "McNamara has said no," Julian told Mark. "He doesn't want someone as a representative in Europe who hasn't already worked for the Bank." Mark was the second choice and so we were able to move to Paris after all. His job now would be to look after the World Bank image in Britain and in various European countries and at international organizations in Paris, Geneva, and Rome. Looking back, we were almost miraculously lucky that the top executive of one of the leading organizations in the world should have micro-managed the decision about a modest staff appointment. The position usually lasted four years, though ultimately Mark stayed on for eleven years—what a run of luck!

I took the overnight train from Paris to Venice knowing I would never have to return to Luxembourg; I could hardly believe it. I was carrying all my cooking equipment for the classes at the Gritti, and as the train chugged across the lagoon into the Santa Lucia Station the French sleeping-car porter said, "Ah, Venice, *on tombe amoureux de Venise, ou ça vous donne le cafard* [either you fall in love with Venice, or it gives you the heebie-jeebies]." As I rode the vaporetto along the Grand Canal toward the Gritti, I was enchanted.

They gave me a curious room at the very top of the Gritti with a window that theoretically overlooked the canal, but I had to climb on a stool to see anything but sky. When the PR woman running the courses showed me the elegant banqueting room with damask on the walls where I would give the classes, I was perturbed to find no water or refrigerator. "We've got people coming for a week at a time, we must be properly equipped," I fretted, but she waved away my concerns. The next day Dottore Natale Rusconi, the charming director of the Gritti, told me he would have his workmen bore a hole in the wall that connected our room to the hotel kitchen and run in a water pipe. Dottore Rusconi, wonderfully courtly, always impeccably dressed in that relaxed Italian style, was kind and universally courteous. When I said, "We need somewhere to put the equipment," he said, *"Non preoccuparti, signora,"* and moments later his workmen were carrying in a magnificent armoire for the equipment. A marble table for pasta, of course, was no problem. For six weeks I taught classes littered with Venetian contessas and contes (the crème de la crème, I learned, did not use the title), and I communicated with the chef in what had been before that moment my non-existent Italian. The students' enthusiasm was encouraging, and one of the contessas made *taglierini* and syllabub for twenty-five at home and was written up in the *Rome Daily American*. It was a fascinating dry run for my own school.

When La Varenne finally launched in 1975, it made news! This picture of Julia was probably taken by her husband, Paul Child.

Chapter Nine

....

PARADISE FOUND

The school [La Varenne] may be the hottest thing since crêpes Suzette.

— *Time*, January 5, 1976

After six weeks of Italian distraction, I returned to Bourg Dun and Elisabeth and Rupert Evans came to visit with their baby, Frances. I was working from my office overlooking fields scattered with black-and-white cows, putting the finishing touches to the recipes, and I gave some of these to Elisabeth to translate into French so that the teacher-chef could use them at the beginning of the courses. I shuttled back and forth to Paris to meet with our partner Sofitel's bureaucrats.

After we found the premises on Rue Saint Dominique and an apartment overlooking the Eiffel Tower, Elisabeth went with me to Paris to tour both places. En route we stopped in at a hypermarket outside Rouen to buy everything I thought we might need, and as we pulled away in our red Peugeot station wagon bursting with ironing boards, lamps, washing-up bowls, and everything else I'd imagined indispensable I felt a surge of joy. Once in Paris, Elisabeth and I somehow managed to unload everything and carry it up in the tiny lift. As we put things away, I felt utterly optimistic, thoroughly determined, and, as I had so often in my life, exhilarated by the prospect of change.

Our Paris apartment at 7 Avenue Émile Deschanel was one street back from the grass-covered Champ de Mars and on the sixth floor, so we looked out over roofs and trees to the Eiffel Tower. The apartment had three bedrooms and the usual French lack of attention to the only bathroom, so it looked as though going to the john would be an experience, since it was the only place to keep the freezer. Still, Mark and I could walk to work and the children were a stone's throw from L'École Bilingue, and in the gutted premises for the school on Rue Saint Dominique some semblance of order was emerging.

For months we had tossed about names for the school. Julia had rejected Bourbon ("sounds like whisky"), Lucullus ("sounds Latin"), and Fin Palais ("a bit cutesy"). We settled on La Varenne, named for François Pierre de la Varenne, an important seventeenth-century chef and author of *Le Cuisinier François,* which felt right. Still, we had no chef. I interviewed two people who had taught in the French hotel schools, but one was too set in his ways. The other seemed ideal and I thought we were ready, but when he declined the offer we were back at square one. My contact at Sofitel, Alain Carric, assured me we had plenty of time, but we had no candidates when he went off on his honeymoon. It wasn't until mid-September that Sofitel finally brought us Michel Marolleau, who seemed unusually adept in both cuisine and pastry.

By now the children were trotting off to school in their blue-and-gray uniforms, as settled as we could have hoped they would be. Our lawyer in Paris, Eliane Heilbronn, introduced us to Jacqueline de Liedekerke, who was exquisitely dressed, bilingual, and low-key. She was the wife of a Belgian industrialist with a new mistress and so Jacqueline was looking for something to occupy her time. She was perfect for greeting people at the door and answering the phone. By late September we had found our staff but we still had only one student registered. I was determined to forge on.

My dear friend Fiona once said to me, "Anne, you always wanted to open a cooking school." I don't remember that as having been true, but I do vividly remember my dismay at being a second-class citizen at the Paris Cordon Bleu, good only for paying money. I had decided that La Varenne would be different from the Cordon Bleu that I knew in every way—light and airy, with plenty of room and good equipment. Students and staff would be treated with respect. And we would never, ever, as we had under Madame Brassart's purview, make students prepare a quiche Lorraine fourteen times. Over eighteen months at the Paris Cordon Bleu we had practiced three hundred recipes; at La Varenne our students would learn five hundred recipes over thirty-six weeks, more than one thousand if one included the demonstrations. The Paris Cordon Bleu ignored the many facets of French cuisine, regional cooking, and classical and historical dishes and their origins that make the subject so enthralling. I would not. The Cordon Bleu was run as a business. La Varenne would run as a vision.

Julia had made arrangements for our New York launch with Tom Margittai and Paul Kovi at the Four Seasons, the perfect setting, with its restaurant a point of intersection between serious food and serious design. We flew to the States in early October, confident the school was on its way. All the important food people were coming to the reception—Craig Claiborne, Jim Beard, Jane Montant, Julia, and Paul, among many others. The morning of the party, Mark asked me what I was going to say. In those days women almost shied away from speaking in public, and I'd not even thought about it. We hurriedly put something together—Mark told me what to say—and in the end the reception was a huge success even if my "few words" were scattered. Jim Beard declared that "such a bilingual school has long been needed in France," and Julia outlined her close involvement from the beginning. We all sipped Champagne and chomped on the *gougères* cheese puffs that later became our signature recipe. I felt as if we had laid up treasure for the future, and many people actually said they enjoyed themselves, which was good to hear. On that visit I even had some time to talk quietly with Julia. Having her as a confidante meant the world.

GOUGÈRES

I often freeze unbaked *gougères* on the baking sheet, storing the shaped puffs in a bag in the freezer so I can bake them just before serving.

Makes about 2 dozen 2½-inch/6-cm puffs

1 cup/100 g Gruyère cheese
1 egg, beaten to mix with ½ teaspoon salt, for glaze
2–3 tablespoons/15–22 g grated Gruyère cheese

For the cream puff pastry dough

1 cup/125 g flour
1 cup/250 ml water
1 teaspoon/7 g salt
½ cup/110 g butter, cut in cubes, plus more for baking sheet
4–5 eggs

Heat the oven to 400°F/200°C and set a shelf fairly low down; lightly butter a baking sheet. To make the cream puff pastry dough: Sift the flour onto a piece of paper. In a saucepan, combine the water, salt, and butter and heat gently until the butter is melted. Bring the mixture just to a boil (prolonged boiling evaporates the water), take from the heat, and immediately dump in all the flour. Beat vigorously with a wooden spoon—the mixture will make lumps, but keep beating for a few more moments until it pulls away from the pan sides to form a ball, 30 to 60 seconds. In a bowl, beat for 30 to 60 seconds longer over low heat to dry the dough. Beat 1 egg until mixed and set it aside. Break the remaining eggs into the dough, one at a time, beating thoroughly after each addition. Beat in enough of the reserved egg so the dough is shiny and just falls from the spoon. If too much egg is added, the dough will be soft and not hold its shape during baking, but if you add too little, the pastry will not rise so well.

Cut the cheese into tiny dice, or coarsely grate it, and beat it into the dough. (Dicing or coarsely grating the cheese allows the dough to rise higher.) Using two medium spoons, drop 1½-inch/4-cm mounds of dough on the baking sheet, spacing them well apart, as they will puff during cooking. Brush the mounds with the egg glaze and sprinkle them with grated Gruyère.

Bake the puffs until golden brown and crisp, 25 to 30 minutes, but do not open the oven door until they have been baking at least 20 minutes. Puffs often seem done too soon, so take one out and let it cool for a minute or two to check if it is ready before removing the rest. The puff should stay crisp on the outside and slightly soft inside. *Gougères* are at their best warm from the oven, but they can be baked an hour or two ahead.

While in New York we had extensive business discussions about tours with our American lawyer, Bill Kosmas, and we signed with a company called Destination France to do our wholesaling. At *Travel + Leisure* some pros turned us inside out in ten minutes but told us they would send someone to do a write-up. And then we flew back to Paris, where from morning to night I was on the run organizing workmen for our final push. Our promotion effort was thin. I had arranged for a lunch on October 26 for a freelance journalist called Suzy Patterson, a dry run to see how professional we were for Craig Claiborne's visit the following week. Sofitel gave a reception in their hotel right next door (they charged for the Champagne). We hoped they would invite *le tout Paris* so that the whole French world of food would open to us the way the American world had.

But when Mark and I arrived, we saw that Alain Carric had invited nobody at all. "Monsieur," I said, "why didn't you ask people from the food world, the chefs? The journalists?" Carric looked away and said, *"Mais ce n'est pas ma fonction,"* and mild-mannered Mark fumed and literally seized Carric's tie and shook him, a display I have never seen before or since by anyone. I've no idea how we made it through that evening, but I should have known then that our relationship with Sofitel would be short-lived.

It was thanks to Yanou Collart, PR woman par excellence, that our fortunes changed. That tense November, she sent a stream of French- and English-speaking journalists to our classes (for free, of course), and gradually the news began to circulate among the food world. "English is spoken here but the cooking is distinctly French," wrote the *New York Daily News*. "Recipes for Success" was a headline in the London *Times;* the well-known food critic Monique de Faucon's story was headlined "At Last Bilingual Classes." "Have Whisk Will Travel," wrote *House & Garden;* "Cooking School Poses Challenge to Cordon Bleu" in *The Washington Star;* "Woman Tackles French in their Own Kitchens" from *The Observer* in London; "A Yorkshire-born girl of great talent," began the story in *The Tatler,* in a syndicated story headlined, "New Paris Cooking School Has Special Ingredient: Bilingualism." *Le Soir, Figaro,* the *Stars and Stripes,* the *London Daily Mail,* the *Financial Times,* the *Toronto Star, The Miami Herald*—newspapers from Elyria, Ohio, to Seattle, Washington, from Brussels to Auckland, wrote glowingly about La Varenne.

Of course the mid-seventies was not like now, when cooking is a popular, fashionable, and lively subject. In those days one of my guiding ambitions was not just to pass on food knowledge but also to expand the whole food world. Cooking is tough, sweaty, unfeminine work—you can't wear makeup;

you must scrape back your hair so it doesn't fall into the food; it's hard on your feet; it's no good wearing even tidy clothes. You do a great deal of heavy lifting. Julia's knees eventually gave out. Later on my hips did. Everybody's backs go. But I was determined that La Varenne students—every one—would learn all they could about French cuisine. When I had been a student anybody who thought at all about the subject thought I was crazy to use my hands rather than my brain. The idea was incomprehensible except to a few people who understood that to be a really outstanding practical cook you had to understand the intellectual side. Now at last it seemed as if the world was welcoming us.

In January 1976, when *Time* published their article and photograph about us, they got it exactly right: "La Varenne is by no means an academy for chefs. Julia Child, citing the eminent Paul Bocuse's definition of a chef as 'a general who commands an army,' prefers to think of the school as a clearing-house for everyone who is even the tiniest bit interested in cooking." And to my delight, even discerning Frenchmen quickly offered us praise. Michel Oliver, owner of Bistro de Paris, son of the three-star chef Raymond Oliver, was quoted in *Time* as saying, "We need something like this in Paris." Bookings at La Varenne took off and by the second week of 1976 Jacqueline was taking calls every few minutes. Tradesmen dropped by to sell us things—always a good sign—and one guy suggested deliveries of sawdust, the traditional answer to grease on a kitchen floor.

Very quickly we were filled up with thirty full-time students and our kitchens were buzzing. We established our routine. In the morning, under the direction of Marolleau, students made the dishes I posted, with no repetition of a dish for three months, and afterward we lunched on their handiwork, accompanied, as *Time* had put it, by "democratic criticism." From the beginning it was important to me that we all sit around the same table, though there was always a certain amount of resistance—few of the chefs liked it, and there were trainees who would much rather have sat only with other trainees. But I felt that sitting together was part of what we were doing—enjoying the same good food and discussing it.

In the afternoon we adjourned to the upstairs demonstration kitchen, where the chef turned out more complicated dishes. On the day described in the article, Marolleau had prepared *chaud-froid de poulet*—poached chicken filled with mousse of foie gras, coated with white cream sauce, glazed with chicken aspic, and decorated with sculptured truffles. Meanwhile, down-stairs under my direction, five American women and one Vietnamese made potage Palestine (root artichoke soup), entrecôte steak flamed in Cognac, and *chaussons aux pommes*. I ran about offering shortcuts, such as a more aesthetic way to slice apples vertically so they tilt into overlapping crescents.

From the start I wasn't thrilled with Marolleau, but I was totally dependent upon him. He was an adequate teacher, but he wasn't the engaged and engaging chef I wanted. Besides, the job quickly grew beyond his control. We put an advertisement in the *Herald Tribune* and also contacted culinary chef associations for help. The Association des Maîtres Cuisiniers de France yielded one elderly man who had been a top chef but sadly had trouble talking as the result of a stroke; he also didn't understand the concept of following recipes I had prepared for the school. Another woman had been a famous model and came to the interview in furs, with her poodle in a basket. She could cook, but she was American and I was determined to have French chefs teaching.

From that same ad, a young man called Gregory Usher turned up. Although Greg wasn't right for teaching—he was an American, from Portland—he was absolutely great in many other ways. Greg had come to Paris years earlier to study at the Sorbonne, but his passion for food led him to apprentice with one or two chefs. He understood that in France the connoisseur is respected as much as the cook. He also was wonderful on public relations. He quickly became deputy director of La Varenne and my right hand.

I soon had my routine day established. Lesley, our au pair, was a serious, earnest girl, and it was she who got the children up in the morning and afterward came to school as a trainee. On his way to work, Mark walked them to the École Bilingue, where Emma was in preschool classes and Simon in first grade. I had already set off for La Varenne, passing on the way four pastry shops on the Rue Saint Dominique. You can tell at a glance if a pâtisserie is any good, for each item—éclairs, *sablés*, macaroons—will be exactly the same size and browned to the same shade. Two of the shops I passed sold acceptable, routine stuff like *pain au chocolat* and the chocolate-coated meringues our children loved—they exploded in a cloud of sugar when poked. A third was a tourist trap with piles of outsized, misshapen lumps laden with margarine. A year or two after we opened, a fourth shop appeared and proved to be one of the finest in Paris. There Jean Millet, the young chef who would become one of La Varenne's favorite guests, displayed his glazed lemon *sablés*, chewy *cannelles*, mirror-like chocolate *tartelettes*, and crisp *palmiers*, each one a feast to the eye. Occasionally I took a few *palmiers* to school and we divided them in slivers, each one a trip to heaven. Every morning by 8:00 I stopped at the café with my copy of the *Herald Tribune*, where I sat among the regulars, among them construction workers who dropped in for a glass of white wine and a well-dressed woman who came for a beer on her way to work. Then it was off across the Invalides to the school.

Quite soon after we opened, we had a group visit for a week from Sainsbury's, then the top grocery chain store in England. They were looking for sophisticated gourmet foods for their frozen offerings, ideas beyond quiche Lorraine and sole Mornay. They latched on to recipes like *poulet au champignons sauvages* and *beignets de Camembert,* and when I looked skeptically at their leader, a jovial old cove who dined in starred restaurants each night in the interest of "research," he twinkled his eyes at me. "You wait and see," he said. "It's all changing." How right he was.

But my search for a chef meanwhile continued. In March Gregory put in a call to Madame Lepaute. She had been head of personnel for the Relais & Châteaux group of luxury hotels and was a down-to-earth, straightforward woman I really liked, and she knew everyone. Gregory was certain she could find us the second chef we needed. One day she mentioned Chef Fernand Chambrette. "He's a difficult man," she said. "Not everyone can get along with him, but you might, and he can certainly cook well."

It was Chef Fernand Chambrette who changed everything for me. By then Chambrette was in his mid-fifties, and his two-star restaurant, La Boule d'Or, had closed. In the 1950s Jim Beard had raved about Chambrette's classic bistro. Back then it had been thriving in a rented space opposite the old covered market in Place d'Aligre on the Right Bank. When the owners developed the premises, they threw him out and Chambrette moved his restaurant to a corner of the Invalides gardens. Although he took his two stars along, the location was only a block from the politicians at the Assemblée—a suave, upscale market that hardly suited Chambrette's rough-and-ready welcome, albeit backed by superb cuisine. He went broke, closed La Boule d'Or, divorced his wife, and married Josette, the love of his life. Gossip had it Chambrette was not faring well with his unaccustomed freedom from the kitchen, and he was curious about La Varenne, so I telephoned him. He assured me he did not need a job but would come by the next day to meet *la directrice.*

It was a bright spring day when Chambrette eased his way into our tiny, crowded office wearing his unobtrusive tweed jacket, cap, and signature thick-rimmed black bifocals. He was short and stocky, with a confidence that filled up that little room. I noticed his hands were huge and awkward looking—I couldn't imagine how those hands could be responsible for any of La Boule d'Or's famous dishes: the *crêpes soufflés aux fruits de mer, filets de sole au vermouth, homard à l'américaine*. I didn't dare inquire about his training or experience, for he was, after all, a two-star chef. But he obliged me with a lecture on how to properly cook asparagus the classic French way, the best way. And this led him on to a lecture on the structure of French cooking.

He was speaking my language. "You don't fiddle around with a recipe until you know how to do it the right way first," he said. After that I asked him to come do a trial class for our trainees. A few days later when he did, I felt that it was myself and La Varenne who were on trial, not the chef. I scheduled a couple of our exam dishes for him to supervise, a *navarin* of lamb with spring vegetables and a *turban de sole*—he was famous for his seafood. Reports the following morning were outstanding, and that afternoon after a brief conversation the deal was sealed. The chef would start next week.

For the first two months Chambrette bided his time—observing the players, particularly me, deciding what this curious place was. The setup intrigued him. He had always been a maverick who took his work very seriously. For instance, when he came to us he hadn't made puff pastry since his apprentice days thirty-five years earlier. Ever since, in his restaurant he had had a pastry chef. For six weeks Chambrette arrived at the school extra early each morning and made puff pastry. In the end his was the best I'd ever had. However, he needed no practice in dishes like *gratin dauphinois;* he had prepared vats of it at La Boule d'Or, to scoop out by the ladleful and bake to order as individual servings.

GRATIN DAUPHINOIS

Chef Chambrette's *gratin dauphinois* is softer and richer than most versions, as the potatoes are simmered in milk and then finished in crème fraîche. I usually make one large dish of gratin, but individual versions, baked in small dishes, are good for a party.

Serves 6 to 8

5 cups/1.25 liters milk
2 pounds/900 g baking potatoes
1½ cups/375 ml heavy cream

1½ cups/375 ml crème fraîche
Salt and pepper
Large pinch of grated nutmeg
Butter, for the dish
¾ cup/75 g grated Gruyère cheese

Mandoline; 8×11-inch/20×28-cm baking dish

Put the milk in a saucepan. Peel the potatoes and cut them in slices ¼ inch/5 mm thick, preferably using a mandoline. Add them at once to the milk so they do not discolor. When all of them are in the pan, bring to a boil and then simmer them until almost tender, 15 to 20 minutes (potatoes take longer to cook in milk than in water). Stir often to prevent sticking.

Drain the potatoes (the milk can be used for soup), and wipe out the pan. Return the potatoes to the pan with the heavy cream and crème fraîche. Season with salt, pepper, and nutmeg, and bring just to a boil. Simmer, stirring occasionally, until the potatoes are very tender, 10 to 15 minutes. Do not let them boil or the cream will curdle.

Butter the baking dish. Spread the potato mixture, which will be quite sloppy, in the dish. (If you are preparing ahead, the sauce should be even sloppier, as it will thicken on standing.) Sprinkle the top with the cheese. The gratin can be prepared ahead and refrigerated, tightly covered, for two days, or frozen.

To finish, heat the oven to 350°F/180°C. Bake the gratin until very hot throughout and browned on top, 25 to 30 minutes.

It took Chambrette a couple of months to come out of his shell in the classroom, but he was clearly an instinctive cook who shone when left to improvise. Indeed, the only problem ever was too much invention. He had me changing my recipes to accommodate his style. But Chambrette's cooking was a revelation—a combination of instinct and knowledge acquired during fifty years in the kitchen. His snippets of learning brought the background of food to life. For instance, he knew that peas should be planted near beans and carrots but never beside an onion or garlic. He knew when basil was at its best and how to test a melon for ripeness. Chambrette communed with his ingredients, poking vegetables to test their freshness, looking fish straight in the eye. He had an extraordinary ability to extract flavor. Again and again he proved that intelligence and education are as important to cooking as they are to any other art.

That May the temperatures in Paris broke all records, and one boiling hot day, just two weeks after we had been frozen by snow flurries on a family outing to Fontainebleau, Chambrette came to my office in the early morning. He sat down and looked me in the eye. "Madame," he said, "I understand what you are trying to do here. I want to do all I can to help you." It is so seldom that one feels truly understood by another person, the memory of that moment still brings tears to my eyes, for that day was the true beginning of our partnership that lasted until he died in 2010 at the age of ninety.

One thing Chambrette at once insisted on, and this was that we buy our food at Rungis, the world's largest wholesale market. Rungis is so large it takes up the entire train station that was built to serve it and remains open around the clock, the hours of different pavilions staggered so that the fish pavilion, for instance, opens at midnight and closes when all the merchandise has been sold. Traders from all over the world buy and sell there. Once a week Chambrette drove off in a little rented van, returning to La Varenne with top-quality ingredients. It was wonderful to see those giant turbots and Dover soles—one per student for them to practice filleting. Once the Rungis runs began, the students' cooking took a quantum leap. Chambrette knew it was technique far more than individual recipes that mattered. He also knew all the tricks, and despite those giant, clumsy-looking hands, his lightness of touch was mesmerizing.

But Chambrette could also prove exasperating. I learned this very early on when one day a health inspector came to survey the premises. By then the chef was in charge of the stockpot. As all cooks know, you have to cool stock rapidly, and if it's a huge professional pot that takes quite a while. In the scorching heat of that spring and summer, cooling stock was no easy task—it can turn sour as it cools. I had no idea how Chambrette had chosen to solve this problem until one day I heard a student whispering and I discovered that Chambrette had come up with a unique solution. The school had two toilets—men's and women's—and the men's had a window. If you left the door open, you would get a cross breeze, so Chambrette had taken to putting the pot in there to cool it more rapidly. It was only by the grace of God the pot wasn't there on that day that the health inspector called. As soon as he had gone, I went to Chambrette and said, "Never put the stockpot in the men's room again!"

"*Oui, madame,*" he said. One week later I walked into the classroom and looked around. Chambrette was not there, and neither was the stockpot. When I asked the students where he was, they fell silent. Someone must have glanced toward the toilet, and sensing the worst, I ran to the door, flung it open, and saw the stockpot in the tiny space. Chambrette was in there, too, having a pee, but when he heard the door bang open he was so startled he turned and peed right into the pot.

Chambrette loved to shock and provoke. One day when the children were eight and nine, our au pair was on her day off and someone requested a last-minute meeting with me. Normally I would never ask Chambrette to help, but I was stuck, so I asked if he could take Simon and Emma along on his trip to Rungis. He agreed, and that evening when I got home the children were unusually quiet. It was much later that Simon told me that he had been sitting up front in the van when Chef asked if Simon knew the difference between eroticism and pornography and went on to define the two in some detail. I don't recall what I replied to Simon, but in truth I cannot think of a better person to have explained to our children the difference.

Chambrette professed to a cynical attitude, but he had to bite his lip to keep from laughing at his own jokes. Sometimes he was biting that lip to keep from laughing at the awkward nature of the wide-eyed students who flocked to us. When his smile turned extra sweet and the twinkle in his eye mischievous, it was time to watch your step. But sometimes a slight nod in your direction with a wink might mean "quick, over here" and he would hand over some trimmed ends from the foie gras terrine he had just unmolded—that is, if he hadn't already determined to take it home to his beloved and very spoiled cat, Léonard. Chambrette was not the least bit elitist. In fact, he was just as happy creating something delicious out of leftovers as he was creating a vegetable terrine layered with veal mousseline. He also understood better than I how to run the school, since it was not unlike a restaurant, with students taking the place of customers. It had never occurred to me before then that I could not allow the students to cook badly in case they were faced with food they had ruined. On that Chambrette was adamant: What is placed on the table must be excellent. When I taught at the Cordon Bleu in London, I was not experienced enough to save the students' mistakes and sometimes we had quite bad food. In Paris, the chef would simply take over and do it himself. But at La Varenne I depended on the chefs to rescue students' mistakes. Chambrette especially knew how to fix things without ever looking as if he was taking over.

Most mornings by the time I arrived at 8:30, Chambrette was already in the little office placing orders, a demitasse of extra-strong coffee by his side. By 9:00 the main staff had arrived. Our receptionist, Florence de Vallette, was there, along with Gregory and the invaluable Paule Tourdjman, our book-keeper, who would prove, time and again, to be a lifesaver, for she watched the accounts with an eagle eye. Soon Marolleau and Albert Jorant, the pastry chef I had hired, were there, too. I insisted on punctuality for classes, start-ing at 9:30. If a delivery hadn't come and the class couldn't start with fish as planned, we made a change. If something was broken, I made sure it got fixed. I checked student attendance. By 9:45 I sat down to a second coffee and tackled the administration.

By the end of spring of 1976 we had the system rolling, meticulously cho-reographed, and we were attracting students and trainees from all sorts of places and backgrounds. In January we had begun with a single class of peo-ple who stayed a maximum of three weeks at more or less an intermediate level. By June we had three classes on the go all the time. Each student had four practical classes and five demonstrations a week. In the fall we extended class length to twelve weeks at three levels, Beginner, Intermediate, and Ad-vanced, all adding up to a Grand Diplôme. Putting all these pieces together was like composing a jigsaw puzzle.

In a practical class the chef opened up with all the ingredients on the ta-ble. For nearly an hour he would describe the dishes, showing any special techniques like filleting a fish, and then he would be off, assigning groups of two or three different jobs in the task of preparing three courses. Folding chairs were stacked, aprons tied and laced with the torchon—the protean French dish towel—sponge, pot holder, and cheesecloth. The kitchens rap-idly became sweltering with ovens hot, fast, and tricky. For three hours knives flashed, pots clattered, oven doors squeaked, and voices rumbled—encouraging, exhorting, reprimanding. At the end of class the counter was cleared and everything was laid out for presentation.

It took me a while to understand that a successful class must be like a theatrical show with plenty of action and education slipped in on the side. Over those first three months, as I translated presentations, I came to under-stand that literally translating words was inadequate (and in the case of someone as inarticulate as Marolleau could lead to long silences). A chef is a cook, not a conversationalist. So I would keep the action going by asking questions like, "Why are you using that knife?" "How do you select the freshest chicken?" "How do you know when that fish is done?" To fill gaps I added comments from my own knowledge, trying always to include the chef in the conversation. The cooked food laid out on the counter for comment was the visual finale. And since assessing taste mattered, too, at last we all, students included, enjoyed a meal together.

Presentations kept the chefs up to snuff because they knew whatever the students were making in the morning would be critiqued at lunch. The chefs, who understood the French approach to food, took this seriously. If anyone began to talk during a demonstration, I would say, "I'm sorry, we can't have that." If Chambrette heard someone whispering, he would bang a lid on the demonstration bench. There was one more delicate dance we learned to do. The building was 150 years old, so naturally we had our share of cockroaches. We had three ways to deal with them. We might say, "Ah, another friend," and casually brush it away or we might pretend it wasn't there, or we popped a lid over it and slid it casually off the table. In short order Gregory also began translating demonstrations, and he was very good. He was also terrific on promotion, with a lot of ideas for how to get the word out about the school. He quickly became an integral part of what I was trying to create, and our reputation and reach expanded. From very early on we were training people who would become not only chefs but also—perhaps more typically of La Varenne—food writers with great visibility outside the kitchen.

In parallel with our student classes, we began to develop our *stagiaire,* or trainee, program, for we clearly needed more help. In the beginning just about anyone who walked in off the street and could speak a bit of French was asked to stay on, but over time the internship evolved into a nine-month, structured program. Eventually trainees divided into two groups—practical trainees who worked in the kitchen and editorial trainees who did research and editing for my books, thus learning how a manuscript is put together. In this we were active in an area that no other cooking school has followed. Usually a trainee was good at one or the other, though that wasn't always the case. From the first, we began to attract remarkable talent. Steve Raichlen was invaluable and in those early days helped write the curriculum. Nina Simonds, one of our earliest trainees, came to us with her long plait of hair stretched down her back and much experience in Chinese cooking. Chambrette was especially interested in hearing Nina's views, for she had much to say on the strong and complex Asian flavorings. Another early trainee, Jane Sigal, later made her name at *Food & Wine,* and Judy Hill, one of the top early trainees, went on to become a first-class food editor at *Martha Stewart*

Living, founding editor at *Cook's Magazine,* and later food director at Rodale.

This was a magical period in Paris for cooking. As Steve Raichlen later said, for anyone interested in food being in Paris at that time was privileged, much like being a writer in Paris in Hemingway's day. Most of the *stagiaires* lived in six-floor walk-ups. They spent every waking moment doing something with food—classes in the mornings, demonstrations in the afternoons, a trainee practical class twice a week in the evenings. Many got unofficial jobs in pastry shops or markets, at restaurants, or catering to the American community. French cuisine was becoming a portal by which Americans were rediscovering the culinary arts after a long dormant period that began in the 1930s with the taming of vegetables in cans, followed by the 1950s and frozen foods. Julia had opened the front and led the battle, and now La Varenne was the place people could have the Julia Child experience, a working laboratory of classical French cuisine. The stagiaires were able to plunge into French culture in a way any other kind of visit to Paris would never provide.

One day a letter came from a woman saying: "I enormously want to learn to cook. I'm coming from Israel with my husband and I can't afford to pay for the class and have nowhere to live." Fortunately I asked Julia what she thought I ought to do, and in her usual democratic way Julia said, "Well, dear, I think you should talk to her." So when Faye Levy appeared, I welcomed her. She was a tiny thing with a high voice and proved to be a shining exception to my rule about such letter writers. We desperately needed help with English documents in the office, and Faye said she could type. I didn't want too many people in our tiny back room overhearing all the private conversations, but within a week, in exchange for classes, Faye was installed at the desk that belonged to Chambrette, typing faster than anybody else. Faye became a gifted cook, a writer and editor, and another invaluable fixture at La Varenne. Her husband, Yakir, an Israeli army veteran, became a treasured babysitter for Simon, whom he would toss in the air to release Simon's energy.

Now and then someone would drop by and say, "I'd love to come to a cooking class; tell me about them," and when I mentioned the cost they might say, "Ah, not a chance." In those cases we'd ask, "Do you speak French?" and quite often we would ask them to stay for a week on trial. If that went well, we would invite them to stay on as a stagiaire, working at various jobs in exchange for classes. Once in a while we had to nip and tuck with someone whose French in the beginning was minimal, but usually within six weeks of being yelled at by the chef people learned to communicate surprisingly well. Translating a good demonstration could be exhausting. The most famous example of a problem was the day Chambrette spent forty minutes skinning a bucket of eels in total silence. If I had been doing the translation, I would have stopped him, but I was the only person around who would dare to do that and certainly not the unhappy young stagiaire who was translator for the day. When questioned, trying to get him to talk, he would say only, *"Mais, bien sûr,"* or "I have no idea." Occasionally Chambrette could be like that, though there always was a reason. I'd probably told him to do something differently from the way he usually did it.

It did help to have a pretty young woman translating; the chefs loved that. It also helped if the stagiaire spoke really good French. Of course some people get along and some don't. On the whole Chambrette was happy with everyone. Albert Jorant, our pâtissier, was a wonderful chef, and I didn't have to tell him anything about teaching—he just knew. Saturday morning was pastry day, and Jorant baked enough pastries in just two hours to completely cover the huge demonstration table. He was from the Picardy, a poverty-stricken northern mining area. When he was very young, he'd wanted to be a hairdresser and made his way to Paris. But the hairdresser he applied to didn't feed his apprentices, so the eight-year-old turned to a nearby pâtisserie. Too short to knead the brioche, he had to stand atop his treasured ditty box of possessions. Now, fifty years later, he had left the Cordon Bleu because they were mean on ingredients—he told me it reminded him of the War, when he'd had to stretch his bread by adding sawdust to the dough. The trouble was that Jorant regularly told his same tedious jokes. While kneading his brioche he would say, "You must be really delicate and careful; *c'est comme une jeune femme mariée* [it's like a young bride]." The first time you heard it you thought, oh well, good for him, but after six times you had to restrain yourself from groaning. The stagiaires (particularly the girls) struggled to find euphemisms, and some got on with him less well than others.

His classic repertoire of recipes was superb. Financiers were my favorites. These odd little cakes are baked in purposely designed rectangular molds so that when turned out they look like small gold bars. They are said to have been invented by an enterprising pâtissier near the Paris Bourse (stock exchange) as a snack for hungry traders who were taking a break.

PETITS FINANCIERS (LITTLE ALMOND CAKES)

Financiers are traditionally baked in special bar-shaped molds, though boat molds can be substituted. The color of the cakes is intensified by browning the butter to *beurre noisette*.

Makes 2 dozen small cakes

1 cup/225 g butter, more for the molds
2/3 cup/100 g whole blanched almonds
3/4 cup/100 g flour, sifted, plus more for the molds
2 1/4 cups/300 g powdered sugar, sifted
7 egg whites (1 cup/250 ml), whisked just until frothy

Twelve 3-inch/7.5-cm bar-shaped molds

To brown the butter: Have a bowl of cold water ready. In a small saucepan melt the butter and heat until it stops sputtering, stirring often. When the milk solids at the bottom are lightly browned and the butter has developed a characteristic nutty smell (and flavor), remove from the heat and at once plunge the base of the pan into the bowl of cold water to stop the cooking—it will scorch very easily. Let it cool to lukewarm.

To grind the almonds, put them in a food processor with the flour. Work with the pulse button until finely ground, 40 to 60 seconds. Put the almond and flour mixture in a bowl, stir in the powdered sugar, and make a well in the center. Add the egg whites to the almond mixture and stir with a whisk until smooth. Put the mixture in a heavy-based saucepan, set it over low heat, and stir constantly until the mixture is just warm to the touch. Take the pan from the heat and stir in the brown butter. Cover and leave the batter to stand at least 4 hours, or overnight, at room temperature so the flour softens and the financiers bake more evenly.

Heat the oven to 425°F/220°C and set a shelf in the center. Butter the molds generously with more melted butter and chill until set. Sprinkle them with flour, then tap them on the counter to remove the excess. Pour the batter into a pitcher and fill the molds nearly to the top, using half the mixture. Set them on a baking sheet and bake in the oven 12 to 15 minutes, until the financiers are risen, golden brown, and firm when lightly pressed with a fingertip. Unmold them onto a rack and leave to cool. Bake the remaining batter in a second batch. Financiers can be kept up to a week in an airtight container, or frozen, and the flavor mellows.

Depending on the personality of the stagiaire, their trainee program would go better or worse. Ris Lacoste, now the chef/owner of an outstanding restaurant in Washington, D.C., is an example. She never managed to learn much French and so was never in the kitchen with the chefs, though she was the best receptionist we had—enormously friendly and organized. I thought she would go into front-of-the-house work in a restaurant, but when she returned to the States she cooked with several chefs, including Bob Kinkead, and eventually became a renowned chef in her own right. Now and then a trainee might be very talented yet cause problems. One young woman who knew a lot about food was intelligent but also sly; one day I walked into the kitchen to find one of the most distinguished chefs in France standing there. No one had told me anything about his coming. *"Chef, grand honneur,"* I said, and on and on. I eventually learned that he was there because he and the young woman were having a flaming affair, and I was not pleased.

Our Japanese associate, Fumiko Homma, knew the restaurant scene inside out and placed students in top restaurants for their study weeks. Fumiko was one of the most beautiful women I've ever known, and endlessly patient. There were places women couldn't work—particularly in Paris so many kitchens were tiny. But Fumiko unerringly placed trainees in just the right spots. One day a trainee, Danielle, took one of the more pliable stagiaires as her girlfriend and chose a day when Fumiko was on vacation to go to their restaurant *stage* together. That evening Danielle called me, furious. "The chef has made improper advances to my girlfriend," she fumed. I thought, well, of course he has; chefs always made advances to any girl anywhere near acceptable looking.

One summer when Steve Raichlen was doing a stage at a Michelin-starred restaurant in Brittany, he reported back that he had done two things that were regarded as heresy in the kitchen where he was working. He asked questions as his co-workers never would have dared to do, and he brought a notebook with him and took notes on everything he saw. It was, he said, a lesson in openness to his French companions, and that openness was something I think all our staff, and so many Frenchmen and -women who came over the years, learned at La Varenne.

The structure we had established within a year of our opening scarcely varied during the school's fifteen years of life in Paris. There was also little change in staff in all those years. From these firm foundations we launched half a dozen major book projects and a string of little ones; we sent La Varenne on tour, with mixed results; we survived a precipitous drop in the value of the dollar and a corresponding decline in enrollments. Mark was happy in his job and was entirely suited to it. The children grew up under our eyes. I enjoyed perhaps the happiest years of my life.

La Varenne had a wonderful band of teaching chefs: (left to right) Maurice Ferré, Patrick Martin, me in my Miss Dior, Albert Jorant, Claude Vauguet, and Fernand Chambrette with school director Susy Davidson.

Chapter Ten

....

LUNCH WITH THE TAX INSPECTOR

One cannot think well, love well, sleep well, if one has not dined well.

—Virginia Woolf

Looking back on those first five hectic years at La Varenne, it was clear that problems were there from the very start and the end might have been anticipated. I was determined that the school should fulfill my vision, but I paid too little attention to budgets and the bottom line. We were a small business with expensive international marketing overheads (not to mention those first-class Rungis ingredients). We had an office in the United States and, by the end of the first year, nine full-time employees, not counting me, entailing high social-security charges, for which France is notorious. We understood promotion was vital, but in those days there was no Internet for marketing, so we had to use our imagination to find other ways to spread the word.

Our partnership with Sofitel ended unexpectedly. Because of those first classes I had given at the Gritti, I came up with an idea based on traveling exhibitions. So far we had no European students. We needed a portable kitchen for cooking demonstrations to attract students closer to home, and without asking anyone at Sofitel—which in retrospect I should have done—I hired someone to build a moveable setup with three modules: a stove and two work surfaces, with a small fridge and shelves underneath. When Alain Carric found out, he was furious. He said it was a useless cost and, even worse, this should have been a mutual decision. At the time, we had a good deal of money on deposit for future classes, money that provided us with a cash flow to pay salaries and buy supplies. Sofitel had an accountant called Monsieur Mouchené. (*Mouche* translates as "fly," and in a Dickensian way the name was perfect for this man.) Mouchené had signature authority with me over our account.

One early morning, I received a call from our bank manager. "I thought you ought to know all the money has been withdrawn from your business account," he said. That left us nothing for outstanding checks, and bouncing a check in France could result in our being declared bankrupt. In a panic, I called Eliane Heilbronn, who charged, "This is *escroquerie* [theft]!" We had to get the withdrawal stopped before the end of the banking day to avoid disaster. Not until Eliane contacted her acquaintance—the senior vice president of the Sofitel Group—was our money restored.

From the start the partnership with Sofitel was odd and we were a tiny enterprise in a vast machine. After that crisis we entered negotiations to separate, and they played hardball: They threatened to force closure of the school and even went so far as to send the *huissier,* a bailiff, to our door with a *summation de payer* if we didn't buy them out of the whole contract. The hasty exit of our influential partner was a warning that La Varenne was treading on thin ice, but I was determined to carry on. Besides, Sofitel had brought us one valuable asset—the long-term lease to our commercial premises. Although the rent was steep, such locations were rare in Paris and we were lucky. After Sofitel departed, carry on we did.

Our first adventure with the mobile unit happened soon after the Mouchené incident. The American army in Frankfurt hired us to upgrade the repertoire of cooks from the mess halls all over Germany. Their aim was to revive their chefs' flagging enthusiasm and to introduce a few new dishes among their repertoire of hamburgers and club sandwiches. Gregory, Chambrette, Marolleau, and I packed up what would become our signature red valise with everything we needed—pots and pans, whisks and sieves. We traveled by train with our mobile kitchen to Frankfurt.

For the next week we were in the vast sergeants' mess surrounded by commercial equipment in industrial-strength stainless steel, doing demonstration and hands-on classes for twenty-five cooks, all male. I was the only woman, and I was in charge. We taught dishes such as coq au vin and *boeuf en croûte*, crème caramel and *mousse au chocolat*. At the beginning of each day, Chambrette would say, "I'll do the fish and the sauces," and Marolleau would claim the soufflés. Not wanting to upset the chefs and to keep everyone happy, I wound up on the deep-fat station, so that by the end of our eighteen-hour day I exuded deep-fried shrimp scampi and beignets.

On our third day, Marolleau began to get surly first thing in the morning; it was very unlike him. By that afternoon as I began the demonstration, he refused to say a word. Even when I asked him a question, he remained stubbornly silent. As we were tidying up after the class, I said to Greg, "What on earth is wrong with Michel?" "I think he's missing his wife," Gregory said, and suggested a visit to a Frankfurt brothel might be in order. Naturally I had never dealt with such an excursion, but that night in a torrential cloudburst Marolleau and Chambrette trudged off to the brothel. The next morning Marolleau was restored to his usual equanimity while Chambrette was sneezing away and did so for the rest of the week. When I asked Greg why Chambrette had even gone he told me he, too, had asked, and before Chambrette answered, "*Je me suis bien débrouillé* [I kept my end up]."

For the final banquet at the U.S. Army base in Frankfurt we planned to serve a seafood pilaf that we prepared the day before. In the morning when we took it out of cold storage, we could smell that it had gone sour. That was the day I learned that a large volume of food stays hot for a very long time, long enough to ferment overnight. If you plan to cool a big pot, anything more than six inches in depth is risky. Chambrette simply waved away my concerns, fished out all the shrimp, washed them in bleach, and stirred them in again. No one got sick, though to a discerning palate the pilaf tasted rather odd.

As we traveled home I realized Marolleau had only been doing his duty, with little joie de vivre. In stark contrast, Chambrette had thoroughly enjoyed his week with the soldiers. Marolleau obviously had talents other than cooking—at school occasionally I noticed a student handing over her hotel room number—but he was unhappy and not long after he returned to Paris he gave notice he would leave before the end of the year. I asked Chambrette if he knew anyone who could be our second chef. "Well, madame," he said—he addressed me always as madame—"I might." At La Boule d'Or his apprentice chef, then *commis*, then sous chef, had been Claude Vauget. "*C'est un très bon chef*," Chambrette said. I telephoned Claude—I always called him Claude, for he was my age. He came in to talk. If Chambrette trusted him, so could I, so I invited him to join us, and our team was complete.

So it was that early in the New Year, 1977, on a snowy day, a flock of dazzling, unflappable, and determined trainees and Claude both began at the school. One of the trainees later said that the requirement for creativity and hard work at La Varenne shaped their future lives. Claude was the perfect teaching chef for these bright young people—a good cook, handsome, cheerful, kind in a teasing way. He loved to joke, in French—he had no English. One of his favorites was "*ça brûle normalement* [it's burning normally]," as he flung open a smoking oven door. A live class has a great advantage over television. In person, performers can sense the audience reaction. Cooking involves all five senses—sight, sound, touch, smell, and taste—and three of those are lost on television. As our afternoon demonstrations became better known, people came just as they went to the cinema, and our audience grew. We offered tastings of every dish, and one fateful day when forty people showed up the chef had to cut a single chicken into forty portions. After that, I increased the budget, while Paule, our bookkeeper, kept a keen eye on the books.

That year, just outside our door they began doing roadwork and we had to shout over the deafening roar. One day just as the demonstration was to begin, I realized with great relief that the horrid jackhammer had gone silent. "*Mon dieu*, it's quiet today," I whispered to Chambrette. When I saw the twinkle in his eye, I understood. Chambrette knew all the dodges; he had bribed the workers with bottles of our wine to silence their machinery from 2:30 to 4:30 each day.

Despite Chambrette's protests, I insisted we explore the contemporary Paris food scene, and this meant nouvelle cuisine ("a little bit of nothing on a big white plate," he called it). By 1978 we had begun to offer a course in the new light style of cooking, and Chambrette led the field with his fish sauerkraut and red wine reduction sauce mounted with butter. We all kept an eye out when using flour—one of the nouvelle chefs declared he had banished it from the kitchen. When we discovered there was scant literature available, we printed a booklet called *The Ten Commandments of Nouvelle Cuisine*, basing our title on an article written by journalists Henri Gault and Christian

Millau, listing the ten characteristics of this new wave. The reclusive cookery writer Elizabeth David wrote from London to ask me for a copy of our booklet and invited me to her kitchen in Chelsea. Naturally I was nervous. She was a classic English intellectual, inquiring and sharp. I need not have worried. I took Mark along and he fielded the tough questions while we all sat around her wooden kitchen table and ate freshly baked apple pie with tea. Elizabeth was most welcoming.

One sidelight of the proliferation of new dishes in nouvelle cuisine was the difficulty describing them. Even Paul Bocuse had protested the bending of precise French terminology to embrace the cuisine's eccentricities—"pâté," "terrine," "rillettes," and other charcuterie names were now being used for fish and vegetables. Michel Guérard calling his duck stew *pot au feu* was equally provocative. And classical shorthand—*à la florentine, bonne femme, normande*—failed in the face of recipes for sautéed Brittany lobster and scallops with a purée of Brussels sprouts or hot pâté of baby wild rabbit with fiddlehead ferns, oak leaf lettuce, rocket cress, walnut oil, and croutons. Such flowery descriptions strayed dangerously close to the absurd. Chambrette loved to play with this notion. When he prepared his steamed fillets of fish with red skin, white skin, blue skin, he dubbed his creation *"méli-mélo de poisson à la vapeur aux arômes orientales, sauces beurre blanc et beurre rouge* [mishmash of fish, steamed with Asian perfumes, red and white butter sauces]."

And the Cuisinart? At the Cordon Bleu it was shunned, but the revolutionary new machine that had been invented in 1971 by an American raised in France, Carl Sontheimer, was simply a home adaptation of the French restaurant gadget beloved by chefs, the *robot coupe*. Why couldn't we use the Cuisinart? If the goal is to teach people to cook, you cannot dismiss what's going on around you. It gave quicker results even if it lacked finesse—a Cuisinart purée was never quite as smooth and silky as a hand-sieved one, and the blade bruised raw meat and fish so the texture became chewy and sticky rather than clean-cut. We also taught students that a hand grinder yields different results from chopping with a knife. One day Chambrette made a terrine by chopping the pork entirely by hand, and the intensity of the flavor startled even me.

One evening as I was leaving the school at 5:30, hurrying home to prepare a meal for people coming to our apartment at 8:00, I turned to Chambrette for advice. "Poach some scallops and make this sauce," he said, handing over a recipe he'd just put together. "Bring it to a boil." I argued that boiling would curdle any sauce that contained egg yolks and cream, but he shook his head and said, "Just go away and do it." To my amazement, not only did it work, it was perfection. Another evening I asked him for a dessert that would take no time and he gave me some peaches and told me to slice them and cover them with red wine and a bit of sugar. It wasn't great art, but it was a legitimate dessert and delicious. Later I learned it came from the Loire and had a name, *chicolle*. There's nothing like immersion in a working kitchen for adding depth and sublety to one's knowledge.

CHEF CHAMBRETTE'S SCALLOPS WITH SAFFRON AND CREAM

As well as flavoring these scallops, a hefty pinch of saffron dyes them a vivid buttercup yellow. Fresh noodles are the perfect accompaniment.

Serves 8 as a first course, 4 to 6 as a main

    6 ounces/170 g mushrooms, cut in julienne strips
    1 tablespoon butter, plus more for the pan
    Juice of ½ lemon
    Salt and pepper
    2 pounds/900 g large scallops
    Large pinch of saffron threads, soaked in 2–3 tablespoons
        boiling water

For the sauce

    1 shallot, finely chopped
    2 tablespoons/30 ml dry white wine
    2 tablespoons/30 ml dry vermouth, or more white wine
    1¼ cups/300 ml crème fraîche
    6 tablespoons/90 g cold unsalted butter, cut in cubes

To cook the mushrooms: Put them in a buttered saucepan with the lemon juice, 2 tablespoons water, salt, and pepper. Press a piece of buttered foil on top, cover with the lid, and cook over medium heat until the juice froths up and covers the mushrooms, about 5 minutes. Set them aside.

Drain the scallops of any liquid and dry them on a paper towel. To cook them, melt the butter in a frying pan—it should be large enough for the scallops to sit on the bottom. Add them and pour over the saffron and liquid. Cover and cook over low heat just until the scallops stiffen slightly, 2 to 3 minutes; turn them and cook 1 to 2 minutes on the other side. They should still be pliable to the touch, showing they are rare in the center. Lift them out with a draining spoon and set aside.

For the sauce: Stir the shallot, wine, and vermouth into the scallop liquid and drain in the mushroom liquid, leaving the mushrooms in their pan. Boil the scallop and mushroom liquid until reduced to a glaze of 1 to 2 tablespoons, 3 to 5 minutes. Whisk in the crème fraîche, add any more juice released by the scallops, and boil until reduced by about a third, 2 to 3 minutes.

Take the frying pan of sauce from the heat and gradually whisk in the cold butter, working on and off the heat so that it softens and thickens the sauce creamily. When all the butter is added, bring the sauce just to a boil (the high proportion of cream prevents the sauce from separating). Taste and adjust the seasoning.

Add the scallops and mushrooms to the sauce; heat gently about a minute until very warm. Serve on warm plates.

When Gregory and I decided to invite the rising stars of the food world to come and offer a demonstration once a week, Chambrette immediately welcomed the idea. Most of the chefs knew one another—they met on Mondays to discuss ideas when their restaurants were closed—and many were young, with boundless energy. The common denominator was their ability to cook well. Greg kept in close touch with the grapevine and knew who might draw a crowd, and the chefs who came loved the informality and the respect we all had for their skill and the way they thought about their cooking. Word spread, and many chefs jumped at the opportunity. A very few turned us down—Alain Senderens, the famed chef at l'Archestrate just blocks away, was too toffee-nosed to come.

We asked those who came to show something the chef wanted to do but also that illustrated interesting techniques or new ingredients. Like everything else, ingredients go in and out of fashion—in the mid-seventies duck was in and, now that air freight services were expanding, so were flavorings such as lemongrass, soy sauce, star anise, and tropical fruit. We kept up with all the magazines and restaurant reviews, and personalities who came through our doors ranged from bombastic to charming to caustic. Our guest chefs included Jean Michel Bédier, whose Le Chiberta is still going strong; Gérard Besson; Maurice Ferré, the pastry chef from Maxim's; Jean Delaveyne at La Camélia, whose restaurant had three Michelin stars; and Joël Robuchon, who was just starting his international career. The guest chefs did things like *blanc de volaille farci à l'étuvée au vinaigre de Jerez*—one of the chic ingredients was sherry vinegar—or *salade d'homard aux petits légumes*, lobster salad with a stylish julienne of vegetables.

When Antoine Bouterin, who later became the well-known chef at Le Périgord in New York, came to us he was just nineteen, a totally unknown chef in a one-star restaurant called the Quai d'Orsay, just across the Invalides from us. He was tall and dark with great big dark eyes and huge eyelashes. He made wonderful Provençal food, very different from the Parisian style, with three times the quantity of herbs and lots of garlic. His scallops with garlic and tomato had to be tasted to be experienced. As Antoine cooked he barely said a word, but he would glance up, terrified and shy under those long eyelashes, and that shyness absolutely wowed the audience. He was a great lesson to me in understanding that all sorts of personalities can communicate a passion.

Though our schedule revolved around classes, not stars, Gregory was ideal at inviting celebrity guests and people who knew about food. Simca came quite often—she lived in Paris. Hugh Johnson gave a class on wine, to my shame wrinkling his nose at the acrid white we were passing around. Craig Claiborne came again, and Jim Beard. Chuck Williams of Williams-Sonoma stopped in for a visit. After several invitations, Alice Waters dropped by with an exhausted-looking sous chef in tow; she had slept in, she said. Dale Brown, a senior editor at Time Life was looking for a writer for his new technique series, *The Good Cook*. Dale and I got along very well and indeed he became a good friend. But he pointed out that I was far too busy with the fledgling La Varenne business to write the books, and it was Richard Olney who eventually created the landmark series. Julia came whenever she was in France, though she never told anyone in advance because she didn't want a fuss. When she came, Greg would ask her to talk about the food the students had made and Julia always knew just the right thing to say: "Oh, I haven't seen that in ages," or, "How utterly delicious. . . ." But if a dish was poorly cooked, she said so.

One year on our Alsatian cooking day, I insisted the class prepare *lewerknepfles*, calves' liver dumplings. From the start there was complaint. Quite a lot of the students didn't like liver, and when it's ground into a dumpling—almost like a matzo ball—it's not awfully popular. This time, added to the general disgruntlement, the *knepfles* failed. Instead of being round, they collapsed into a kind of gray pancake. As the presentation began, Julia looked at the dish and said, "Oh dear, it looks like the cat's been sick." Everyone collapsed with laughter and looked at me with a kind of "I told you so!" expression. I was never allowed to forget it.

There were, on occasion, some rather funny misunderstandings. It became a joke in the office that I spoke English English, not American English. For instance, I might look at a trainee's dish and say, "That's not bad"—by which I meant, "That's quite good"—though I learned that to an American ear I was sounding critical. "Oh, incidentally, by the way," I might say to a student, meaning, "The primary purpose of our discussion is what I'm about to say." "I'm sure it's my fault" meant "It's your fault," and there were dozens of other examples of turns of phrase that, when interpreted, had us laughing. There was also my favorite line that said so much: "It'll be done in its own time." All too often a student would neglect to test if a dish was done, and simply remove it without checking. "Oh, but the recipe says . . ." was the standard reply, and how difficult it was to convince inexperienced cooks that cooking times would vary almost every time.

Still more journalists continued to come to see what the fuss was about, and before long we were on the tourist route. One day, to my delight, Jane Grigson, the well-known food editor at the London *Observer* newspaper, wrote to say she would be in France for the summer and would like to visit. In the summers, Jane and her husband, the poet Geoffrey Grigson, lived in an authentic troglodyte dwelling, a cave hollowed in a cliff overlooking Le Loir, the river north of the famous La Loire. They were the only people I knew who lived in such a place. When Jane and I met, we got on right away, discovering quickly how much we had in common. As she would write in an article for *The Observer,* "Some coincidences would not be acceptable in a novel: They would seem too contrived. It was by a coincidence of this kind that I came to know Anne Willan well." Jane was a decade older than I, but she, too, grew up in Yorkshire and went to Cambridge and she and I shared a love of cooking and of France. We also shared a similar personality—we just got in there and did it.

As fate would have it, less than a week after Jane's visit her editor at *The Observer* asked her to produce a weekly cookery course for the paper. It was the days of supplements in Sunday newspapers, and Jane suggested I contribute a part of it. The editor had never heard of me, but the paper committed to the idea if Jane agreed to write the glossary at the end of each issue. Once we began, they were impressed with what I sent them and started to put money into what became *The Observer French Cookery School*, offering trustworthy information and recipes on the full meaning of such techniques as braising, sautéing, and grilling and such details like the difference between shortcrust and *pâte brisée*. Sunday circulation of the newspaper increased by 10 percent and the series became a landmark in food journalism in England.

From the start, illustrations for the series proved more troublesome than the text. *The Observer* sent a photographer to take the pictures in Normandy because there was no room at the school in Paris. Despite my advance warnings, the young man had to be bailed out at French customs because he did not have the right papers for bringing his equipment into France. After two whole days at Bourg Dun where we had La Maison Blanche, he had completed only a single shot of sole meunière on a gray, stony beach. I knew he had to work faster and told him so. The next morning he was standing in the hallway with his suitcases packed. "I'm leaving. I won't be treated so poorly," he said. I realized that I couldn't afford to cause trouble with one of *The Observer*'s freelance photographers given that I was a total unknown to their experienced staff. Thankfully, Judy Hill, the trainee who had come along to help, mediated and he agreed to continue if he never had to "take orders" from me again. We did, in the end, complete the assignment, though several days late.

When the inserts began to appear in the paper, all my parents' friends and neighbors read them. My mother had always been pleased with what I was doing, since Paris embodied so many of the things she loved. But this helped my father to understand that his daughter was doing something he could be proud of. It also helped us recover from the flop of a celebration we'd arranged in New York for the publication of *Great Cooks and Their Recipes*. At terrible expense we had used the kitchen of a well-known New York restaurant, and Chambrette came over and cooked. We invited a dozen movers and shakers, but nobody ended up writing about the dinner of historical recipes from the book. It had been a mistake to bypass a PR person in New York.

There was one good outcome. We had included one of the finest cookbook editors of the time at that dinner, Narcisse Chamberlain at William Morrow. She wanted an American edition of *The Observer French Cookery School*—a rather more flossy version, though the book was written to be used in the kitchen. Under the name *The La Varenne Cooking Course* it came out beautifully, and it had the La Varenne name on it, too. Thankfully, Jim Sherer from Boston was the photographer, and his photos looked as lovely as he was to work with. One of them starred on the back cover, a petit four of mounded vanilla butter cream, topped with a dot of candied cherry, all veiled in transparent white fondant icing. Of course soft porn lurks often in food photographs; Betsy Balsley of the *Los Angeles Times* had a whole wall plastered with dubious images from free handouts sent to the newspaper. To this day I do not know what Narcisse's intention was, but the photo was a perfect symbol of a breast.

While we were in New York, I had an opportunity to work with my friend Peter Kump, who had opened a cooking school in the cramped kitchen of his Upper West Side apartment. Before the class, as he recounted the trials he had endured in launching his school, I said, "Keep your pecker up!" a common English expression but one he had never heard. It left us both collapsed in laughter. Peter had been unable to negotiate any electricity hookup, and we had to use gas burners, the roaring dragons used on building sites, for heat in near-zero outdoor temperatures. In the class we explored the difference between French and American ingredients, and I was surprised to discover it was not just the meats and fish nor even the flour that were so very different. It was the French cream and butter that were irreplaceable.

Naturally we had our grumblers at La Varenne. In early January 1977, while visiting my parents in snow-swept Yorkshire—my father had just had emergency surgery for removal of a kidney stone—I received a letter from Julia with a copy of her letter to a Mrs. Pettibone who had written to grouse to Julia about her three-week course at La Varenne. Julia defended us with as much conviction as she always had. But I knew Mrs. Pettibone was right about a few things—late deliveries sometimes, possible lack of equipment. But her complaint that our *femme de ménage,* our cleaning-up woman, didn't speak English seemed petty minded. The main problem was that the school wasn't what Mrs. Pettibone had expected.

We worked to bridge this communication gap by sending out descriptions of the school and its staff and orienting students when they arrived. And most students were enjoying themselves. Julia also passed on to us the encouraging letter she'd had from someone saying he'd be back next year. By the early eighties the Culinary Institute of America and Johnson & Wales

University and other professional schools had begun to offer reliable introductions to French cuisine. Francois Dionot had opened L'Academie de Cuisine in Bethesda, Maryland, in 1976, and soon after, the French Culinary Institute in New York was going strong. As a result, our student body began to change, with fewer novice thirty-six-week students and a more mixed group coming for twelve weeks—those seeking the French sophistication and making a junior chef investment that would take them two notches higher as they sought work. Career changers in their late thirties began to appear, often from the financial sector, exhausted by the stresses of their profession. Students also became more demanding, for now they had other good schools to compare with La Varenne. For the most part the students were terrific, though there were so many over the years, it's difficult to remember everyone. While they were there, I was engaged with them, commenting on their cooked dishes, and insisting they learn the theoretical side for their exams. And then a whole new group of students would arrive, and inevitably I would move on.

Some imprinted themselves on my memory—Toni Allegra, for instance, who spent just one month with us in 1976 but was such an excellent cook and took such a lively interest in what was going on in the Paris food world, she was unforgettable. Our paths have crossed many times since—she was, in fact, the inspiration for the food editors and writers symposiums we later held at The Greenbrier. Susan Broussard had an artistic streak that she transposed into a career in food styling, while Mark Tarbell came to us for a year in his late teens and now runs a string of restaurants in Phoenix, Arizona. Others imprinted themselves for less pleasant reasons, like a young American couple who came for a three-month course and immediately began complaining of translators not knowing what they were doing, recipes they didn't like, and a lack of freshly washed chefs' jackets every morning. They wanted their money back. I explained our policy explicitly stated we did not offer refunds and promised we would do our best to resolve their problems. But the problems were endless. The grumblers continued to attend classes but taught me that it takes just one person in ten to sour the goodwill of an entire group. I understood only then that we hadn't reserved the right to ask a student to leave the school and that would have to change. We also had our share of people suffering from bulimia and anorexia—diseases that are the dark side of enjoying food. We had one otherwise charming woman who would wolf down nearly a whole baguette topped with slabs of butter at a single meal. This was before I had learned something about crisis management.

We tried to keep every candidate on equal footing in every way, notably when it came to exams. We combined an easy entrée with a difficult dessert and vice versa, though inevitably some dishes were harder than others—consommé being the prime example. In an Escoffier-style kitchen, you'd have had one cook whose entire job was to make consommé. The stock alone takes six to eight hours to simmer. For the exams we prepared the stock ahead, but even then it had to be carefully clarified with an egg white "raft" or the broth would turn the color of city smog. Pepper, and even salt, can dull an already-clarified consommé. Toilet paper—unscented—was my secret weapon; when you run trails across the surface of warm consommé, it miraculously absorbs any trace of fat.

You cannot master the art of French cooking in a week, a month, or a year. That's what the chefs told the students, and every day they learned new techniques and recipes, each day growing a little more confident. Of course not all students had the same level of commitment as the stagiaires studying for their Grand Diplôme. On exam days both students and trainees were put to the test, a trial for everyone as students crammed outside the kitchen and staff made up their exam packets. What exactly was in that *marinière* we made eight weeks ago (white wine, shallots, garlic, and a shower of parsley)? *Bonne femme, basqaise, diable,* Dubarry, lyonnaise, Rossini—how could one cuisine have so many garnishes?

For the practical component of the exams everyone was required to make two dishes in three and a half hours, not a minute more. They might be asked to toss up some *crêpes aux champignons* or *blanquette de veau* or perhaps a chocolate soufflé. One day one young woman we had nicknamed the Watering Can for her tendency to burst into tears exploded into full hysterics in the middle of her practical exam. Helpless, the other examinees shifted from foot to foot. We tried to calm her, but when I realized words were useless I administered a classic slap on the cheek. Thankfully, that pulled her together and everyone could continue their work.

Her recipe assignment had not been the problem. My flour-less chocolate soufflé dated back to my days at the Paris Cordon Bleu when my parents agreed to an extravagance, dinner at Le Grand Véfour, the restaurant in the seventeenth-century Palais Royale that everyone was talking about, headed by Raymond Oliver. The Véfour is still there, installed in a belle epoque café at one end of the Palais, its velvet banquettes and mirrored walls creating a nostalgic intimacy, though its culinary glory has faded. I remember nothing of the food except the dark chocolate soufflé, which was a revelation.

CHOCOLATE SOUFFLÉ

Chocolate soufflé is so easy, 15 minutes prep and 15 minutes to bake. One reason I love a soufflé is that there is always the challenge, the element of risk like the high jump that you can trip and fall with no halfway of saving face. If it flops, you have to eat chocolate soufflé flat as a rather odd warm pudding. A relatively hot oven is important in creating a crisp outside and runny center that forms its own dark chocolate sauce.

Serves 4

4 ounces/110 g dark bittersweet chocolate, chopped
½ cup/125 ml heavy cream
3 egg yolks
1½ tablespoons/45 ml rum or cognac
Melted butter, for the dish
5 egg whites
3 tablespoons/45 g granulated sugar
Confectioners' sugar, for sprinkling

1-quart/1-liter soufflé dish or four 1-cup/250-ml soufflé dishes

For the soufflé mixture, put the chocolate and cream in a saucepan and warm over low heat, stirring often with a wooden spoon until the chocolate is melted and the mixture just falls easily from the spoon. Take the pan from the heat and beat in the egg yolks so they cook and thicken the chocolate slightly. Stir in the rum or Cognac. The soufflé mixture can be prepared to this point 3 to 4 hours ahead, covered, and kept in the pan at room temperature.

To finish, heat the oven to 425°F/220°C and set a shelf low down. Butter the soufflé dish, chill in the freezer until cold, and butter a second time. If using individual dishes, set them on a baking sheet. Whisk the egg whites until stiff in a copper bowl or using a heavy-duty electric mixer. Gradually add the granulated sugar, whisking to form a light, glossy meringue, about 30 seconds. Warm the chocolate in the pan until just hot to the touch, take from the heat and stir in about a quarter of the meringue to lighten it. Add the chocolate mixture to the remaining meringue and fold the mixtures together as lightly as possible. Spoon the mixture into the prepared soufflé dish and smooth the top; the dish should be almost full. Run your thumb around the inside rim of the dish so the soufflé will rise evenly.

Bake the soufflé at once until puffed and almost double in volume, 12 to 15 minutes for a large soufflé or 7 to 9 minutes for small ones. If you shake the dish, the soufflé mixture should wobble slightly, showing it is still soft in the center. Meanwhile, line a platter with a napkin so the soufflé dish cannot slide. Take the soufflé from the oven, sprinkle quickly with confectioners' sugar, and set the dish on the plate. Serve at once; a soufflé cannot wait. When serving a large soufflé, use 2 large spoons to scoop up both the crisp outside and soft center onto each plate.

La Varenne required a lot of infrastructure. Everything cost a great deal, and some months were slower than others. Business also went up and down, depending on the value of the dollar. We seemed to be paying a vast retainer to Bill Kosmas in New York, and now that we were established he had less to do, so we severed the connection. Fortunately, with an eye to the future, Julia introduced us to her lawyer, Bob Johnson, who was excellent and a wise advisor. Bob was based in Boston, partner in one of the old firms, and he became a dear friend over the years. It was he who once said to us, "One should never trust a man with a Mercedes and no fixed address." That became a motto I'll never forget because of an American called Michael Prince.

I had met Charlotte Turgeon, the translator of the first American edition of *Larousse Gastronomique*, when I did a story about her son's wine tasting group for *The Washington Star*. Charlotte was an honored member of the food community (she'd been at Smith College with Julia), and when she learned we were looking for help with the business aspects of the school she told us of someone who might help us raise money. Michael Prince, she assured us, had a good business sense. Mark and I went to meet Michael, who moved around. He also drove a Mercedes.

Michael proved charming and spun a convincing yarn about how he would help us develop La Varenne. After lunch we passed by one of those big old-style banks, and Michael said, "I'd like you to meet a good family friend. He's one of the bank vice presidents. Let's say hello, but don't mention just yet what we're doing. It isn't the time." I put on my best English accent, and we chitchatted with the vice president, then departed. Later I understood Michael had done this to impress us with his banking connections and because he enjoyed playing risky games.

Michael seemed a bit of a manipulator, but he was also plausible, with his fast talk of balance sheets and restructuring, and we needed money if the school was going to survive. We had repaid Simca her original investment and we wanted to return their start-up capital to Paul and Julia. At the end of three years the pressure was heightened when Nick Brown mentioned that when it was convenient he would like to take out his money, too. We began to count on Michael to help us raise the additional capital we needed, and he introduced us to a number of people and diverted us with an idea of parlaying the La Varenne name by developing a line of La Varenne copper pots and aprons. But the investors he promised never materialized. Bob Johnson was not the only one to question whether Michael was the great businessman he purported to be. Nick Brown also cautioned us. Fortunately we remained firm that we would not sell Michael a share in the La Varenne trade name until he had lined up investors, though we did sign an agreement giving him a share in some of my books. As month followed month we realized he was a sham. Bob fortunately negotiated us out of the tangle.

Bob came to the rescue again with a presentation in Longview, Texas, an oil town. By then I had visited Longview several times, having been invited to give demonstrations by the rich oil ladies in town who, as an amusement, had created the gem of a cooking school. The ladies had their pecking order: The wealthiest woman had Chinese export porcelain and Impressionist paintings displayed in her mansion; another bought her clothes from Dior and had just been voted one of the best-dressed women in Texas. She kindly welcomed even our children into her luxurious ranch house and took them shopping for Texas duds at the cowboy store. The ladies' school was a huge success because all their society friends came. One of the women we met expressed interest in a charcuterie we were hoping to open in Chicago—this was long before anyone in the United States had heard of charcuteries. "Your budget is about what it costs to drill a trial oil well," she said, "so we might take the gamble." We hadn't yet come to understand that people who are investing money also want to be directly involved with the project, and this time our Longview investors decided the charcuterie ought to be in Dallas. We tried to explain that Texans wanted barbecue, not fancy French charcuterie, but the investor said no Dallas, no dough.

Bob was wonderful about helping us whenever we called on him, and we were devastated when, years later, we learned he had been diagnosed with AIDS. This was still in the days when such a diagnosis was always fatal, and for someone like Bob, who was in the closet, it meant opening unimaginable vistas. He quickly disappeared from sight, but when we were in Boston we learned he was in the hospital and immediately went to see him. He was obviously terribly sick, but psychologically he seemed to have faced the situation and we were glad of that. We saw him several more times before he died, but watching the decline of such a good friend, someone who had been so invaluable to us, was terribly painful.

Not only was I not very good at selling myself; I've also never been good at promotion. In 1980 when President Reagan and his wife, Nancy, were coming for a state visit to Paris, the embassy called us and asked La Varenne to produce afternoon tea in the Grand Palais, one of the grandest of all Paris monuments. Gregory was thrilled and had great ideas about what this would do for the school. We put together a group of a dozen students with two or three trainees, drawing straws from the most advanced class, and off they went with Gregory. They brought along some lovely cakes and fruit tarts, and the reception went along very smoothly. Indeed, Mrs. Reagan so enjoyed her chocolate pear tart, she asked for a second. There was a flurry because the Secret Service had to taste everything before she ate it, but we wound up with a rather misty picture of Mrs. Reagan enjoying her time, surrounded by some of our students. Quite rightly Greg stressed we must promote this wonderful opportunity.

But how do you do it? Greg tried, but not a single magazine wanted to touch the story. The only real English newspaper in France that might conceivably have carried such a piece was the *International Herald Tribune* and it had a limited social column and thus no place for it. Much to Gregory's chagrin, the story simply disappeared. I felt guilty for failing to do more, but I had opted to channel my energies into writing cookbooks and running the school and Mark was busy and often traveling for his work. I could not, and would not, further sacrifice our family life at a time when our children were so young.

CHOCOLATE PEAR TART

This pear tart has a secret filling, a simple sprinkling of chopped chocolate that dissolves in the juice from the cooked pears to form a creamy
sauce. Easy when you know how, but it took half a dozen tests to get it
right! The best pears for this tart are juicy Comice when you can find
them, or else ripe Bartletts.

Serves 6 to 8

4 ounces/110 g dark chocolate
3–4 pears

For the pâte sucrée dough
1²⁄₃ cups/200 g flour
½ cup/100 g sugar
4 egg yolks
Pinch of salt
6 tablespoons/90 g butter, plus more for the pan

For the topping
2 eggs
1 egg yolk
¾ cup/175 ml heavy cream
½ teaspoon vanilla extract
1 tablespoon sugar, for sprinkling

Pastry scraper, 9–10 inch/23–25 cm tart pan with removable base

Make the *pâte sucrée* dough: Sift the flour onto a work surface and
sweep a wide well with your fingertips. Put the sugar, egg yolks, and
salt in the well. Pound the butter with a rolling pin to soften it, add it to
the other ingredients, and work with the fingers of one hand until thoroughly mixed. Using a pastry scraper, gradually draw in the flour from
the sides of the well and continue working with both hands until
coarse crumbs form; they should be soft but not sticky. Gently press
the crumbs into a ball; the dough will be uneven and unblended at this

point. To blend the dough, set it on a floured surface and, with the heel of your hand, flatten and push the dough away from you. Gather it up, press it into a rough ball, and flatten it again. Continue until the dough is as pliable as putty and pulls away from the surface in one piece, 1 to 2 minutes. Shape it into a ball, wrap, and chill it until firm, 15 to 30 minutes.

Roll out the dough to a round 2 inches/5 cm larger than the tart pan. Lift the dough around the rolling pin and lower it into the pan, pressing it into the sides of the pan and draping the edges over the rim. Roll the rolling pin over the top of the pan to cut the dough edge neatly, then flute it with your fingers. Chill the tart shell until very firm, about 15 minutes. Heat the oven to 400°F/200°C and set a baking sheet low down.

With a large knife, chop the chocolate into very small chunks. Spread the chocolate in the tart shell. Peel and halve the pears and scoop out the cores and fibrous stems using a melon baller or the point of a paring knife. Set the pear halves cut side down on a cutting board and cut them very thinly crosswise without separating the slices. Gently flatten the slices to make elongated ovals that keep the shape of the pear halves. Still keeping the slices together, lift them on the flat of the knife and arrange the halves, stem end inward, on the chocolate layer in a circle like the petals of a flower. To make the topping: In a bowl, whisk the eggs, egg yolk, cream, and vanilla to make a custard. Spoon it over the pear halves so they are lightly coated.

Bake the tart on the hot baking sheet for 10 minutes. Lower the oven heat to 350°F/180°C and continue baking until the pastry is brown and the pears are tender, 25 to 35 minutes longer. The tart should be shrinking from the sides of the pan. If the tart is done but not browned on top, brown it briefly under the broiler to highlight the scalloped pattern of the fruit slices. (You may need to shield the pastry edge of the tart with a strip of foil.) Serve the tart at room temperature.

As the years passed, we grew preoccupied by the financial situation at La Varenne, but until we hired a certified accountant, Emile Jacob, neither Mark nor I understood that in France corporate tax actually paid and corporate tax owed could be far apart. Emile Jacob explained that there needed to be a negotiation. Since La Varenne was such a strange animal, Emile told us to expect a tax inspector to approach for a *contrôle,* an audit. He explained that we would need to leave missteps on our books for the authorities to discover.

Soon Emile's prediction came true when an agreeable, experienced tax inspector began to come to the school to investigate. The last thing we wanted was for the inspector to see all our trainees with their questionable residential status traipsing in and out and enjoying a free lunch. So we tucked the inspector and Paule up in an old maid's room on the fifth floor—the part of the building where a few old tenants still lived, among them Sonya, a Russian woman who collected newspapers left over from the newsstands and hid money inside. Indeed, when the Social Services finally came to take Sonya away they found a small fortune in notes hidden between those pages. For three months, twice a week, the inspector came and sat with Paule upstairs going over the books. The inspector soon turned up what we had left for her to find and she departed to do her calculations.

When she returned with her findings she demanded a sum much larger than we had anticipated. Mark and I were horrified, but Emile assured us there was no need to worry. "Now we'll take her out to a very good lunch and negotiate." He deemed a three-star restaurant too pretentious—it would suggest too many rich foreigners ready for the plucking—a two-star would be more suitable. And so one day Emile, Mark, Paule, the tax inspector, and I went to lunch. Our first course came and went as we made polite conversation and sipped our wine. As I was finishing my main course, a delicious Dover sole, I began to worry. What was Emile up to? He hadn't said a word about business. By the time we had ordered dessert and he still hadn't said a thing, I was feeling restless and nearly chimed in when the coffee came. At last, to my relief, Emile leaned forward and said, *"Eh bien, si on peut regardez les choses* [let's look at things]." Somehow, in very few minutes Emile and Paule had beaten the inspector down by half. I was greatly relieved.

Unfortunately, our financial problems did not end there. The franc was fluctuating wildly and with it the number of students who came. La Varenne had been losing money each year for five years, and future bookings were depressing. After long conversations, Mark and I agreed we had to cut back on staff. We had three chefs, two overlapping office staff, and two directors, myself and Gregory. The notion of cutting staff was distasteful and went totally against my instincts. I hate having to ask people to leave when they're doing a good job, and everyone was. But I had to face the fact that we had to cut back or close La Varenne altogether.

In France one can sack someone only for dishonesty or incapacity or because of the employer's bad financial situation. To let go of anyone we had to get permission from a government authority, and so Paule and I went to meet with a woman at the Conseil de Prud'hommes, the labor court that has jurisdiction over employment contracts. Paule and Florence had gone over and over the accounts, and we took these along to our meeting, which lasted quite a long time. In the end, slightly to my surprise, the woman agreed that our decision was correct. By law, the four let go would receive up to one year's pay, depending on length of service.

Back at the school I immediately called everyone to a meeting. Fortunately, both Jorant and Chambrette were eligible for pensions and when I explained the situation Jorant, who had brought his wife along, quickly said, "I've had to let people go in my time; you don't need to explain to me." Chambrette instantly understood, and it was agreed that both men would return to teach occasional classes. As for Florence, she had known how dire the situation was and knew that Paule must stay—the bookkeeper is always the last to go. Then came Gregory. When I explained the situation, he said he needed time to think. Early the next morning a mailman arrived with four registered letters from the Conseil de Prud'hommes requiring signature upon receipt. When I saw those letters, I was relieved I had had the good sense to forewarn everyone. Now that they had those letters, by law they each had six weeks to put forward any argument they might have against dismissal. Gregory told me that he was thinking of putting one forward.

La Varenne was housed in a building that had been part of the grand houses that backed on to the Invalides. On the ground floor were the coach houses and the curved archway entering into the mews, the porte cochère. Our little office was so small, there were no secrets, so when the weather was good we sometimes held private consultations downstairs, using our code requesting privacy: "Oh, we'll be under the archway." But that day it was cold outside, so Paule and I invited Gregory to come sit in Paule's car. I took the backseat, and Paule and I again explained the circumstances. Gregory was not sympathetic. In the first few years he was employed at La Varenne, he had worked without a permit. We had eventually obtained one for him and he was very happy, but now he told us he was prepared to tell the government we had hired him illegally. He also said he might also tell them about informal arrangements we had with Chambrette and Jorant. It did not seem to matter to Gregory that he would be implicating not just me but also his fellow staff members.

When I asked Greg what he needed, he told me he had never had any money to spare, and over the next hour we negotiated a cash settlement of $10,000, which in those days was quite a lot. I explained I would need to know he wasn't going to go to the authorities. The windows fogged; the sky grew dark and menacing. Gregory was quiet for a long time. At last he said he needed the six weeks to think about the figure. I felt sick about this, but I was about to leave for a trip to teach in the States. I asked Greg if he would carry on with work while I was gone, and he agreed he would.

Three weeks later, when I returned to Paris, I found that Gregory had moved his desk into an empty room we called the Goldfish Bowl, a tall, well-lit space with turquoise wallpaper—we were about to sell this valuable real estate to raise cash. Greg sat there doing nothing but talking on the phone to his friends. I was particularly upset because we had once worked together in such harmony. Everyone else had understood our dilemma. Yes, we'd differed with each other a few times, but only in the way a family does. Now we were in the midst of a family breakup, and on top of the sadness, I had to worry about the authorities and the impact of rumors it seemed Gregory was spreading. Just before the permitted six weeks was over, he accepted our offer, and over time things settled down. Madame Lepaute, who was in frequent contact with Gregory, was not upset with me, though she exclaimed, *"Ah, vous êtes une vraie Madame Thatcher* (Ah, you are a true Madame Thatcher)!" All the same, I know that others, among them Patricia Wells, the *Herald Tribune*'s esteemed restaurant critic and cookbook author and someone whom I considered a friend, felt that I had abandoned Greg. I was relieved when he found a position with the Cordon Bleu and it was even better when he was asked by the Ritz Hotel to found the Ritz-Escoffier cooking school. After that I saw Gregory from time to time, but our relationship as close colleagues and friends was over, and a few years later he died of AIDS, a distressing end to a promising future.

Despite all these reverses, I knew Mark and I would carry on.

As we wrote and collected more and more books,
Mark and I were in our element.

Chapter Eleven

....

MOI, ARTISTE!

*I'm a great believer in luck, and I find that the harder I
work, the more I have of it.*

—Thomas Jefferson

We were fairly certain that Mark's father would not last long without his wife, Mary. She had always been the family leader.
One story had it that when they first married, the bank manager called her and said, "Mrs. Cherniavsky, there has been some consider-
able drawing down on your account." When Mary asked, Mischel confessed

he'd been gambling. She asked how he could be so irresponsible and he said, "But Mary, I only gave them one of those check things. . . ." Truthfully Mischel was sharp as a needle, but he liked to play those kinds of naughty games.

They had married in 1919 after first meeting in Fiji, where B. T. Rogers, Mary's father, leased sugar cane plantations. The Cherniavsky brothers' trio happened to be playing in Fiji at the time, and Mary and Mischel fell in love. B.T. didn't want his daughter marrying a Russian Jewish musician and put his foot down. Then, three years later very suddenly and quite young, he died, and Mary and Mischel married.

Mischel remained an incorrigible eccentric. He had never had a driver's license, and he was a wild, dramatic driver, talking and turning to people in the backseat, waving his arms. One day Mark was in the passenger seat when a gendarme pulled them over and politely knocked on the window. Mischel lowered it and listened as the policeman cited his infractions, but before he could finish Mischel said, *"Moi, artiste!"*—not even proper French—rolled up the window, and sped away. Mischel was an *originale*. He talked at you, grabbing your arm and pulling you in so you couldn't escape. A distant cousin of Mary's once told us she had happened to meet Mischel enjoying his morning walk on February 6, 1952. She remembered precisely the date because it was the day King George VI died. She had been stunned when this handsome man with his impenetrable Russian accent and wearing a large black cravat suddenly said, tears in his eyes, "Our kink is dead!"

Sadly, just as Mark and I were weathering the troubles at the school, both Mary's and Mischel's health began to fail. Mary suffered a stroke in the winter of 1980 and for an entire year was nursed at home by their devoted housekeeper, Françoise. When Mary died in 1981, we were surprised how well Mischel did. Françoise cooked him nice meals, and he took three-mile walks every day and continued to drive. Indeed, the house was on a rectangular plot with a gate that opened straight out into a T-junction, and the locals called that spot Russian Corner because Mischel always drove straight out without a moment's hesitation.

In January 1982 Mischel started to slow down and died very quickly. I happened to be in the room when Mischel's breath stopped. It was a peaceful death, and we were grateful he had not suffered. But this was a Sunday in the heart of the countryside, so I volunteered to help Françoise lay out the body. The only other person I saw die was my father, though that would not be for many years, and both times I was struck by the emptiness, the departure of the spirit. With Mischel's death, our lives changed once again.

La Varenne was my ongoing project, and writing books was becoming another passion. At the school we began with *La Varenne Basic Recipes,* the core collection of essentials we have issued ever since to each student who has been through the school. We financed this booklet, but when we moved into bigger books publishers' advances allowed us at least to cover the costs of the ingredients for recipe testing. By the time Linda Collister arrived in our life, I had annexed the little kitchen in our apartment for testing.

Linda was one of many young women who over the years acted partly as au pair for Simon and Emma, partly as a trainee, and then as an assistant at La Varenne. But Linda had by far the most experience of any of our previous au pairs. She was English, and we interviewed her at the Oxford and Cambridge Club in London, overlooking Pall Mall. When she came for the interview she was wearing a white chef's coat. "Please excuse me," she explained. "I work just around here." "Here" turned out to be Clarence House, residence of the Queen Mother. Linda, however, was the opposite of grand: down-to-earth, with a lively sense of humor. She asked the children to keep secret that her middle names were Ariadne Flowerpot. Three happy years with us and an emergency appendectomy later, Linda returned to London. Among other jobs, she interviewed for the newly married Prince Charles and Princess Diana. Much later she revealed to me that she hadn't taken the position as their cook because she didn't want to deal with the Princess's dietary demands.

One of the recipes Linda had learned at Clarence House was for Russian *pojarski,* a kind of ground veal cutlet enriched with cream and served with mushroom sauce. The recipe had been passed down from the family of Tsar Nicholas, who was married to Alexandra of Hesse, a granddaughter of Queen Victoria of England.

VEAL POJARSKI

Pojarski look like hedgehogs, coated with cubes of brioche bread, then deep-fried; how luxurious can you get? If your brioche is very fresh, let the cubes dry in the kitchen for half an hour before you use them. An earthy whole-grain pilaf of buckwheat is the perfect accompaniment.

Serves 6

1-pound/450-g loaf of firm brioche bread, sliced ⅜ inch/8 mm thick
¾ cup/175 ml milk
1½ pounds/675 g ground lean veal
⅓ cup/75 ml crème fraîche
Large pinch of freshly grated nutmeg
Salt and pepper

For coating

½ cup/60 g flour, seasoned with salt and pepper
2 eggs
Vegetable oil, for deep frying

For tomato and mushroom sauce

2 tablespoons/30 ml vegetable oil
1 medium onion, finely chopped
2 pounds/900 g tomatoes, cored, seeded, and chopped
2 tablespoons/30 g tomato paste
2 cloves garlic, finely chopped
Bouquet garni of 2 bay leaves, 2–3 sprigs thyme, and a few parsley
    stems
Salt and pepper
¾ pound/330 g mushrooms, sliced

To make the tomato sauce: Heat half the oil in a frying pan and sauté the onion over medium heat until browned. Stir in the tomatoes, tomato paste, garlic, bouquet garni, salt, and pepper, and sauté, stirring occasionally, until quite thick, 8 to 10 minutes. Let cool slightly, then work the tomato mixture through a strainer into a bowl, pressing well to extract all the pulp and discarding the bouquet garni. Wipe out the frying pan, heat the remaining oil, and fry the mushrooms until tender, 2 to 3 minutes. Stir in the tomato pulp and taste for seasoning. Set the garnish aside.

For the veal mixture: Put 3 slices of the brioche bread, including crusts, in a bowl, pour over the milk, and leave to soak 5 minutes. Cut the remaining brioche into a ⅜-inch/2-cm dice, discarding the crusts. Squeeze excess milk from the soaked bread with your fist. Put the ground veal in a processor with the soaked bread and work briefly to mix. Add the crème fraîche, nutmeg, salt, and pepper, and work again just until well mixed. Sauté a small piece of the mixture and taste it—it should be savory but lightly seasoned.

To shape and cook the *pojarski,* prepare the coatings: Spread the seasoned flour on a plate; break the eggs onto a plate, add a pinch of salt, and whisk with a fork until frothy; spread the diced bread on a tray. Dip your hands in water and shape the veal mixture into 6 equal patties, flattening them slightly. Roll them in seasoned flour, patting with your hands so they are evenly coated. One by one, coat the patties in egg, using a brush and turning them with two forks until evenly coated. Transfer each patty to the diced bread and toss and turn them until evenly coated, pressing in the bread cubes with your hand. Chill them 30 minutes.

To finish: Heat the oven to 375°F/190°C. Heat a 1-inch/2.5-cm layer of fat in a deep frying pan to 350°F/185°C—a piece of bread should sizzle at once. Carefully lower a *pojarski* into the hot fat and deep fry until brown, 2 to 3 minutes, turning it once. Drain it on paper towel. Deep-fry the rest in the same way. Transfer the *pojarski* to a baking sheet and bake in the oven until a skewer inserted in the center is hot to the touch when withdrawn, 15 to 20 minutes. Reheat the tomato garnish. Transfer the *pojarski* to serving plates and spoon the sauce on the side.

Meanwhile, Mark and I were launched on a food lover's dream. *French Regional Cooking* was inspired by the weekend drives we were taking to the farthest corners of France. Although nowadays nobody ever talks about it, two journalists called Henri Gault and Christian Millau had produced a most amazing gastronomic guide (known as *Gault-Millau*) to the regional food specialties of France. We relied on this tubby little book to tell us what to look for on the spot in obscure places. Also, at La Varenne I began to understand that where a chef was brought up or had spent his apprentice years is seminal to understanding his cooking. Chef Chambrette spoke of the chowders of Brittany where he went for his yearly vacation, and Claude described the fruit tarts of the Loire where he was raised.

Wherever we went, Mark and I did not just visit. Rather, we sought out food stories and those explorations immersed us in the culture of the place. For *French Regional Cooking* we had a 1935 map of the regions of France by Curnonsky, a Frenchman whose real name was Maurice Edmond Sailland.

He had appropriated a Russian-sounding name for himself in 1895, a time of nostalgia for Old Russia, and he became known in Paris as the prince-elect of gastronomy.

It was Curnonsky's map backed up with *Gault-Millau* that guided us in our journeys. The density of type on the map, which measures a meter square, shows ingredients and dishes particular to each place and today many of the recipes Curnonsky named have become anchored to those places. For instance, down south on the Mediterranean with its blue water and brilliant sun, the specialty is bouillabaisse bursting with saffron and the bonier fish of those waters. The fish stew called Cotriade comes from the land of cold water much farther north and features the region's delicacies—whitefish, mussels, good butter, and the richest cream.

COTRIADE NORMANDE

Mackerel would be the rich fish of choice for this simple fish stew, plus any whitefish, including cod, haddock, sole, or flounder. But traditionally Cotriade uses up the leftovers from a day's catch, so almost any fresh fish is appropriate except salmon. The cider should be alcoholic hard cider that is not too sweet. For a last-minute pickup, I like to serve the stew with lemon wedges and a bowl of sea salt.

Serves 4 generously

1 pound/450 g rich fish fillets, without skin
1 pound/450 g whitefish fillets, without skin
1½ pounds/675 g small mussels
2 tablespoons/30 g butter
2 leeks, white and light green parts, sliced
4 garlic cloves, finely chopped
Salt and pepper
1 pound potatoes, cut in 1-inch chunks with peel
3 cups/750 ml dry hard cider
3 cups/750 ml water, more if needed
Large bouquet garni made with 2 bay leaves, 2–3 sprigs thyme,
    and stems from a medium bunch of parsley
Juice from ½ lemon
½ cup/125 ml crème fraîche

For serving
½ lemon
Sprigs from medium bunch of parsley
Sea salt

For fried croûtes
2 tablespoons/30g butter
2 tablespoons/30ml vegetable oil
½ baguette, sliced
Garlic clove

Make the *croûtes:* Heat half the butter and half the oil in a pan until quite hot—a slice of baguette should sizzle when dipped. Add half the baguette slices and brown them over medium heat, 30 to 60 seconds. Turn them, brown the other side about 30 seconds, and drain the *croûtes* on a paper towel. Fry the rest in the same way. Rub them all with a cut garlic clove and set them aside.

Wash and dry the fish fillets on paper towels and cut them in 2-inch/5-cm chunks. Discard any damaged mussels, or gaping shells that do not close when tapped on the counter. Melt the butter in a soup pot. Spread the leeks and garlic over the bottom and sprinkle with salt and pepper. Add the potatoes, cider, and enough water to cover the potatoes. Simmer until the potatoes are almost tender, 20 to 25 minutes (they take longer than usual because of the cider).

Lay the fish on top of the potatoes, putting firmer fish in first and more delicate ones on top. Push the bouquet garni down into the fish, sprinkle with salt and pepper, and spread the mussels on top. Cover the pot, bring the Cotriade to a boil, and simmer until the mussels open and the fish is just tender, 4 to 6 minutes. Meanwhile, halve the lemon and cut one half in 4 wedges. Chop the parsley sprigs.

When the potatoes and fish are ready, discard the bouquet garni. Stir a ladleful of hot broth into the crème fraîche, squeeze in the juice from a half lemon, and pour this liquid back into the Cotriade. Taste, and adjust the seasoning of the broth. Spoon the Cotriade into bowls, sprinkle with chopped parsley, and perch a lemon wedge on the edge of each bowl. Serve very hot, with the *croûtes* and sea salt passed separately.

On our explorations, Mark and I always drove our Peugeot station wagon packed with books and we sought out back roads. We learned to recognize crops—up in the cold, rough north, for instance, we were mystified by the five-foot-high mounds covered with black plastic until we learned that Belgian endive was grown inside these mounds. The green leaves bleached in the dark. We booked ahead only for the better restaurants and slept wherever we liked the look of a modest hotel. We stopped at little places for coffee and a bite to eat and sought out market days listed in the green Michelin guide. Many of these markets had medieval roots and were a useful source of local produce and cheeses. For pastries we scanned pastry shop windows, and charcuteries for pies and sausages. Restaurants were less helpful; at that time local dishes were being displaced by ill-executed versions of nouvelle cuisine.

France is nearly two and a half times the size of Britain but with virtually the same population, and driving on back roads felt like stepping back a hundred years. In France people often live their lives where they were born. Western Brittany, for instance, was a land lost in time where most people still spoke Breton. The mountainous interior of France, the Massif Central, was equally remote, with the timeless quality of my Yorkshire childhood. Those journeys immersed me in France in a way I hadn't experienced since I was a girl.

Over the years Mark and I have collected more than seven thousand books, the vast majority on cooking; we have a small but definitive collection on nouvelle cuisine by the leading French chefs of the 1970s and some thirty books on cooking with wine (a surprisingly esoteric subject, as I discovered when I wrote a book about it). We picked them up all over the world, from *Boozy Food Australia* to *100 Recetas con Cava* from Spain. As for the country cooking of France, until the 1870s there wasn't a single cookbook that could be remotely described as regionally based. Even Brillat-Savarin didn't write about local food, although he was famous for living in Belley, in Burgundy. Then came the railroads and the motorcar, and travelers began going out to enjoy the countryside and eating things local. By the turn of the century Michelin was writing its guides to encourage people not only to drive but also to wear down their tires from the Michelin factory. By the thirties, regional food had become a great fashion. On our travels Mark always sought out books on the food and recipes of the region and not uncommonly would find locally printed treasures. Arriving back in Paris, I would launch at once into a portrait in text and recipes of the region we had visited.

GÂTEAU BRETON

Gâteau Breton sums up the best of Brittany with its world-class butter and outstanding pastries. The pure flavor of the cake, made with equal weights of butter, flour, sugar, and egg yolks, deserves the very best butter. No other flavoring is needed, not even salt.

Serves 6 to 8

1 cup/225 g butter, plus more for the pan
1¾ cups/225 g flour
1 cup plus 2 tablespoons/225 g sugar
6 egg yolks

8-inch/20 cm tart pan with removable base

Butter the tart pan. Sift the flour onto a work surface and sweep a large well in the center with your hand. Cube the butter and put it in the well with the sugar and egg yolks. Using the shell of one yolk, scoop a teaspoonful of yolk into a small bowl, add a teaspoon of water, and set aside for glaze. Work together the central ingredients in the well with the fingertips of one hand until smooth. Gradually mix in the flour with the fingertips and heel of your hand to make a paste that is very smooth and sticky; you will need the help of a pastry scraper, as the paste is so soft.

Transfer the dough to the pan and smooth the top with your fist, dipping it in cold water so your fingers do not stick. Brush the surface of the gâteau with the reserved egg yolk and mark a lattice in the glaze with the tines of a fork (this lattice marked in the glaze is the signature of Gâteau Breton). Chill the gâteau for 15 minutes. Heat the oven to 375°F/190°C and set a baking sheet on a rack in the center.

Place the tart pan on the hot baking sheet and bake for 20 minutes. Reduce the heat to 350°F/180°C and continue baking until the gâteau is firm, deep golden brown, and the sides shrink from the edges of the pan, 20 to 25 minutes longer. Let it cool to tepid in the pan, then unmold onto a rack to cool completely. Gâteau Breton is equally good freshly baked or kept in an airtight container for 2 to 3 days, when the texture softens and the butter flavor develops.

In all of my books I have had a fictional reader as a character in my head. When I wrote *Entertaining Menus,* Mark and I nicknamed her Mrs. Housewife. She had done a bit of cooking, didn't want things too complicated, and liked having people around to cook for. For *Great Cooks and Their Recipes,* Mrs. H. transformed to be slightly more sophisticated, a cook with some knowledge of cooking and an interest in learning more. This book was fathered by Mark, the first of us into old cookbooks and culinary history, which inspired my realization of how much we owed to cooks of the past, many of whom had led lives of adventure. Nearly all would have echoed the sentiment of Robert May, who, looking back on six decades in English kitchens, informed readers that "God and my own Conscience would not permit me to bury these my Experiences with my Silver Hairs in the Grave." For the next book, Mrs. H. changed again and became a student. *The Observer French Cookery School* (known in the United States as *The La Varenne Cooking Course)* was designed to be like the school itself, with shorter explanations that assumed readers wanted to do things professionally.

For all my books, Mark always did the overall editing and he was quite strict; we argued often about too-long sentences and finding just the right adjective. But I always had others on my team as well, trainees like Judy Hill and Tina Ujlaki and Linda Collister, friends like Elisabeth Evans and Margo Miller. When we were doing French Regional, Linda Collister tested every one of the 350 regional recipes and a whole lot more that we rejected and every night Mark and I ate the recipe tests for dinner. After two years of this, one night Mark said he was absolutely sick of regional cooking and pleaded with me to please try something new. At the school, to Chambrette's dismay, we had just begun to experiment with nouvelle cuisine, so I told Mark I would draft some recipes. Within two weeks of eating my efforts at the new style, Mark said, "You're not seriously thinking of putting this muck in a book, are you?" I kept going, trying to make the recipes work, but I quickly discovered what I had already suspected: Really innovative nouvelle cuisine recipes required the very best and freshest vegetables, fish, and poultry, and on the whole these were prohibitively expensive. They also called for expert restaurant-style cooking. Simple dishes with just a few ingredients are far more difficult to perfect than are more elaborate recipes. With nouvelle cuisine you couldn't add a good shot of booze or boil something down to hide a mistake. If a dish was overcooked, it was ruined.

This intransigence of the recipes was one reason traditional eaters never took to nouvelle cuisine. Julia strongly disliked it and Mark did, too. Once when Julia visited, we three went to La Côte d'Or, a three-star in Burgundy, and ordered the tasting menu. We were taken aback when we were told that Chef Bernard Loiseau's soups and sauces were based on water only—he refused to countenance the stocks and broths on which traditional French cooking is founded. When the third or fourth dish came on a large, square plate, it showcased an inch-thick hunk of duck breast that had its skin slashed lattice-wise to get rid of the fat. Julia took one bite, pronounced it flavorless and tough, and refused to eat the rest. It was, she declared, reductio ad absurdum. After that I gave up the idea of a *La Varenne's Nouvelle Cuisine*. Julia and Mark, the two most influential people in the development of the school, so strongly objected to it, I felt I must listen. They turned out to be right; nouvelle cuisine was too elitist and expensive and lasted only two or three years at the top before it was drowned in a sea of poorly cooked, insipid imitations.

Simon and Emma were always closely involved in the kitchen. They started by decorating the Christmas cake I had learned to make as a child, then whisking the vinaigrette dressing, and graduating to chopping, slicing, and gathering parsley and thyme from the herb garden. They had discriminating tastes, and when they went to boarding school in the States they insisted whenever we visited them that we smuggle in Mars bars because the French variety are far richer than the American ones and make the world's best hot chocolate sauce. Now, at age eleven, Simon was too old to continue at the Holy Fathers school in France and it was time for us to find him a good boarding school. We settled on Les Roches in Normandy, but Emma could not bear the idea of being left without her beloved older brother and insisted she had to go, too. Fortunately, Les Roches accepted girls, unlike most British boarding schools at that time. And so in 1981 both children went off to school, coming home often for the weekend. They called regularly. At the beginning nine-year-old Emma wept into the phone, "Mummy, I'm missing you." To ease her homesickness, the headmistress bought Emma a little stuffed chicken she called Le Poussin, the baby chicken, for that is what the youngest child in a French family is called.

The children enjoyed their summer holidays in Paris. One year Calvin Trillin passed through for a visit and nominated Simon and Emma to be a part of his gastronomic research team. Bud, as he is informally known, was doing a comparative survey of *hamburger à l'américaine* for *The New Yorker* and so, kids in tow, he went out to the Champs-Élysées and Boulevard St. Germain. Bud always makes even the most mundane event funny, and as he and the children traveled from Whataburger to McDonald's to Burger King, Simon the gastronome made pronouncements. He and Bud agreed that the triangular burgers in one aspiring establishment did not make the grade. The balance of the interview was tipped by Simon's statement that though his favorite food was French fries, he also liked squid.

After Mischel's death, Mark and I sold Maison Blanche and began to look for somewhere near enough to Paris to be accessible for school holidays and summers. Mark drew a one-hundred-kilometer circle around Paris and defined our requirements—an attractive building in good repair with a caretaker nearby; a location south of Paris for more sun; relatively close to a highway; and express trains close by. Of course the price had to be right. And I added a further stipulation—it had to be a beautiful, old house. Note the word "house."

In the early winter months of 1982 we visited a dozen or so places, each one a pathetic wreck, stripped of paneling, fireplaces, doors, anything that might be worth money. In one splendid eighteenth-century mansion complete with chapel and dairy, we counted more than fifty-seven rooms. We couldn't understand why a charming Directoire pavilion only forty kilometers from Paris and surrounded by idyllic woods remained unsold after two years. Then, standing inside, we heard the trickle of water and learned the place was built atop a marsh.

When we first heard about Château du Feÿ, we headed to Burgundy. The road nearest the château, Route Nationale 6, had been a stagecoach route from Paris to Lyon, intersecting the river property below the château. It was also near, but not too near, the new Autoroute du Soleil that headed south. Within an hour of the place we could be in Beaune sampling the finest wines, or in the Morvan mountains eating hams, or on the Loire buying goat cheeses at Sancerre. The region and the nearest town, Joigny, had changed little since the 1600s, with an open market twice a week where vendors had gathered since Roman times, when Joigny was known as Jovinium, dedicated to Jove.

It was a chilly March day when we first drove up the hill that led to Château du Feÿ. Mark's back had been bothering him, and there was sheeting rain. At the top of the wooded hill, we found the wrought-iron gates tightly closed and the château's shutters barred. The only sign of life was the thread of smoke sliding down a lean-to roof of one of the many outbuildings. We had read that the place was inhabited and for sale, so the abandoned look surprised us. We retired to the nearby Côte Saint Jacques restaurant and fortified ourselves with a two-star dinner (its third star came a decade later).

The following day we were taken round the property by Philip Hawkes, an English real estate agent who was already an expert on châteaux and lived in a splendid one himself. We'd found the Peugeot wagon to be reliable, built as it was for heavy terrain, and so we decided to drive into the woods—Mark was unable to walk far because of his back. But we got stuck. That was how we first met Monsieur Milbert, who appeared as if out of nowhere—a squat sixty-two-year-old man in blue overalls and weathered skin, an unlit cigarette dangling from his lips. He offered to help us push the car, but that was useless. Ultimately Milbert had to get his tractor and pull us out. He was nearly wordless the entire time, seemingly amused by these hopeless city dwellers.

We drove back toward Paris, just two hours away by autoroute, mulling over what we had seen. From the outside Château du Feÿ had everything we wanted—including buildings we could rent out if they were renovated, the former farmhouse, the gardener's and gamekeeper's cottages. From the terrace was a magnificent view, something I cherished from my childhood, and the eighteenth-century paneled reception rooms were breathtaking. The château itself was classified a *monument historique* in recognition of its architectural merit and was grander than anything we'd lived in but cost the same as a three-bedroom family apartment in central Paris. We couldn't get the place out of our minds.

One week later, we decided to return. This time we brought along a new friend, George Wanklyn. We had met George through his brother Fred, who by happenstance was taking a class at La Varenne when Mark was putting together a family tree. When this unusual name showed up on a list of students, Mark thought he must be a relative since the name Wanklyn was on the tree. Fred led to George, who knew much more about Mark's maternal ancestors, and so one evening George came to the house. When he walked in and saw Mark dressed in a beautiful silk dressing gown, George smiled. He told Mark he looked Edwardian, and thus began what would become a lifelong friendship with both George and his first wife, Liza, and later his second wife, Varena Forcione. George and Liza's daughter, Amy, was between Emma and Simon in age, and they quickly became friends, calling one another *cousin(e)*.

George was teaching courses at the American College (now the American University) in Paris in his specialty, the art and architecture of France. Because of this expertise, Mark and I asked him to join us to see Château du Feÿ and to give us his opinion as to whether it had any architectural distinction and was worth the price. This time the day was sunny, and as we approached through the dense wood all three of us were quiet. At the top of the slope where suddenly everything cleared we looked at the straight alley lined with centuries-old linden trees. At the end stood the house. It seemed almost a dream.

This time there was another realtor with a potential buyer taking a tour, and right away the property was even more attractive than Mark and I had remembered. While not as dazzling as some châteaux, it seemed to embrace us with its rosy brick and buff Burgundian stone. Philip Hawkes was standing outside on the front steps and led us through the front doors and into the main hall. There he theatrically flung back the tall window shutters and the room was flooded with light. Here in the central part of the château it was only one room deep, but mirrors were placed at either end. As Philip opened the blinds and flicked on the lights, the mirrors worked their magic, doubling and redoubling the twinkling chandeliers to infinity.

Le Feÿ, Philip told us as he led us on a tour, was built around 1640. Each of the two wings that flanked the two-story central block, the *corps de logis*, had a staircase, three floors, and an entresol, with mezzanine rooms tucked in here and there off the staircase. George speculated to us, privately, that the current owner hadn't the means to keep up a place this size, and perhaps we should have paid more attention to his comment. George studied everything with an artist's eye—even down to checking the roof carpentry.

George and Mark talked about how those old French estates were really villages, enclosed by an outer wall and self-sufficient. At their peak, Mark told us (he had been doing his research), between fifty and sixty staff resided at a château like this to give it independence, in this case by earning revenues from oak trees in the forest behind and the vines planted on the sunny slopes in front. On we walked, more and more excited, exchanging looks as we passed through one room after another. The electricity and water were in working order and, we assumed, the drains. Out on the terrace we inhaled the panoramic view—rare for châteaux. Places this size had been built as working farms, so most were sheltered in the valley and near attendant villages that could supply the needed labor. But Le Feÿ was on this hill, and from the terrace we had a dazzling view that included nine villages, two on what had once been château land, all of them with that rich Burgundian soil.

That sloping ground in front had been planted in grapevines, but George explained that phylloxera had destroyed Burgundy's vines in the late 1800s. Mark knew about phylloxera, a pest that was introduced accidentally in France when infested American vines were brought to Europe by English botanists. Ultimately a native American vine stock resistant to phylloxera was discovered and vintners began to graft European vines to their roots. It was too late for Château du Feÿ. By then the high-alcohol wines of southern France could be transported cheaply on the new railroads and the thin wines of this part of Burgundy were condemned to extinction. In 1824 a young British observer, John Cobbett, had remarked, "The whole country, indeed, except the meadows by the river's side, is vineyard, but now and then planted at the same time in standard fruit trees, such as peaches, apricots, apples, pears and mostly in plums." Today, as Mark and I looked, we saw that some cherry trees remained, but most of the land was a patchwork of arable fields, winter brown tinged with green. Sheltering the château to one side were the towering oak trees of a forest (now belonging to the state) that dated back centuries and were the source of masts and spars for Napoléon's warships. It's possible that even that day Mark was beginning to imagine the black truffles that grow at the root of oak trees that we would, years later, plant just down the hill.

George also drew our attention to the clock out front overlooking the central courtyard. It no longer worked, but, he explained, those clocks were designed to ring on the hour, loudly enough to wake the dead, and then to ring a second time five minutes later for those who might be walking the property and had missed the first chimes. Mark right away knew he would find a way to restore that clock. We toured the stables, barns, dairy, a battery of rabbit hutches lining one wall. I almost failed to notice the swimming pool and tennis court—both of which were on pre-teen Emma and Simon's wish lists. Mark and I saw the massive stone wheel for crushing walnuts in one of the outbuildings, a huge oak winepress beside it, and noted the date on the crossbeam of 1756, and the huge well that was medieval and turned out to be ninety meters deep.

In the eighteenth century, estates were measured not only in acres or hectares but also in pigeons, because they are succulent birds, excellent eating, and supply valuable guano for fertilizer. Landowners had the right to a pair of pigeons per arpent—about an acre—of land. But pigeons are also greedy, without respect for property, and if set loose they gobble up ripe grain. And so, during the Revolution, in 1789 the droit de seigneur (seigneurial right) to a pigeon house was suppressed and many were demolished. Now they are prized possessions, admired as architectural curiosities. Le Feÿ's soaring *pigeonnier* crowned with the image of a pigeon was intact and could have housed ten thousand birds, reflecting the vast spread of the original property.

As Mark and I discovered that day, the rooms abreast of the pigeon house also housed two people. We were making our way across the gravel courtyard toward the vegetable garden when a familiar figure in blue overalls came toward us and Philip Hawkes reintroduced us to Monsieur Roger Milbert, the property's caretaker, who again had a dead cigarette in his mouth. We exchanged handshakes and thanked him for his help the previous week as we walked on to the enormous walled vegetable garden, a hectare (2.4 acres) in immaculate order and Monsieur's pride. He was just about to seed the potatoes, working from neat piles at the end of each well-tilled trench. I thought of my mother—this was a garden she would admire. She had given me just a small idea of the daily, backbreaking work involved.

Inside again George studied an eighteenth-century vellum map on the entrance hall wall that showed the property dimensions from 1751, the year it first changed hands. However, he said, he could tell from the architectural style that the house and some of the barns dated from the 1640s. Tiny stakes were drawn on the map to mark thousands of acres of vineyard running down to the Yonne River valley, while on the upland curlicues indicated the oak trees of the neighboring Forêt d'Othe. The outlines of the property indicated forty-seven hundred acres, a number confirmed by the grandeur of the pigeon house. Now scarcely one hundred acres remained of the original property, just enough to protect the magnificent front view, with some woodland to the rear.

Over time Mark and I would learn that Nicholas de Baugy, counselor and officer of the household to King Louis XIII, had built the château and in the eighteenth century handsome paneling had been added to the main rooms.

But in 1756 the owner, Baron Philibert de Chamousset, died, leaving a young widow. In her turn, in the 1790s she sold the property under a peculiarly French arrangement called a *viager*, in effect a wager, under which she had the right to remain on the property in return for a lump sum plus an annuity (in current jargon, a reverse mortgage). Madame de Chamousset certainly won that bet, as she died at ninety-nine, well after the end of the Revolution; she outlived the buyer. His son-in-law, Admiral Meynard de La Farge, finally inherited the property in 1819.

At the end of the tour, as Mark and I walked off, we turned to George: "Okay, what's your opinion?" By then I think we knew we were going to make an offer, but we were glad when George told us the place had a lot of potential and distinction. He pointed out that we had got to be prepared to put in an enormous amount of time, love, effort, and money. But once again we had fallen in love. Besides, we both relish the challenge of a project.

We offered the asking price, our offer was accepted, and thus we became the seventh owners in Château du Feÿ's 360-year history. This was the third great gamble I had taken in my life with flying off to Costa Rica to marry and opening La Varenne being the first two. In signing for Château du Feÿ we both kept wondering just how crazy we had been. Did we really want a château, and a large one at that, with all the responsibilities that entailed? Yes, we did! Perhaps my mind drifted back to the excitements of that year I spent in the garrets of the Palace of Versailles.

We came to understand that a great property like Château du Feÿ abounds in vegetables and fruits and flowers.

Chapter Twelve

....

SEVENTH HEAVEN

Live in each season as it passes, breathe the air, drink the drink, taste the fruit, and resign yourself to the influences of each.

—Henry David Thoreau

Soon after Mark and I put in our offer for Château du Feÿ we invited the previous owners, Baron Fernand de Drouas and his wife, Clothilde, to lunch. "It's wonderful that you Americans [they thought we were both Americans] want to keep up Le Feÿ and that you love it like it ought to be loved," they said, with no resentment at our being foreigners. They were ten years older than us, and he worked as a banker in Paris. They had bought Le Feÿ because she came from a family, the de Saint Phalles, who had lived in the nearby hamlet of Cudot since 1275. But the château, Clothilde said, had become too much for them. They invited us to their farewell party and with

French élan introduced us to the neighbors. Everyone seemed to know everyone else, and there were people with such unlikely names as Pissepot Chassy, people whose forebears were seen off by the British at Waterloo (there were some jokes about that). Other guests included Henri de Montesquieu, scion of the great philosopher, who doffed his Panama hat to salute us. Mark rapidly dubbed the circle "the château mafia," and we called them that forever after.

We found that in France château owners (*châtelains*) jockey for position and those who live in a château that has passed down within the same family for ages are usually at the top. Still, over the years Mark and I were invited to many château parties, and some châtelains became good friends, like Robert and Geneviève de Fleurieu, who had a charming nineteenth-century château with peaked roofs and ornamental brickwork; an ancestor had been a world explorer and gave his name to the Fleurieu Peninsula in southern Australia. Many of the couples were older than us, but Arnaud and Mona de Bontin were about our age, and their property had been in the hands of the Bontin family since 1152. But far from excluding us, they welcomed us and offered congratulations on our having acquired the most attractive place in the neighborhood. There was an entertainment circuit. Each family held a reception once a year in summer for everybody else. I especially loved the invitations—we were always addressed as *Chers Amis*—and I was careful to keep track of correct spellings of names, though I never managed to emulate the casual elegance of their handwritten invitations.

The French are ideal guests, launching into any occasion with gusto, and so they did. I rapidly found that not only were all our neighbors comtes and comtesses, but they were interested in food and cooking, too, so different from England where gardening was the preoccupation. Emmanuel and Huguette de Sartiges lived in a château whose chimneys had a tendency to collapse; he told us how he had saved the local private lycée from extinction by a Communist city council by converting it into a widely respected hotel school, and he was a governor of École des Roches, where Simon and Emma were at school; General Jacques Massu, who lived in the neighborhood and retained his status as a famous Gaullist, would relive his own campaigns, alluding to the battle between Charlemagne's grandsons in A.D. 841 at nearby Fontenay-en-Puisaye. The creator and publisher of an ingenious encyclopedia called *Quid* was Dominique Frémy, who warned Mark and me that there was a Madame de Broglie in our midst—she was the one whose husband had been inexplicably gunned down on a Paris street in the mid-seventies. All this, needless to say, was strong meat for us.

Still, we couldn't wait to move in, and on July 20, 1982, the children and I left Paris at dawn. We paused at the nearby truck stop for *café crème* (the brioche bread was free) and arrived at the château just as the first moving truck was edging its way under the wisteria into the courtyard. Mark had stayed in Paris at my insistence, as he was still recuperating from back surgery; I knew if he was on the spot he would risk his recovery. From the front steps I directed traffic while Simon and Emma galloped up and down the twisting staircases, directing the movers to the bedrooms—the Oak, the Green, the Dutch, and half a dozen others. Each room had rapidly acquired a personality and a name.

That summer we lived like gypsies. The château was habitable only because it was summer. Most of the rooms had peeling walls and the occasional disquieting hole in the floorboards, and we had no serviceable kitchen. We had learned in France to expect that when a house or apartment changed hands the cooking stove would vanish, leaving only a stone sink, but I thought it odd that no one had cooked in a château this size until I learned this was because recent châtelains came down from Paris only for weekends and summer vacation and they relied on charcuteries and pâtisseries, backed up by the homey skills of the caretaker's wife.

Right away friends began to visit—I suppose to assess our folly. Very early on Steve Raichlen came to help us unpack our china, and while he was there Joy and Joe Billington arrived. Joy was an English journalist we'd known in Washington who insisted they were coming though we were just camping and nothing was installed. I decided to put them in the downstairs bedroom, but when I went into the bathroom I found the bath absolutely deep in grime. The de Drouases had been very good about cleaning up but apparently had missed this bath. I stripped off my dress, climbed in, and scrubbed away.

When Joy and Joe arrived, I suggested we all go to supper at a nearby restaurant that would become a favorite. The Pavillon Bleu was a simple little place and perfectly comfortable and the *pommes dauphine,* half *choux* pastry/ half puréed potatoes made into balls and deep-fried, were absolutely delicious. But Joy insisted we stay in. "I'll cook," she said, and in Joigny she bought the cheapest fillets of fish. She boiled these in milk and served them with Tater Tots. I knew I'd never let her cook again. In our twenty-five years at the château, that was the last time we had a shameful meal.

I hated to admit we'd bought a house with no real kitchen, but I was also glad to be able to plan a new one from the floor upward. There was one catch. We had just nine working days before August, the month when the French are dedicated to vacation. In those few days we had to knock down a wall and install plumbing, electricity, and appliances. The cabinets were open shelves, and the floor tile was partly cement. One day into the work, we discovered the hidden doors of a giant hatch from the future kitchen into the dining room that had been blocked for at least a hundred years. This thrilled me, it seemed an example of our empathy for the place and it was only the first of treasures we would discover. Quickly a makeshift kitchen did emerge, one that would last us for the next twelve busy years.

Clothilde de Drouas had warned me about Monsieur Milbert: "He doesn't like working in the house." I soon learned he hated even being asked to help. Mark and I had big ficus trees from Luxembourg we wanted to put in the alcoves of the salon in place of the Grecian statues the de Drouases had had. But the trees were too big, so I asked Milbert to please trim them. Two days later when nothing had happened, I said to Monsieur, "Oh, there are still the trees to trim." Still nothing happened. The third day I said, "It really is important to trim the trees." He cut them back to skeletons. Thus I learned my first Milbert lesson, one that would recur quite often: If he didn't want to do something, he was not going to do it.

Le Feÿ stands on the edge of a dry, chalky plateau, and the buildings were originally constructed on the foundations of a fort that relied for water on an immense medieval well. It was still there in the farmyard—dug down for a dizzying three hundred feet, as deep as a twenty-five-story skyscraper. The flints of the medieval masonry still hold and the water is pure, but to augment the well water the eighteenth-century owners had channeled rain run-off from the immense roofs (over an acre) into three great stone cisterns dug underground near the main buildings. Until World War II, these kept the château supplied with water—although the previous owner, who had lived there when he was a boy, said that in summer he turned his undershirt inside out for lack of water for laundry. He also told us that in 1940 German troops occupied the house for three months but, fortunately, moved on when the taps ran dry. Many years later Simon and friends actually discovered a soldier's helmet in one of the crawl spaces between the floors.

But the flow of water could not keep up with a twentieth-century lifestyle. Mark and I had inherited a water system cobbled together in 1947—two kilometers of private uncharted line. To find a leak you had to cast outward from each end to find a wet spot. For years when the supply failed, in an emergency we made do in the kitchen with water from the swimming pool. In the late 1980s, we got together with the village administration to build a modern installation that pumped unlimited water up to the château—"low nitrate and not a drop of chlorine," boasted Claude, the village water man. The installation came just in time to supply an increasing flow of visitors, all of whom became beguiled by the place and almost always wound up staying for at least a week. All that first summer the children played in the pool and slept until noon despite complaining of the crowing of the cockerel in the dry moat at 4:00 a.m. Mark and I often had ten people or more around the table. Dessert was invariably fruit from the garden. I would send the children to pick whatever was ripe, sometimes wild peaches that Monsieur Milbert propagated from cuttings or late-ripening gooseberries, a member of the currant family.

GOOSEBERRY TORTE

If you can't find gooseberries, blackberries or pitted cherries are good in this torte that takes no more than 15 minutes to mix.

Serves 6

⅔ cup/140 g butter, plus more for the pan
1 cup/125 g flour, plus more for the pan
2 cups/250 g gooseberries
1½ teaspoons/10 g baking powder
½ teaspoon/4 g salt
¾ cup/150 g granulated sugar
1 egg
1¼ cups/150 g ground almonds
Confectioners' sugar, for sprinkling

18-inch/45-cm springform pan; parchment paper

Butter the cake pan, line the base with parchment paper, and butter and flour it. Wash the gooseberries, dry them on paper towels, then snip off the blossom ends and stems. Sift together the flour, baking powder, and salt. Heat the oven to 350°F/180°C and set a shelf low down.

Cream the butter until soft in an electric mixer with the beater attachment. Add the sugar and continue beating until soft and light, 2 to

3 minutes. Beat in the egg until well mixed, about 1 minute. Stir in the ground almonds with a metal spoon, followed by the flour mixture. The batter will be quite stiff.

Spread half the batter in the cake pan. Sprinkle the gooseberries on top and dot with the remaining batter so the fruit is almost covered. Bake until the torte starts to shrink from the sides of the pan and the top is firm when lightly pressed with a fingertip, 45 to 55 minutes. The top will be rustic looking, like a crumble.

Let the torte cool for 10 to 15 minutes in the pan, then loosen the sides and slide the cake onto a rack to cool completely. Serve it warm or at room temperature, sprinkled with confectioners' sugar.

One late summer night the beautiful Burgundian weather broke suddenly in a storm of tropical intensity. The lights failed, and it emerged that the transformer stuck on a telegraph pole had been struck by lightning. So there we were with no electricity and with immobilized water pumps. We saw that life at the château would not always be everything we dreamed. Fixing the transformer, like so much else, took time and was expensive, and once the rains came the kilometer of avenue that had seemed so scenic with its great lime trees framing the entrance turned out to be hell to maintain as a public right-of-way.

Something close to forty-five hectares, over one hundred acres, of woodland surround the Le Feÿ buildings, including a hunting forest that still has the same rides, with the turnarounds that were drawn on the vellum map of 1751. Mark learned that the paths radiating out from a center were designed for hunters to drive their game—in this case deer and wild boar—from circle to circle, almost like playing chess and totally different from the straight runs of England. In spring and fall we often saw a deer or two with a fawn cropping the grass in the front pasture, while in the woods there would be clods of earth overturned by rooting wild boars looking for truffles. The woodland, what the French called the park, was in truth a forest, and when we got two Rhodesian ridgebacks, first Zulu, then Zoltan, they loved long walks in those woods. During hunting season one morning I woke to find a hunter with his rifle right outside our window—property lines didn't seem to matter—and I would have chased him away, but I was stark naked at the time. Still, Mark and I took to the property, indeed to the whole area, almost at once.

Monsieur Milbert's province was the outdoors, but Madame Milbert was happy to help about the place. Their gatehouse, though, had that deep-down grime and smell of earth, so I knew she had never washed the floor. With the best will in the world, Madame was not good at housecleaning. In the early weeks I was on my hands and knees scrubbing plaster dust, desperate for someone to help. Clothilde had given me the name of a hairdresser, Dominique in Joigny—*"c'est comme à Paris,"* she had said—and when I went to have my hair done Dominique suggested Madame Maria. Maria took over and she introduced us to the Portuguese community in Joigny, all hard workers and wonderful artisans.

Maria was forty-five at the time, compact, wiry, and dark skinned, enormously muscled, her black hair parted in the middle and scraped back into a bun. Milbert collected her in Joigny every morning, agreeable to doing this because we paid him for each round-trip; he kept impeccable accounts and hoped we would not notice he charged a margin on the gas. Maria stayed only until lunchtime, but she cleaned the whole château and did all the laundry. Mark and I hadn't yet converted the bedrooms on the upper floor, but there was our wing in the south and the far wing and all the main rooms downstairs, the steps, the windows. In France there is a five-page, single-spaced contract for housekeepers that includes all their obligations and ours—by law the cleaning lady is not allowed to clean windows. But Maria couldn't be stopped.

She had started work in a household before she was ten and in her early teens peddled breakfast rolls in the streets of Lisbon, toting a flat wicker tray on her head. She was a good cook, too. Even after twenty years in France her cooking was Portuguese—feasts of cuttlefish in its ink and suckling pig, salt cod with fried potatoes, and soups of kale, chorizo, and potatoes. It was a while before I realized she couldn't read or write and she became a glimpse for me of a different way of organizing life—when literacy is closed to you, you function differently. Maria remembered everything—how many towels we had, everything that needed buying, anything that was broken. She was a powerhouse of nature.

Over the fifteen years she was with us I learned more about Maria's life outside the château. She did her best to live off the land, buying cheap fowl that had reached the end of their egg-laying life in the fall. She cleaned and plucked them and stored them by the dozen in the freezer. She also raised rabbits in her backyard and had an electric grinder for the corn kernels she collected in the fields with which she baked *broa,* the cornmeal and whole-wheat bread that is a staple of life in Portugal. She had no garden where she lived, but her family's rented allotment, as they are called, was on fertile soil near the river, right next to the one belonging to Jean-Michel Lorain, the chef owner of Côte Saint Jacques, one of France's top restaurants. They would exchange gossip over the fence. She had two sons—one who was difficult to get along with and the younger, as in so many families, beloved. He worked in the local granary and tragically smothered in a cascade of grain when still in his teens.

My parents visited to cast an eye over the magnitude of our indiscretion—my mother especially knew well the unexpected costs of maintenance since her father had dealt in such properties. My father winced as we hit potholes on the kilometer of private road. Mark recalls my father saying one should never buy a place with a private driveway or private water supply, but of course that's what we'd done. But never once did my parents criticize. My mother was a meticulous housekeeper and recoiled a bit at the mess indoors, and Mark and I knew they thought we were crazy to have bought such a place. But I'd become conscious of the fact that both my parents were very cautious and thought I must have inherited some of my grandfather's more adventurous genes. Not his financial acumen, though.

The work at Le Feÿ was daunting. In one courtyard we pushed open the door of the farmhouse and found no plumbing at all. The last tenants, it seemed, had quit in a temper and taken the bathtub with them. We had to adjust to the country way of business when we thought to do our current neighbor a good turn. Monsieur Pinta was a bullheaded farmer, and we offered him use of one of the barns at a modest rent; one year and five registered letters later he was still pushing for an even smaller sum based on the yearly price of a bushel of grain. In another corner there was a gardener's cottage, a perfect rental property if renovated. The roof was sound, but when it rained the ramshackle gutters overflowed in ragged jets of water: *"Ça pisse partout!"* crowed Milbert. By providence, a local artist volunteered to repair it in return for a year's tenancy. There was also the gamekeeper's house we named the *garçonnière*, bachelor's pad, and we set it aside for Simon in a few years.

Le Feÿ—with its windows everywhere—makes you feel as if you're living out of doors. In any case, in summer Mark and I did exactly that, the first year and on into the twenty-five years we lived there. We ate all our summer and autumn meals on the terrace, overlooking an endless, rolling landscape of golden wheat fields in the distance, darkening into plow as the season changed. We made constant trips to the vegetable garden, took long walks in the woods. Every evening I swam laps in the pool. It was a wonderfully friendly house and property, built for the people who were living off the income of the surrounding vineyards and forest. Eventually, at least to some extent, we would, too.

Each year for our château neighbors, the "mafia," we had seated lunches; one year Lisa and Holly, two of our stagiaires, hadn't finished the sausages, called bangers in England. They woke early to finish, walked downstairs, and turned on the stove to get started. Mark and I were upstairs in our bedroom—we normally couldn't hear a thing in the kitchen, but we were woken by a booming explosion. I recognized that sound from the London Cordon Bleu, where students occasionally put on the ovens without lighting them. I rushed downstairs in my dressing gown and found Madame Milbert standing stock-still at the sink and the girls huddled near the far door. The boiling stockpot had been thrown from the stove to the floor, and the door of the oven had blown off. Miraculously no one was hurt, and with nearly fifty guests expected we kept going. It wasn't until after the party that I went into the bathroom that backed on to the kitchen and found the entire wall had been blown into the bath.

One day when I had stayed down at the château and Mark was away working, Mark Williamson, who had recently opened Willi's Wine Bar in Paris, dropped by with friends and a crate of wine. Back in the kitchen we scouted around for food. After all, it was summer and a great big salad from the garden was no problem, nor were generous dishes of peach and raspberry crumble for dessert. The main course revolved around a huge pot of red wine risotto, imbibed with a couple of the bottles Mark had so kindly brought. I had recently discovered that risotto is improved by adding double the amount of red wine suggested in traditional cookbooks; here I'm proving my point.

RED WINE RISOTTO

This recipe needs a full-bodied red wine—the Italian original calls for Barolo, but a less expensive Valpolicella or Chianti will do, too. I like my risotto very fluid—the Venetians call it *al onda,* on the wave—and it should not be left to stand, as it will become sticky. Red wine risotto, with or without a sprinkling of grated Parmesan cheese, is a great opener to a winter meal of braised beef or pork, and any leftover is perfect for *arancini,* small balls of rice reheated in a frying pan.

Serves 4

2 cups (500 ml) robust red wine
2 cups/500 ml vegetable stock, plus more if needed
4 tablespoons/60 g butter
1 onion, finely chopped
2 celery stalks, finely chopped
Salt and pepper
1 cup/200 g risotto rice such as Arborio
Parmesan cheese (for serving)

Heat the wine and stock in separate pans. Heat the butter in a sauce-pan and sauté the onion and celery over medium heat with a little salt and pepper until translucent and very soft, 12 to 15 minutes. Stir in the rice and cook, stirring constantly, until it absorbs the butter and looks transparent, 2 to 3 minutes. Add about half the wine and simmer, stir-ring, until the rice starts to dry, 2 to 3 minutes.

Add a couple more ladlefuls of hot stock and continue simmering, stirring constantly. When the rice starts to dry again and needs more liquid, continue with more wine, then with more stock, alternating wine and stock until all are used. It's important to stir the risotto constantly and add liquid often so the rice does not get dry.

The rice is done when very tender, with only the slightest bit of re-sistance when you bite into a grain. It should be very creamy. The starch leaches from the grains, and don't hesitate to add more stock, if needed. Total cooking time for the rice is 25 to 30 minutes. Serve it as soon as possible, with a sprinkle of grated Parmesan cheese.

———————

When everyone had gathered around, I asked Simon to take his dad's place at the head of the table. Simon was just fourteen, but in an instant he was extending a welcome to our guests. Halfway through the meal he came up to me and said, "Mum, we're going to run out of wine; should I open more?" I could see he was a born host as well as a boy with an adventurous streak, so like my father's father, who had friends everywhere and was always talking.

———

As much as I loved our time in Paris, to keep the school going I was expanding my outreach. When Gallo Wine announced they would be bringing their wines to Paris and were looking for three well-known cooks to do a television commercial for their ultra-cheap white Chablis, Mark and I agreed I must get more experience as a TV performer. I would compromise my purity in return for a healthy amount of money. The school needed a boost. The ad was my introduction to Hollywood, and I asked our excellent trainee Charles Pierce to be the cook.

We met in a grand turn-of-the-century paneled Paris apartment. The wardrobe lady bought me a lovely cream silk dress by Céline with long sleeves and a little bow with streamers at the neck. I wore a gold chain Mark had given me, and the makeup person did up my hair and full makeup. The shoot wound up taking three whole days, but we began with seven of us around a table holding up wineglasses (the camera made an intrusive eighth). We were directed to toast one another, again, and again. To my right a French actor was to say, "*C'est disponible* [it's available]?" The wine was their cheapest "Chablis," but Gallo wanted to make it appear high class.

I had been in charge of the menu, and I made one bad mistake. I thought shrimp would be lovely—pink, pretty, an interesting shape—but under those terribly hot lights the shrimp started to stink. Ultimately we did seventy-three takes on just those two short sentences—I counted. Time on the shrimp ran out. I was to say, in response to, "It's available?" "Why, I should think just about anywhere you like," but each time the director changed the way I ought to say it. "Why, *just* about anywhere you like," "Why, just *about* anywhere you like," and so on, seventy-three different intonations. It gave me a real respect for the pros like the accordion player on my left at table, very French, an old music hall veteran who knew how to do nothing more than precisely what was needed. The minute anyone wanted a response, he was on, while amateurs like myself took much longer to get it.

The clincher was this, and I've never told a soul: Gallo did not have customs clearance for their Chablis, so we were drinking French wine. Of course it had to be the right color, and of course we were not allowed to take a sip from our glasses in case we should be drunk by the end of the day. But most of what I learned was that such shoots are terribly boring. We sat around ninety-five percent of the day eating dreary junk food and waiting for a camera call, though I had to wait less than the others as I was on camera more. The ad ultimately ran on prime time on Sunday afternoons during sports because Gallo wanted their wine to rival beer. The week it aired, when Mark was at the World Bank he was much teased. His friends were amused to find Mark's wife suddenly appearing in the middle of a football game.

The same year we bought the château, I was invited to become a member of the board of the International Association of Culinary Professionals. The organization was composed of many people I admired tremendously, including of course Julia and Jim and François Dionot, who was always down-to-earth and practical, and Nathalie Dupree, who was very bright and had lots of ideas, though sometimes she could become overly emotional. I was caught by total surprise at one of the meetings when Nina Simonds, who had been one of our trainees, stood up and nominated me to the board. I was really touched by her support. IACP's mission was to serve as a resource and support system for food professionals worldwide, and being a board member gave me a different look at American institutions and brought new friends into my life. Among the most lively of these was Irena Chalmers, an Englishwoman who was my age and with whom I felt an instant kinship. By the early eighties she was living in Manhattan and, as well as being an author herself, amusing, sharp, and witty, running her own book company.

Four years after I joined the board I became treasurer, running up to vice president and president, and at one stage helped to run the IACP Scholarship program as well as the Cookbook Awards. Around the same time, one of my great joys was to be elected as an early member of the Who's Who of Cooking in America, the same time as Simca. When my name was announced I was elated, and later Judy Hill told me I was very lucky to have been chosen. "It was a very difficult choice," she said. I felt still more greatly honored—she had been on the selection committee. I wasn't idealistic about IACP but did hope to expand its scope. This was just the beginning of the explosion in food careers, a time when terms like "food stylist" were being coined and when food television was entering its adolescence and food photography was rapidly expanding. And, of course, everybody wanted to write a cookbook.

La Varenne Archive

On stage with the all-stars: Shirley Corriher, Emeril Lagasse, me, Julia, Johanne Killeen, and Martin Yan.

Chapter Thirteen

....

THE PERKS

The primary requisite for writing well about food is a good appetite.

—A. J. Liebling

By 1984 Mark had squeaked out his maximum time from the World Bank in Paris and we learned he would soon be posted back to Washington. The children were turning twelve and fourteen and Mark and I wanted them to do their secondary education in English, so we began to look around for boarding schools. Bedales in southern England was more liberal than traditional schools like those Mark and I had attended—we were adamant that the children should attend a co-educational school, as we felt we had suffered from segregation of the sexes. But when we went to see Bedales, our hearts quailed at the sight of all the children arriving for interviews and carrying instruments. This didn't seem the right place. All the same we were taken aback when our intelligent, bilingual children were politely but firmly rejected.

We adjusted our perspective to the United States, and thanks to Margo Miller's help we were lined up with advisors. In the States we found much more tolerance for the children's international background. We had hoped they would attend the same school, but ultimately Emma was accepted at Groton, one of the few boarding schools that would take someone so young, and Simon was accepted at St. Andrew's in Delaware, a school just starting to become prominent, and as it turned out perfect for Simon because it was in the countryside and had good sports. Simon rapidly adjusted his accent to become part southern, part clipped English, which sounded very odd until it lapsed over time into mid-Atlantic.

To occupy Le Feÿ in the long periods we would be away, Mark and I began to look around for tenants. Right away shady characters appeared—a smooth-talking couple with Libyan connections, a fine arts dealer who dreamed of bringing clients to France to view his antique statues of dubious provenance, a currency broker whose only reference was a numbered Swiss bank account. Then Dale and Lorraine Perkinson arrived. Mark and I hadn't really done things up, but as Dale gazed at the moon rising over the pigeon house he said, "This château sure makes a statement. Mind if we make some renovations?"

So the Perkinsons took over the whole of the southern part of the château and it was as if we suddenly had fairy godparents. Before we knew it the plumber was competing for space with designers and electricians and painters who swarmed over the reception rooms that emerged shimmering in a color a friend kindly described as vanilla. Upstairs disused doors were reopened to reveal the original configuration of suites, each with bedroom, a bathroom, and a salon. Mark and I began to see that great houses like these were designed for extended families—for grandparents, maiden aunts, and broods of children. In just six weeks the Perkinsons redecorated the entire southern end. We began to refer to them as our "perks," and when they paved the driveway Mark dubbed it "the J. Dale Perkinson Memorial Parkway."

We still needed someone to take over as director of La Varenne, and one of our finest trainees, Susy Davidson, came to mind. She was working in New York at *Cook's Magazine* ("the magazine of cooking in America," as it was called at the time). During a trip to New York we met with her at Teachers' Restaurant to ask if she would be interested. She tells me she remembers floating down the street after our lunch, wondering if this was a dream, and for us Susy was a dream come true. The bonus was that she and Chambrette got along well. The school had finally begun to make a little money, and Mark and I bought a nice apartment for Susy on the Right Bank, near the Palais Royale.

Not long after she began as director, Susy discovered Chambrette had a white leather bag into which he often stashed "extras"; Susy's strategy was to wait until after the demonstration, when Chambrette would empty food into that satchel. Later she went downstairs and emptied it, without saying a word. He would fill it again, and she would empty it until eventually he stopped. They never said a word about this to each other, but they both understood that a line had been drawn. That was how Susy was, handling everything with intelligence and aplomb.

In the fall of 1984 Mark and I settled into a classic small railroad apartment in the Georgetown area of Washington, D.C., and suddenly we were back with no children just like when we got married. I was determined to be a hands-off boss to Susy, but once again I needed something to do. Mark chimed in with an idea: In four years I would turn fifty; why not write a book full of recipes and anecdotes from half a century in cooking? And *Real Food* was born, with a clear vision for the British market. There was at the time something a little George Orwell–ish about the excesses of nouvelle cuisine, kitchen artistry turned on its head—colors that fooled, textures that deluded, tastes that confounded, and food that did not nourish—so I decided *Real Food* would include recipes that appealed to all the senses. Since real food is so often associated with a personality, I introduced the teachers, cooks, writers, and gastronomes who had touched my life.

My time filled up rapidly. I was again writing newspaper columns, thinking of future books, working with IACP, and giving dinner parties. This time Mark and I enlisted the services of a butler of the old school. Portly, smiling Clay Wilson helped set the atmosphere; in his black or cream tuxedo, depending on the season, and his crêpe-soled shoes, Clay recalled a more leisurely era of servants and stately charm. He freelanced at *The Washington Times* and the White House and regaled us with anecdotes about the nobs. Best of all, he loved cooking. Clay and I exchanged recipes. Every time he served, I felt challenged to try a new dish, dishes he was forever tarting up—adding turnip roses to fish or forests of lettuce to roasts. Once he even carved a whale out of an eggplant. When we had smoked

salmon rillettes, he sculpted the soft pâté into a swimming fish with scales
of cucumber.

SMOKED SALMON RILLETTES

Rillettes are very rich, with equal amounts of fresh and cold-smoked
salmon that are cooked and then beaten with butter for serving with crusty
bread, toast, or crackers. They are good for canapés and I can happily
devour a small ramekin of them as an appetizer, particularly with a handful
of arugula on the side. Other options for serving are chopped chives, capers, and wedges of lemon. To keep the rillettes for a day or two, smooth
the surface, seal with melted butter, and store in the refrigerator.

Serves 6 as an appetizer

½-pound/225-g piece of salmon fillet
½ pound/225 g cold-smoked salmon
1 cup/225 g butter
Salt (if necessary) and pepper
Grated nutmeg

To poach salmon
½ cup/125 ml dry white wine
½ cup/125 ml water

Lay the salmon fillet in a frying pan and pour over the white wine and
water. Cover and simmer until the salmon just flakes easily, 5 to 7 minutes. Let cool for a few minutes, then lift out the salmon and set it
aside. Add the smoked salmon to the pan, cover, and cook 1 to 2
minutes, until the slices are no longer transparent. Leave to cool in the
liquid, then drain and discard it.

Finely shred the fresh and cooked salmon with two forks, discarding skin and any bones; you may need to trim brown edges from the
smoked salmon. Cream the butter until very soft and stir in the shredded salmon, still using a fork (be sure the salmon is cool or it will melt
the butter). The texture of rillettes should be rough and slightly flaky,
so do not overstir. Season the rillettes to taste with salt (if necessary),

pepper, and nutmeg—salt may not be needed, as the smoked salmon contains salt. Pack the rillettes in individual ramekins or in a pottery mold and chill thoroughly at least an hour or two before serving with your chosen accompaniments.

Two years into our stay in D.C. we had a shock in store when Susy decided to return to the States and Mark and I had to find a new director. For those couple of years La Varenne had prospered, but Susy's departure turned out to be a turning point for the school. Not only was she hard to replace, but at the same time the dollar began to fall in value. By now the Cordon Bleu had been purchased by André Cointreau of the liqueur family. With his unlimited funds he was transforming the school, which was now becoming serious competition. Susy gave plenty of notice, so Mark and I were able to install an interim director, but soon I began to receive disturbing reports from Paule, our bookkeeper, that bookings weren't going well. So I returned to Paris to look things over, and we began again to search for someone new, eventually hiring a former stagiaire, Dewey Markham, the son of a New York jazz musician, extremely bright, fluent in French, and good with food. The students liked him, and so did I. The only problem was our management styles wound up being far too different for the arrangement to last.

In the meantime, Peter Kindersley, creator of Dorling Kindersley, had developed a concept of how-to books with literally hundreds of titles and a huge range of subjects and came to me with an idea he wanted me to develop. He was looking for a definitive guide for someone who already knew how to cook, with lots of technique photographs included. In England this project became *Reader's Digest Complete Guide to Cookery*; in the United States it was *La Varenne Pratique*, an enormous task with chapters on everything imaginable—from sugar and chocolate to fats and oils, from vegetables to fruit and nuts, with chapters on bread and soups and even one on kitchen equipment. Once again the key was to stay on deadline. Peter knew I could keep up because of the *Grand Diplôme Cooking Course*, but for this new project we had just fifteen months. Each chapter required immense amounts of research and recipe testing. We faced innumerable other issues, for instance in the technique pictures—since this was to be an active cook's guide—we needed a working kitchen and utensils, clean but not brand-new, and hands that looked professional. We decided the château was the place to do much of the photography and that Chef Claude would be the perfect model. We did intensive two-week bursts of work, dining on leftovers from the shoot. During the first chapter on shellfish we ate lobster, oysters, and clams. Great! But when we got to vegetables and eggs, it wasn't nearly as much fun.

I did the research and writing in Washington. The terrific Amanda Mannheim, young as she was, because her mother was a publisher turned out to be a stellar editor. Once again we ate the results of Chef Randall Price's recipe tests for supper. I wrote most of the book on a Sony desktop computer with a vertical screen, cutting-edge and perfect for drafting recipes and so different from my electric typewriter; without it we could never have written the book to deadline. Squeezed into that small apartment, we worked at a terrific pace. Some chapters went like clockwork—"Sauces" was one—but others, like "Preserving," were dogs and took far longer than expected. Somehow I managed to distill into words my twenty-five years (was it already so long?) of work in food and cooking in three countries, with each chapter instructing the way to choose ingredients, how to store them, how to identify them in the first place. We covered hundreds of skills, from chopping an onion to boning a rabbit to tempering chocolate. My core belief was, and still is, that with the knowledge of techniques and ingredients recipes flow naturally and everyone can enjoy the pleasures of the table, inside and outside the kitchen.

One weekend while we were at work on this project, Mark and I were in England, traveling the tedious train ride from London to Yorkshire. Mark was editing the chapter on fruits. At one point he complained my opening text was unclear, and I began to try to explain what I was getting at. Our argument was growing heated when a total stranger sitting across from us intervened, saying, "Perhaps I can help you, I'm a plant scientist." Geoffrey Palmer, it emerged, was an academic working on the molecular biology of plants. "You're confusing the difference between maturity and ripeness," he said, and he went on to explain. By no means all fruits, it seems, are ready to eat when they are mature. Raspberries and melons, for instance, go on ripening and developing sweetness after they are picked, but pears picked when mature do not continue to ripen—they must ripen on the tree. Hence the disappointing quality of so many pears. Mark and I learned a great deal on that journey.

We were also tremendously lucky to have Jill Norman in London as our editor—she had been Elizabeth David's editor and had a clear vision of the book as well as an excellent grasp of the material it should cover. Earlier I'd done two other charming little books with Jill that were her idea—the highly illustrated *Classical French Cooking* and *Anne Willan's Desserts and Pastries*—so I knew she was a pleasure to work with. As *La Varenne Pratique* neared its deadline, one of our trainees, Martha Holmberg, and I traveled from Washington to London so that we could be virtually at Jill's side as pages needing last-minute fine-tuning poured out of the fax machine. We didn't sleep much on that trip, but I felt proud of the resulting book, and it proved to be a great global success. *La Varenne Pratique* was translated into nine different languages, sold over a million copies worldwide, and broke the price bar for illustrated cookbooks. It also garnered me a prized award, one of several I've received from IACP. That same year Julia also had a general cookbook nominated. We were sitting at the same table listening to the announcements when my book was selected over hers. I was slightly embarrassed when I heard my name, but as always Julia was nothing but gracious and pleased for me.

With the publication of each new book came the requisite tour. When I signed book contracts these always seemed far off, but usually following a long silence after seeing the book to bed the publisher's PR department would contact me, demanding a list of my contacts in cities everywhere. When I was lucky the tours followed a logical route through the States from coast to coast, but more often than not travel was a zigzag from climate to climate, time zone to time zone, a whirl of airplanes and chain hotels, crammed into the shortest space possible. I learned to dress not just for weather but for region—makeup, pastels, and high heels in the South, a more muted look for New England. I pressed the flesh, and from questions journalists asked I grasped an understanding of the audience's interests. It is true that I never thought I would tire of potato chips until one morning when, jumping on an early flight in Chicago, I found myself eating them for breakfast.

It is lovely to be looked after, and quite often the publisher lined up a perfect handler who led me on time to shows I had to do. Still, it's tough out there. One always hoped to make the big shows—*Good Morning America*, Martha Stewart, *The Today Show*—and I was lucky enough to snag several appearances on these. Martha had a reputation for sharp remarks, but I always found her wonderful to work with, and over the years she became quite a friend, perhaps feeling a kinship with me because we were fellow entrepreneurs, however modest La Varenne's scope. She treated me like an equal and told it like it was. And just sometimes I was the "talent" for whom limos and five-star restaurants and an entourage of acolytes was appropriate. At times like that I thought I could happily settle into celebrity status.

But there were tricky moments, too, like the early-morning show in Texas, at an evangelical television station where I was surprised to find a very smart set. I saw clearly there was money here, and as I began to prepare my demonstration I climbed up two steps to the stage to set up. Stepping back to have a look at the camera angle, I forgot about those steps and went flying. Without thinking I cried, "Jesus Christ!" I'm not sure I looked at the camera crew's faces, but I can imagine.

Throughout this time I had had a British agent, Andrew Nurnberg, a colorful character who also represented Boris Yeltsin. This was a tough job according to Andrew, involving overnight stints at the bath house whenever he visited Moscow. By the mid 1990s I was publishing more and more in the United States, and was looking around for an agent on the spot. So when I heard Lisa Ekus was opening her own literary agency, I was thrilled. I had known Lisa as a cookbook publicist from as far back as the late 1980s. On behalf of various publishers she had sent me (and many other authors) on ten-day, coast-to-coast tours, and she always tackled things with aplomb— like the time I prepared a raw chicken on *Good Morning America* and then shook Charlie Gibson's hand. I barely noticed having done so, but Lisa told me after the show aired the producer, Jane Bollinger, received many calls from viewers—the salmonella scare was in full bloom at the time, and Jane called Lisa to let her know I was to be more careful in the future.

In 1987, while I was still in the middle of *La Varenne Pratique*, Mark had the chance to take a golden handshake from the World Bank. Within two weeks his job was ended and he came home and occupied our sofa, the only spare seat. Within a day he was answering the phone; within a week he was absorbed as an integral part of the team. He and I talked of returning to Europe as soon as the book was finished. The school needed me, and now we weren't tied to the States. The children were approaching college age, more than capable of crossing the Atlantic on their own—after all, Emma had first done so at the age of eleven.

Also, Mark and I were beginning to glimpse more possibilities for Le Feÿ. We knew it was a wonderful place to work, and with some investment in a teaching kitchen, and more bathrooms, we were convinced it would make an ideal haven for the in-depth study of French cooking surrounded by restaurants and top chefs, in a region brimming with outstanding ingredients and within cracking distance of Chablis, the Côte d'Or, Champagne, and the Loire, all those world-class wines.

The Perkinsons were still in the south wing, and with their windfall rent Mark and I created a country kitchen for teaching, added a couple more bathrooms, and squeezed a half-dozen students into the north wing. We shortened our courses, made them more diverse and more demanding. We started with just a few courses in the summer, inviting some extraordinary guest teachers, like the tall, bearded Jean-Michel Bouvier, whose increasing girth made him appear almost Rabelesian and who thought nothing of leaving his restaurant in Chambéry at midnight and driving at high speed the four hours to the château only to appear bright eyed at 8:00 a.m. in the kitchen. "*Le goût du terroir* [the taste of the soil], that's what matters," he would say. Another guest was Frédéric Gauvin, a young pâtissier who at twenty-two was in charge of pastry decoration at Fauchon, one of the leading caterers in Paris. "I'm the SAMU [ambulance driver]," Frédéric joked about his work for Pierre Hermé, the top pastry chef and his mentor. Frédéric would bounce to a grand reception in the back of a truck carrying multi-tiered, intricately decorated cakes and his pastry tools, "prepared for emergency surgery."

Once in a while, Mark and I treated ourselves to a three-star restaurant meal. "Great chefs have no taste," Mark noted, looking around at some of the dining rooms with their brassy chandeliers, felt on the walls, and nude sculptures resembling a chocolate confection, all piling up debt. And some of the excesses did cause terrible problems. Jean-Michel Lorain at the nearby Côte Saint Jacques had expanded early and thus survived, but later some were ruined in the ups and downs of the world economy. Among the most tragic stories was that of Bernard Loiseau at the Côte d'Or in Saulieu, an acknowledged master of thirty years' standing. He expounded his difficulties on television. "How can I create good food when I have to worry about finding fifty thousand francs every single day of the week to pay back the bank?" he lamented. Sadly, in 2003, when his restaurant was threatened with the loss of its third star, Loiseau committed suicide.

One year after a regional IACP meeting in Paris, Mark had an idea to offer a special option to fifty attendees to come down to Burgundy for a reception at Château du Feÿ. Julia and Patricia Wells stayed with us at the château while forty other people were lodged in local hotels. We embarked on a gastronomic odyssey and in a single day we ate at three three-star restaurants. We had lunch at the Côte d'Or, with Patricia commenting knowledgeably on the meal. Afterward we drove over to Vézelay and Marc

Meneau's L'Espérance for tea, where remarks were up to me. Meneau created an unforgettable repast with each table set in eighteenth-century style with a galaxy of pastries. We started with a bowl of hot drinking chocolate made with whole, unpasteurized milk and whisked for an hour over the lowest possible heat. Ethereal toasted brioche came separately for dunking, and then there appeared tiny tartlets of dark rose petals in fresh cheese, the perfume of rose harking back to the Renaissance. The pièce de résistance was his grandmother's apple gâteau, baked overnight to achieve an essential essence of apple with a hint of orange and butter. Including a bit of sugar, that's just four ingredients—classic superstar simplicity!

MARC MENEAU'S APPLE GÂTEAU

You'll need a tart apple such as Granny Smith or McIntosh for this spectacular gâteau, a masterpiece that demands lots of time for slicing and arranging the slices in the mold. Before baking, the apples tower at least 8 inches/20 cm high, and they cook down to about two-thirds of the height. You'll need to keep an eye out during the 10 to 12 hours of cooking, as the oven must remain very, very low. Meneau has a classic accompaniment, salt butter caramel sauce.

Serves 6 to 8

1–2 tablespoons butter, for the mold
2 oranges, for zest
5–6 large lumps of sugar
4 pounds/1.8 kg tart apples

1½-quart/1.5-liter tall soufflé dish

To prepare the soufflé dish, generously butter it. Prepare a wide double strip of foil to form a collar extending at least 3 inches/7.5 cm above the rim of the dish. Press the collar against the inside of the dish. Now butter the inner side of the foil and chill until the butter is set and the foil sticks to the dish.

To extract the zest from the skins of the oranges, rub them with the sugar cubes so the cubes soften and turn bright orange. Wrap the orange-flavored cubes in plastic wrap and crush them with a rolling pin.

Peel the apples and scoop out the stem and flower ends. Halve them and scoop out the cores with a melon baller or the point of a knife. Set a half cut-side down on a board and cut it crosswise into the thinnest possible slices. Alternatively, slice the apple halves on a mandoline.

To assemble the gâteau: Arrange a layer of apple slices in a flower pattern in the bottom of the mold. Top this first layer of apple with more slices arranged across the others like the ripples in a pond. (This crossed pattern of slices ensures that the cake holds together when unmolded.) Sprinkle the second layer with some of the crushed orange sugar. Continue filling the mold until the apples, held in place by the foil collar, extend at least 2 inches/5 cm above the rim. (They will shrink down into the mold during cooking.) Cover them with a round of buttered foil.

Heat the oven to 150°F/66°C and set a shelf low down. Set the mold on a baking sheet. Bake the gâteau in the warm oven until the apples are much reduced and meltingly soft when pierced with a skewer, 10 to 12 hours. Tear off the top of the foil collar and let the cake cool to tepid. Unmold it onto a warm platter—the top should be lightly caramelized with a little syrupy juice running down the sides. Serve it warm, with salt butter caramel sauce on the side.

SALT BUTTER CARAMEL SAUCE

This version of a butterscotch sauce is great with ice cream, too.

Makes 1½ cups/375 ml sauce

1 cup/200 g sugar
½ cup/125 ml water
Squeeze of lemon juice
½ cup/110 g salted butter
¾ cup/175 ml heavy cream
Pinch of salt (if needed)

For the caramel: Heat the sugar, water, and lemon juice in a heavy pan over low heat until the sugar is dissolved. Bring to a boil and boil the syrup rapidly without stirring until it starts to turn golden around the edges. If you stir, the syrup may crystallize. Meanwhile melt the butter with the cream and prepare a large bowl of cold water.

When the syrup begins to color, lower the heat and continue boiling a few seconds to a deep golden color—it will darken rapidly. Take the pan from the heat and dip the base in the cold water to stop the cooking. Add the butter and cream, standing back, as the sauce may sputter and bubble up in the pan.

Put the pan back over the heat, stirring until the caramel is completely dissolved. Let the sauce cool, then taste it and add a pinch of salt if needed to sharpen the flavor. Serve hot or chilled.

———

After Vézelay we all retired to our rooms for a few minutes of rest and to change clothes before Champagne at Château du Feÿ in the grand salon, where the chandeliers twinkled and Simon, at six-four, who happened to be at home, towered over the assembled guests. He did not come with us to dinner at our local gastronomic wonder, Côte Saint Jacques, headed by Jean-Michel Lorain. "No, no," said Simon, who had worked there at age sixteen. "I know the inside stories!" Chef Michel Lorain and his son Jean-Michel had always had a keen sense of style and created dishes with just that touch of novelty that compels attention. It was Julia who took the lead in commenting on yet another spectacular meal in an astonishing day. I'd done similar marathons in Australia, so I learned how—you simply don't eat everything on your plate, you don't eat bread, and you drink lots of water and go very slowly on the wine. Most important, you don't just sit on the bus and stagger to the ladies' room and back to the table; you get some exercise somewhere, even if it's just a walk thirty yards up to the riverbank and back.

Need I say that we ourselves visited these starred restaurants only once in a while? Too much grazing in top restaurants just leads to disappointment. After all, it was Escoffier who said, "*Faites simple* [keep it simple]," and I believe this is a lesson all cooks should take to heart. In search of simplicity, we explored new restaurants in the area like La Madeleine in Sens that the young Chef Patrick Gauthier started on a shoestring budget when he was only twenty-six. Patrick soon became one of our most beloved visiting chefs, full of energy, always with a joke and a smile. Within ten years La Madeleine had gained two stars, and Patrick has deservedly kept them for the freshness of his cuisine, grounded in local ingredients. His three-tiered cheese trolley is a visible reminder of the wealth of cheese available in Burgundy. These days Patrick travels regularly to Japan, where he acts as consultant to several French-inspired restaurants.

In 1987 everything was happening in multiples of seven—Mark and I both were forty-nine and preparing to celebrate our twenty-first wedding anniversary. And that summer when we arrived at the château, we had a special piece of good news. We had half-wished the Perkinsons might consider leaving so that we could move back into the south end of the château, where the sun was such a delight. Mark had decided he would go discuss things with them, when that very morning Dale Perkinson came to let us know they'd decided they wouldn't be staying. To celebrate this good news as well as all those sevens, Mark and I decided to throw a party on the seventh day of the seventh month. A couple of weeks before the party we counted over eighty acceptances and saw we needed all the help we could get. Chefs Chambrette and Claude promised to come down from Paris for the occasion, and for days before the party they folded, shaped, and baked puff pastry edibles with zesty stuffings run up by Chambrette from cans of olives and anchovies years beyond their sell-by date—I've never thought those dates amounted to much. We had real potato chips, using garden potatoes freshly deep-fried. Guests were invited for 7:00, with seven guests to a table.

Pink-cheeked Monsieur Branger, our former mailman, was in charge of service. He knew the house well from the Drouas days. Maria washed up in one kitchen, Madame Milbert in the other. Monsieur Milbert had brought out his hand-painted Parking sign he used once a year and opened the gate to the dry moat. Before the party Mark and I had a formal photograph taken under the great oak tree. My father stands upright, despite his arthritis and eighty-four years (another seven), and my mother is, as always, elegant in navy chiffon with a discreet twinkle of diamond. Emma had turned fifteen that year and wears her first strapless dress, Grandma's earrings, and my pearls around her neck, and I display puffed sleeves and polka dots. Simon wears his first tuxedo, a carbon copy of his dad, whose thirty-year-old outfit shows the strain. I was so excited I was ready to bounce out of the lens and into the kitchen, anywhere so as not to stand still.

As the sun descended we were downing Champagne on the terrace; by some blessing the weather was always benign when we entertained. Only once in all the twenty-five years at the château did we have to retreat indoors for a party. Mark opened the festivities with an elegant speech in French and English on the theme of the number seven and read one well-wisher's message: "May you all be in seventh heaven." We settled down to a concert of chamber music in the salon, a Burgundian tradition evidenced by the horn and lyre that were carved into the paneling above the fireplace. The paneling in the dining room was adorned with a glass and a carafe. We listened to Mark's nephew, Nicolas, playing Mozart on the cello as a pleasant cross breeze carried the scent of lavender and rose. I had asked the chefs to create a personal dessert. Not surprisingly, they turned to wine and made a red wine tart that Chef Chambrette came across in an old Burgundian book.

RED WINE TART

The raspberry-tinged local Pinot Noir of northern Burgundy blends unexpectedly well with cinnamon in this recipe. I like to border the dark red filling with rosettes of whipped cream.

Serves 6

2 eggs
½ cup/100 g sugar
2 teaspoons/12 g cornstarch
2 teaspoons/10 g ground cinnamon
1 cup/250 ml fruity red wine
1 cup/250 ml heavy cream, for decoration

For the pâte sucrée
1½ cups/185 g flour
½ cup/100 g sugar
3 egg yolks
Pinch of salt
5 tablespoons/75 g butter
Dry kidney beans or rice (to keep foil in place while baking)

9-inch/23-cm pie pan with removable base; pastry bag and small star tip

Make the *pâte sucrée* dough and line the pie pan as for Mrs. Reagan's chocolate pear tart (page 190). Chill the pie shell until firm, at least 20 minutes. Heat the oven to 375°F/190°C and put in a baking sheet low down.

To blind bake the tart shell, press a sheet of foil down into the corners of the unbaked shell and fill with dry kidney beans or rice to keep the foil in place. Bake in the oven until the pastry is set and browned around the rim, 15 to 20 minutes. Let the tart cool for 5 minutes, then remove the foil and beans, but leave the shell in the pan. Leave the oven on.

For the filling, whisk the eggs with the sugar, cornstarch, and cinnamon just until mixed—any froth will spoil the smooth surface of the tart. Stir in the wine. Pour the filling into the tart shell and continue baking until the filling is set, 15 to 20 minutes. Unmold the tart and let it cool completely.

Shortly before serving the tart, beat the cream until it holds a stiff peak. Fill it into the piping bag fitted with the star tip and pipe very small rosettes of whipped cream around the edge of the tart, inside the pastry edge.

Later the band struck up for dancing. In his day my father had been a champion waltzer, and that night he looked on with nostalgia. Simon tried not to tread on his grandmother's toes. I danced with a neighbor who had learned the steps of the Gay Gordons, a Scottish reel. After midnight it was darker—though never too dark, since the drive and walks were lit up like fireflies with little five-franc candles. Toward dawn someone sighted Chambrette naked in the pool, and in the wine cellar Emma received her first improper proposal from a guest—she complained indignantly about it for a week afterward. The house was full—more than thirty—though many never went to bed.

Trainees and staff on the steps at Château du Feÿ include Chef Randall Price, Chef Patrick Gauthier, and course director Debbie Orrill.

Chapter Fourteen

....

LA VIE DE CHÂTEAU

Show me another pleasure like dinner which comes every day and lasts an hour.

—Talleyrand

So many characters came into our lives at the château, but none were as ever present or important as the Milberts. They gave us a view of what it means to live off the land. In France, to call them *paysans* (peasants, literally inhabitants of the *pays* or countryside) sums up their instinctive knowledge of the earth and what it offers. Without the smallest sense of deprivation, the Milberts lived almost entirely off the land. Both had been born in this corner of the Yonne region. Many times over the years Monsieur told the story of how at the start of World War II he and the young men of our nearest village, Villevallier, had been marched to the southwest, to Périgord, and on the way were billeted in an orchard where he had had the sense to pick the apples and live off them. Eventually he made his way back and he and Madame married. For lack of a permanent home they lived in a barn. What they earned they saved.

Slowly, as Mark and I came to know them better, we learned their history, one that included much tragedy particularly as regards their four children—two committed suicide, one died of multiple sclerosis, and only one of them remained. They had spent most of their lives near the little town of St. Julien, farming with a horse and plow and selling the milk their cows produced to the local dairy. In 1977 they sold all they had and moved to Le Feÿ to "retire," as caretakers. But retirement for Monsieur meant working long, hard days cultivating our more than two acres of fruits and vegetables—we never asked him to do it; it was his pride and joy. And his garden was extraordinary. Surrounded by seven-foot stone walls, the inside temperature was 5°C higher than outside. It was divided into quarters, with a water pond in the center. A grapevine draped the north wall (to catch maximum sun), and the walls inside sported iron hooks lodged in parallel rows running their length to support panes of glass that sheltered the vines. The scene was similar to one that had unfolded for centuries in the garden drawn meticulously on the 1751 map. In its day that garden would have nourished fifty people or more.

Milbert's specialty was peaches he grew from ungrafted cuttings, watering them devotedly in summer and feeding them with potash from his wood fire in the spring. The taste of those tiny, perfumed peaches is imprinted forever on my palate. Mark and I also learned very early that Milbert was far more reliable than were the French weather forecasters. *"S'il pleut à la Saint Benoît, il pleuvra trente-sept jours plus tard* [if it rains on Saint Benoît (July 11) it will rain for thirty-seven days]. *Si la lune monte, les légumes montent aussi* [if the moon is rising, so will the vegetables]." As a rule his predictions were right.

Milbert had that classic slow, steady, slightly bowed plod of the gardener, and his life revolved around growing things, while Madame picked them. Her province was the gatehouse, where she washed the produce, prepared their meals, and watched television. She left the château just once a week, on Saturdays, to go to market with their produce. (Strictly speaking the fruits and vegetables were ours, as we paid Milbert's salary, but that was a gray area and so long as our table was amply supplied we asked no questions.) More important for us, Madame Milbert also raised rabbits, ducks, and chickens and always had a plentiful supply of eggs. When I first tasted her duck and hen eggs, freshly laid, I understood just how good an egg can be.

On a secret little plot of land the Milberts had somewhere, there were cider apple trees. Every year they gathered the apples and piled them on a tarpaulin in the dry moat, leaving them there to ferment. Once a year our neighbor Bernard Gionnet turned into our backyard clad in oilskins and rubber boots for the business of crushing apples—his family had been doing so for generations. He had a mobile ancient, clanking apple crusher run by water hydraulics that he had been using for fifty years. The crusher shuddered into action powered by a tractor, and I watched the pitted little red, green, and yellow apples mount a chain of buckets to be pulped, then pressed between layers of thick, porous linen so the juice for cider streamed out, leaving mats of crushings to make the earthy local liquor, marc, the French equivalent of Italy's grappa. Milbert handled the hose through which the apple juice was piped into decrepit oak barrels. Fermentation began within days and lasted a month or more, depending on weather. The heady, alcoholic vapor pervaded the winter farmyard. "All natural," Milbert said. When the fermentation stopped, the alcohol content was 6 to 7 percent and the cask was topped up, sealed, and left to mature. "Leave it alone," Milbert cautioned. "If its bed is disturbed, it turns acid."

Milbert was proud of his right to distill hard alcohol—a license he'd been granted in the 1930s and one that would die with him. Each year he took two hundred liters (fifty gallons) of year-old cider to the traveling still in Joigny. The resulting Calvados was legendary in our family—it could clear the head and ward off the meanest bronchitis. We understood why Milbert called it *eau de vie*. Every year at Christmas he gave Mark a bottle and I would be presented with a bottle of Madame's amazing black currant liqueur, the local specialty, which she made from the garden's black currants. Mark and I also had a walnut tree or two on the property, and the Milberts gathered the nuts, dried them, and had a friend press them. The intensity of that freshly pressed oil was amazing.

The Milberts also gathered the chanterelles, black trumpets of death (though deliciously edible), and porcini mushrooms that sprouted in our woods and alleys—the area has just the right climate and the right, very fertile terrain. At the railroad junction to the south of Le Feÿ, Laroche-Migennes, there is an exhibit every year of up to seventy varieties freshly gathered in the region and trained policemen label them *comestible, nocif* (harmful), and *mortel* (deadly). Mushrooms were another Milbert lesson: Once I asked to accompany him when foraging. He said, "Not today," and the following morning when I asked again he declared, "Oh, they're all picked." No way was he going to reveal his sources. Every night I left a note for Milbert telling him what I needed from the garden for the next day, always careful about how I worded it. If he didn't think something ought to be picked, he wouldn't, but when I was lucky I came downstairs at 9:00 to find what I'd asked for.

Sometimes there would be steaming, freshly killed rabbits on the kitchen sink, too, though it was Madame who killed them; Monsieur couldn't face it. Indeed, I once needed a dead rabbit in its skin for a photograph for *La Varenne Pratique*. Madame brought in two live rabbits, one white, one brown, and asked which I wanted. As she did one of them seemed to realize something terrible was going to happen and it started to scream. Madame took them away, but I've never forgotten that.

SUMMER VEGETABLE PISTOU

In this recipe I've used various kinds of squash, eggplant, and multi-colored peppers, all with a base of ripe tomatoes and thinly sliced onion— all vegetables that grew in the garden at Le Feÿ. As a change from classic basil in the pesto, you might like to try spearmint, cilantro, or the familiar parsley, which is a far more versatile herb than you might think. Here's the basic blueprint to ring changes with what is in the market.

Serves 4 to 6

2 medium zucchini (about ¾ pound/330 g)
2 medium eggplants (about ¾ pound/330 g)
1 pound/450 g tomatoes
3 onions, thinly sliced
Salt and pepper

For the pesto
Large bunch (about 1½ ounces/45 g) of your favorite herb
3 garlic cloves, peeled
½ cup/45 g grated Parmesan cheese
2 tablespoons/30 g pine nuts or shelled pistachios

¾ cup/175 ml olive oil, plus more for the dish
Salt and pepper

8×11-inch/20×28-cm gratin or baking dish

Heat the oven to 350°F/180°C. Wipe the zucchini and eggplants with a damp paper towel and cut them into ¾-inch/2-cm chunks, including skin. Put them in a bowl. Core the tomatoes, cut them also into chunks, and add to the zucchini and eggplants with the onions, salt, and pepper. Brush the gratin dish with oil.

To make the pesto: Tear off the herb leaves and discard the stems; set aside a few sprigs for decoration. Purée the leaves, garlic, Parmesan, and pine nuts in a food processor with 2 to 3 tablespoons of the olive oil. Gradually add the remaining oil with the blades turning so that the sauce emulsifies. It should be a rather loose consistency, thinner than mayonnaise but thicker than vinaigrette dressing. Season it to taste with salt and pepper.

Add the pesto to the vegetables and toss so they are well coated with sauce. Spread them in the baking dish and bake until they are very tender and brown, 40 to 50 minutes. Serve the gratin hot or at room temperature, topping it with the herb sprigs.

For many years every morning except Tuesday the baker arrived to deliver baguettes and dark country loaves. Once a week the charcutier came with a load of country pâté, hunks of the local parsleyed ham, strings of black and white boudin sausages, and sheets of extra thinly sliced country ham, all cured and cooked on his premises. Sadly, over the years the convenience of supermarkets ousted these vendors, and only the yellow postal van continued to call at the gatehouse, timing his delivery to the minute to catch Monsieur and Madame Milbert at lunch, as that came with an offer of Calvados, homemade of course.

All the big local towns—Joigny, Villeneuve, Sens—have covered markets, and seventy or so sellers had a circuit they traveled each week. In Joigny market, the minute we pushed open the entrance doors the flood of sound and sunshine beaming down through the nineteenth-century arched glass roof enveloped me. We came to know the sellers well. I established a routine—first to Madame Durville, poulterer extraordinaire, who quickly sold out of her farm-raised ducks that came with heads and feet as proof of authenticity; they were double the supermarket price but worth every centime, with huge, meaty breasts and a minimum of fat to serve half a dozen people.

There was a multi-national crowd—Arab, Turkish, Portuguese, Italian, a Tunisian who displayed fourteen different olives. At the door Roma gypsies sold baskets. One day the cheese man overheard Mark and me talking and piped up with a few words in English. When we complimented him on his skill, he explained that for a year he had driven a truck between the north of England and Auxerre, and to our amazement it turned out he had lived in Northallerton. We invited him to come and give some classes at Le Feÿ, and when he pulled up in his little truck with *Chiens Chats* (Dogs Cats) emblazoned on the side we'd say, "Oh, look, there's the cheese man." Anyone who read French was confused, but we knew he also ran an animal shelter. We much regretted when he gave up the cheese in favor of the dogs and cats.

Summer is wedding time in Burgundy. One year Mark and I were invited to the marriage of the daughter of the Bontins, a high point for the neighborhood because Château de Bontin was a seventeenth-century masterpiece, just a tad younger than Château du Feÿ. Young Claude Godard, whose father had a one-star restaurant, catered the affair and had some of our trainees in the kitchen helping. With three hundred people to feed on one of the hottest nights of the year, Godard looked harassed trying to keep little shrimp molds and squid salad and shellfish in aspic cold. One of our trainees later told us that life in that kitchen hadn't been happy. The pastry cream for the monstrous wedding cake, a yard long in génoise sponge, had been made three days ahead, and in the torrid heat it turned sour. But with the wine flowing and candles flickering, no one gave a damn.

One of our famous neighbors, Leslie Caron, had begun to buy up derelict warehouses on the waterfront of Villeneuve, which was once called Villeneuve-le-Roi and marked the northern boundary between Burgundy and France. One house was known as the Owls' Nest, the Lucarne aux Chouettes, because owls used to nest in its rafters. Leslie renovated it and opened a restaurant, a charming place to go, and Leslie became a good friend. At her place I always seemed to pick the same dishes: foie gras terrine with toasted spice bread on the side, followed by roasted pigeon in a wine reduction sauce, and finally, if I was going for the gold, crème brûlée in just the right shallow dish that provides a maximum of caramel topping.

Many of our visitors appreciated that Mark and I tried to maintain the château grounds as well as the house as they had been when the property was self-sufficient. One of those who understood was Paul Levy, the author and columnist for England's *The Observer*, whose abundant energy put most of us to shame. He was always a trifle portly, but he was indefatigable in pursuit of the very best in fine wine and dining, and his capacity to talk about food matched even mine. One year he came through for a visit, and he and I spent between noon one day and sundown the next, and in a heat wave, too, visiting and eating at several two- and three-star restaurants. Such a marathon would puncture most gastronomes, but the very next morning I woke to find Paul at his typewriter in the blazing sun, with a coffee mug and ritual breakfast of whole-wheat bread spread generously with fresh cheese, writing up our experience with gusto.

Jane Grigson was another visitor. It was she who, in her classic *Vegetable Book*, pointed out that it was not until the mid-eighteenth century that vegetables acquired their own identity (earlier they were called simply herbes), and she especially appreciated the garden. My most vivid image of her remains a sturdy figure in rubber boots firmly planted among the vegetables at Le Feÿ with Milbert beside her leaning on his hoe, the hand-rolled cigarette affixed to his lip. The planter's moon had risen early that year, and Milbert was explaining that this was an inauspicious start to the season. Watching them, I wondered how many times in that 250-year-old garden precisely the same kind of encounter had taken place, though I suspect there had rarely been two such experts.

Julia and Paul Child were also repeat visitors, and Julia especially enjoyed the hands-on aspects of château life and the way everyone pitched in. In August of 1988, when Emma heard Julia was coming for a visit, she reminded me it was her birthday, her seventy-sixth, and Emma insisted she would cook dinner all on her own—an outsized salad of greens from the garden, roast duck with Milbert's tiny potatoes cooked in fat from the bird, and a birthday cake of homemade génoise filled with strawberry ice cream and topped with hot chocolate sauce. And half a dozen candles, of course. Julia was particularly touched because she so fondly remembered Emma's birth sixteen years earlier. When Emma was older, she and Julia often saw each other alone. Neither Julia nor I expressed emotions easily, and Emma tells me that she feels that we sometimes conveyed more easily the pride we felt in each other's accomplishments to her alone. That particular celebration was lovely since Julia ordinarily didn't bother much with birthdays (me, too;

that's not how I mark the passage of time, though I did recently pass my seventy-fifth in style).

By the late 1980s, the bank manager kept telling us it wasn't healthy to be weighed down by the debts we had accrued at La Varenne in Paris. Already we had begun sending Grand Diplôme students down to the château to live there for three weeks and study with the local chefs, going to wine tastings and local markets. We were also offering one-week summer courses with a stay at the château, but this expanded focus was not enough to improve the Paris bottom line. Gradually we were coming to understand that we could not keep going.

Thankfully, just around this time a letter came from Rod Stoner, food and beverage manager at The Greenbrier resort in White Sulphur Springs, West Virginia, a resort that first opened in 1778 when people came to "take the waters" at the natural sulphur springs. Julie Dannenbaum had been giving cooking classes there during the winter months, but this letter let me know that Julie was leaving and they wondered if I'd like to take her place. I knew at once I would say yes, as I always enjoy a change of working environment. Not only did this professional connection turn out to be important—La Varenne at The Greenbrier mushroomed into a fifteen-year association—but the new location turned our failure in Paris into a long-term plan for success. La Varenne had a new permanent home in the springtime, and we would expand classes in Burgundy over the rest of the year. And Rod Stoner turned out to be an outstanding boss, perceptive, decisive, and with that touch of vision that would transform a routine program into a memorable one.

Still, I will never forget that last day in Paris. I locked the door behind me and stepped into the car—Mark had come to pick me up. Tears streamed down my face. "Anne, lovey," Mark said, "don't regret it. You've put such a great deal into it." I knew he meant what I had done was not wasted, not remotely, and though I went on crying, I was beginning to see all the possibilities ahead. I seem to be attracted to grand properties, first Versailles, then the Gritti Palace and Château du Feÿ. Now The Greenbrier became the place I anchored La Varenne classes in the Americas. When I joined, the school was already established, but we brought in our former staff member, Martha Holmberg, to expand classes. In that first season we were set up in one of the grand reception rooms lined with gold damask (so familiar from the Gritti Palace) and hung with giant gilt mirrors—hardly a kitchen setting, but it worked surprisingly well.

The Greenbrier calendar filled up right away, and after the first year I taught for two months every spring. Classes were especially popular when Julia was our guest teacher. Julia, as I already knew, was notorious for planning ahead but changing plans in the kitchen at the last minute. Well as Julia and I got along, her visits could be nerve-wracking, with audiences of up to one hundred and the typical surrounding media hype. And Julia herself was, quite rightly, demanding. Thankfully, her assistant, Stephanie Hersh, was always prepared, but I clearly remember crawling on the floor in the middle of class looking for a dish under the demo bench while Julia boomed: "A cauliflower is round; I want a round dish!"

Even in her eighties, Julia kept everyone spellbound. For one class she and I displayed every imaginable example of variety meat—from pigs' tails to the ears and snout, lambs' tongues, veal sweetbreads, testicles (bulls' balls, as Julia called them), lungs, liver, and lights (intestines). All these were laid out on a carpet of crushed ice. Julia had a field day, bending over the counter and trilling out comments as the audience peppered her with questions.

Over the years I became especially indebted to Brenda Rose, the steward who had been at The Greenbrier for years and understood my priorities—she always made sure I had my bacon and coffee when I arrived in the kitchen at 7:00. As we expanded our horizons, instead of teaching five straight days each week, I stepped back to three, and for intervening days we invited a guest teacher and a guest chef—among them Rick Bayless and Graham Kerr, André Soltner, and dozens of others. Riki Senn, who had already worked for years in the Greenbrier kitchen, took over from Martha and turned out to be a natural as coordinator. We welcomed an astonishing variety of personalities, but Riki quickly knew everyone. Ahead of time she would talk at length to up to sixty new students each week for eight weeks and could alert me to what I might expect. I got to know the Greenbrier chefs well, particularly Walter Scheib, who later became chef to Presidents Bill Clinton and George W. Bush in the White House. When I later interviewed Walter for a column, we sat in one of the White House side parlors lined with cabinets of antique porcelain while the prim junior secretary listened in to make sure we covered nothing personal. Then Walter and I went down to the kitchen and relaxed over a glass of wine, off the record! In the Greenbrier teaching kitchen there was also a stream of young apprentices including Michael Voltaggio, who later won the television show *Top Chef* and would become a good friend.

One year Michel Richard came as a visiting chef and famously sprinkled boxes of Rice Krispies over the trays of white asparagus he had prepared. When the dish was served, everyone gasped, "Look at this new grain . . ."

Richard's giant whole roast sea bass, clad in a golden crust of brioche and served with hollandaise sauce, was the hit of the season. At another demonstration, Ariane Daguin captured us all with her dissection of a duck, using the meat (breast as a steak, legs as confit), bones (for soup), skin (a crispy topping for salad), and innards (braised to serve with bitter greens). When Jean-Louis Palladin was doing oxtail, he pulled it from beneath the table and slapped it down. Blood splattered everywhere. When Shirley Corriher visited, she did an entire class on killers in the kitchen—rhubarb leaves (oxalic acid) and the kernels of peaches and apricots (cyanide), though to be poisoned you have to eat a lot of all of them. Her favorite story involved the question of whether or not a person smelled asparagus pee—turns out it depends not on the pee-er but on the smell-ee. When she began, I could see that many in the audience were not amused and was reminded of something that has never ceased to surprise me: how easily people in America are shocked by everyday facts of life.

In partnership with The Greenbrier, I was also lucky enough to teach at the famous Turnberry hotel in Scotland. I was amazed the first night when Riki, her husband, Tony, Mark, and I sat down to eat. For as long as I could remember genuine Dover sole had been disappearing from our menus. I often had to go to England for my fix of the delectable flatfish. But there on the menu was Dover sole meunière, the emperor of Dover sole, a magnificent one and one-half pounds of aromatic meat on the bone, golden with toasted butter. When I asked the waiter not to bone my fish, he was affronted, but since that childhood encounter with a kipper, I have always enjoyed the challenge of boning a fish on the plate so as not to miss the delicious, buttery swimmerets at the edges. A few nights later we were invited to dinner at a nearby castle. The castle's remaining descendant, a larger-than-life character, was clad in full Scottish tartan, and as the meal was carried in, pipers played. After supper Riki was cross to learn we would be segregated, men from women. I explained the custom—the term "drawing room" comes from the idea of "withdrawing." Mark, Tony, and the male students stayed with our host in the dining room having cigars and brandy while we women "withdrew."

I was also still giving classes all over the place from Florida to Alaska to Japan. In 1993 I was asked to judge the Rémy Martin Cognac/Australian Gourmet Traveller Restaurant of the Year award, offering us the opportunity to travel from Perth, in western Australia, with its fresh salads and grilled fish, to Adelaide and good wine country, where the candidate for the award was a pioneer in *mezzes*. Everyone thought I would choose the restaurant Paul Bocuse in Melbourne, the city traditionally regarded as Australia's gastronomic capital, and where the chef was executing fine French cooking. But I had hoped for more originality. We traveled on to Tasmania, across the island from Hobart, where we were welcomed to a cheerful family meal at everybody's ideal neighborhood place, but hardly great art. "Oh, we've known you were coming for weeks," they said when we arrived, although these visits were supposed to be a secret—they had sussed out the advance booking. In Brisbane dinner was disappointing—beets leaking into an insipid aspic. At last we arrived in Sydney.

I had been told about Tetsuya Wakuda, a Japanese Australian, who was creating a buzz with his restaurant in a former coffee shop in a working-class suburb. He had hung Aboriginal art on the walls and had no liquor license, so we brought our own wine. Tetsuya's food was based on the Japanese philosophy of using natural seasonal flavors, and the freshest possible ingredients, enhanced by classic French technique. He had designed an on-site test kitchen to enable him to constantly evolve dishes such as chilled cucumber soup with sheep yogurt ice cream, an array of fish, including fillet of jewfish with asparagus and pil pil, and his signature confit of Petuna ocean trout served with seaweed, celery, and apple. We had a clear winner. Tetsuya's cooking never overstepped the knife-blade line between creativity and flamboyance, and he has become famous worldwide as one of the leaders of Modernist Cuisine. Three years later, when we returned to Sydney, I was immediately aware that Australian chefs with Tetsuya at their head had joined the elite masters who shuttle the world from kitchen to kitchen in the manner of star orchestral conductors.

Back home at the Château life was busy, too. *La Varenne Pratique* had led quite naturally to another idea from Peter Kindersley, who now envisioned a definitive series for total beginners that became known as *Look & Cook*. These books were designed to be the simplest, most informative cookbooks anyone could own, each one illustrating everything needed at the beginning— so the cook would see at a glance how long a recipe took, how many servings it made, what the finished dish would look like, and how much prep could be done ahead. Each one included easy-to-follow steps, each stage color-coded and everything photographed. We had a contract for three books when Peter said, "Okay, we're off. Now we want a new book from you every two months for the foreseeable future." We agreed that on the job there would always be a French-trained chef and a La Varenne consultant. Once again the legacy of

La Varenne training proved invaluable, and without our former trainees I could never have written the series so quickly.

I was a pioneer on one aspect of all my illustrated books. At the time we were writing *Look & Cook* almost all the food one saw in magazines and books was not real: shaving cream took the place of whipped cream, meat would be blow torched to look as though it had roasted but without shrinking. This may not be obvious to the eye; more often it creates an uneasy feeling that something is not quite right. These days photoshop manipulations can have a similar effect. I insisted that the *Look & Cook* technique photos must lead directly to the finished dish. If a topping was slightly scorched or the vegetables were sliced unevenly, that was the way it was in a working kitchen and that was the way we would do it. Something on the plate will never actually look exactly the same way twice. I wanted dishes we had prepared to be used in the final photograph, and I was determined we would cook the food on camera from start to finish, then plate it and take the picture. At first Dorling Kindersley told me this was impossible, but we did it, with cost saving (the team did not have to cook anything twice) and with great success.

Just as we were deciding who would be the chef, Peter Kindersley's daughter Rosie, who was working for her dad, asked if she might visit the château. She brought along "Eric, the chef," Eric Treuille. When they arrived I was struck by the sight of this tall beanpole of a girl with this small guy beside her. As it turned out, Eric was a marvelous food stylist as well as a chef and cooked for the whole series. Rosie and Eric married and became the happy owners of the highly respected bookshop in London, Books for Cooks.

We called in all sorts of consultants and assistants—Steve Raichlen, renowned for his books on barbecuing and who was involved with La Varenne books from the beginning; Henry Grossi, who wrote the book on Italian cooking; dear Val Cipollone, a born editor. One of the last of the series we did was on classic breads, and because bread varies so enormously in different countries—so much depends on the flour—we first tested the recipes in Washington, then froze the loaves and took them with us in a suitcase over to the London studio because I wanted Eric to copy the shapes.

I did have one real fight with the woman whose London company produced the books. Amy Carroll wanted only my name on the book covers, insisting my name was what would sell them. I was equally insistent that wasn't fair to all the other hands involved, but she ultimately allowed me to include others' names only in separate acknowledgments in the back of each book. It angered me for many reasons—for example, I'm ignorant about

Asian cooking and Lucy Wing wrote that book from start to finish and Carroll axed her name. Years later at the Book and Cook Fair in Philadelphia I ran into Lucy, who said very sweetly, "You probably don't remember, but I wrote a book for you." Of course I remembered and we both laughed, but I was still unhappy about what had happened.

By this time, when I was in my early fifties and courses at the château were in full swing, I could no longer supervise all that cooking and editing and all those students and trainees coming and going without some help from a resident chef. Two La Varenners stood out as gifted cooks eager to share their knowledge. First there was Alex Bird, distinguished by his massive mop of gray hair, which streamed out behind him when he roared the nearby Route Nationale on his Harley-Davidson. He was stopped once by the police, who refused to believe he lived in the château and followed him all the way home to the gates, where Milbert vouched for his veracity. Alex was followed by Randall Price, who way back in the seventies had won a competition from *Chocolatier Magazine* to study at La Varenne. Later he joined us in Washington to work as a recipe tester for *La Varenne Pratique*. Randall was far too lively to remain in his hometown of Middletown, Ohio. He settled happily into the château *garçonnière*, commuting on weekends to Paris. He and I worked together with the tolerance of long-standing colleagues, though I drove him distracted by my insistence on planning and exactitude and he made me nervous by leaving so much to the last minute, but always, in the end, delivering on the line. Randall's penchant for château gossip was equaled only by Madame Milbert's—most days they shared a little chat. Randall was indispensable and had an uncanny knack for sensing food trends—he began brining his turkey at least a year before everyone else was doing it, and he was in early on the craze for biscotti. His are still the best, crunchy with almonds and fragrant with aniseed and vanilla.

RANDALL'S BISCOTTI

Randall rings many changes on these biscotti, adding different spices, even chopped dark chocolate and sometimes substituting toasted hazelnuts or walnuts for the almonds. As the name implies, biscotti are baked twice, first as a cake that is baked and sliced and then baked again to dry out as cookies.

Makes 2 dozen biscotti

½ cup/90 g whole blanched almonds
2 cups/250 g flour, plus more if needed
½ teaspoon finely ground black pepper
½ teaspoon ground aniseed
½ teaspoon baking powder
Large pinch of salt
1 cup/200 g sugar
1 egg
2 egg yolks
Grated zest of ½ orange
½ teaspoon vanilla extract
½ teaspoon almond extract
6 tablespoons/90 g butter

To brown the almonds: Heat the oven to 350°F/180°C. Spread the almonds on a baking sheet and toast them in the oven, stirring occasionally, until lightly browned, 12 to 15 minutes. Let them cool.

To make the dough: Sift the flour with the black pepper, aniseed, baking powder, and salt onto a work surface and make a large well in the center. Put the sugar, egg, egg yolks, orange zest, and vanilla and almond extract in the center. Set the butter between 2 sheets of plastic wrap and pound it with a rolling pin to soften it. Add it also to the well. With the fingertips of one hand, work the ingredients in the well until evenly mixed and smooth. Using a pastry scraper, gradually draw in the flour, working with your whole hand to form a smooth, slightly sticky dough. If it is very sticky, work in a bit more flour. Knead the dough, pushing it away with the heel of your hand and gathering it up with your fingers, until it is very smooth and peels easily from the surface, 2 to 3 minutes.

Pat the dough to a rough, flat rectangle, sprinkle it with the toasted almonds, and roll it up. Knead it lightly to distribute the nuts. Don't worry if some nuts remain on the surface of the dough; it should be rough looking. Divide the dough into two portions, lightly flour the work surface, and shape each piece into a log about 2 inches/5 cm in diameter and 7 inches/16 cm long. Wrap the logs in plastic wrap and chill them 4 to 5 hours.

For the first baking, heat the oven to 350°F/180°C. Unwrap the logs, set them on a baking sheet, and bake until lightly browned and firm on the outside but still soft, almost cake-like, in the center, 50 to 60 minutes. Let the logs cool on the baking sheet and lower the oven temperature to 325°F/160°C.

When cool, cut the logs on the diagonal in ½-inch/1.25-cm slices, cutting vertically downward so the slices have a firm base (the end pieces are the cook's reward). Space the biscotti out on a baking sheet so they can dry, leaving them upright. Rebake them until they are dry and lightly browned on the cut surfaces, 30 to 35 minutes. Let the biscotti cool on a rack and store them in an airtight container.

As one of our stagiaires, Emily Crumpacker, put it, "Food can be anything, and that's why it attracts so many different audiences," but at Le Feÿ I felt responsible for the young people we had brought to this isolated place. We were careful with the stagiaires we selected, fortunate to have Janis McLean in Washington vetting candidates. Still, we had our problems. There was Eliza, who somehow was never around when we needed her. Jason's driving was so erratic the children refused to ride with him and he ended by crashing the car into a ditch. Sheila became a byword, as in "she's going to be another Sheila." On her first evening when handed a dish towel, Sheila complained she was too tired, and the next morning she was late. She had no concept of being part of a team. Eventually I taught her how to wash lettuce—always one of the first jobs I taught trainees—but when I found her at the sink gazing into space, washing so slowly, I reprimanded her. "Faster," I said. "Faster, faster, faster . . ." She did not last long. Thankfully, problematic trainees were by far the exceptions.

We got a huge mix of people coming for one-week classes—wealthy ladies, pastry chefs, couples who wanted a vacation but didn't want to travel from place to place, even a boy of twelve who loved to cook and came with his mother, as well as a British hotelier escaping from his job in Dagestan, and an undertaker from the Midwest who came because, he said, he couldn't enjoy himself in his hometown. One day I was taking a vacation group on a tour of the property. As I led them into Milbert's cider cellar, a tricky gray-haired lobbyist from Louisiana looked at a rack of bottles and asked, "Aren't those the same wines you have in your cellar in the château?" Indeed they were; that was how I discovered the little racket Chambrette had going on with Milbert, exchanging wine for rabbits. For twenty-four hours sparks flew while I sorted out the situation.

One week was particularly festive when Linda Gray came with her new boyfriend. At the height of her fame playing Sue Ellen Ewing in *Dallas,* Gray was the nicest woman. She had come to celebrate her birthday and was delighted when we presented her with a cake. We often had writers. Another week I discovered after three days that one of our guests was Thomas Harris, whose *Silence of the Lambs* had just been made into the film. In advance of one class Mark and I noticed one couple was coming from Gaza and another from South Africa; we wondered what we were in for, but from the start we all got on like a house on fire—no one mentioned politics. Another surprise was Nathan Myhrvold. I knew he worked at Microsoft, though I had no idea of what he did—Microsoft was not yet a household name. It was obvious right away that Nathan really understood what was going on in the kitchen. He was full of curiosity, bombarding Chef Chambrette, who to my surprise seemed to welcome him.

Years later, I was astonished when Nathan published *Modernist Cuisine: The Art and Science of Cooking,* in which he takes a further step on the scientific, surrealist approach of chefs such as Ferran Adrià at El Bulli in Catalonia and Grant Achatz in Chicago. Nathan's brilliance is enthralling but I suspect, like nouvelle cuisine before it, the modernist cuisine movement will wither in the face of the tricky techniques it uses and the demands it makes on an intrepid eater. Some inspirations will remain, like the foams and pearls that dazzle the eye, but by the end of a meal, most of us like to feel, deep down, that we have been nourished rather than intellectually challenged by what has appeared on our plates. Long after Nathan had been at La Varenne, I asked Debbie Orrill, who had been a trainee at the time, if she remembered him. "Remember him?" she asked. "Who could forget him?"

Each year we all became an extended family because we were in this together, and the place, in summer especially, was paradise. The Internet did not exist and phone calls were expensive, so trainees were isolated in the depths of the countryside for months at a time. Occasionally they went to one of the cafés in town, but they found them full of smoke, with slightly drunk Frenchmen trying to pick up the girls. Most of life happened on the grounds and the constant amusements of life at Le Feÿ were the subplots of almost Shakespearean intensity. Sometimes the consumption of wine mysteriously doubled from one week to the next, or we'd wonder what had happened to the cherry tree laden with ripe fruit yesterday and stripped bare today. Madame Milbert swore the birds had got them. There was always the question of which students were romancing together. (Madame Maria was the expert on who occupied which beds—the housekeeper always knows secrets—but she kept her mouth shut.) One year someone in residence shredded favorite dresses and stole personal belongings—it had to be a trainee—and by the end of that season Maria and I had eliminated all suspects but two; to this day I am not absolutely certain who was the culprit.

Most trainees, though, were more like Virginia Willis, who so memorably walked straight off the plane and into the kitchen and within thirty minutes was at the sink—the true test of someone I knew would succeed. Virginia and I both laugh when we recall the day she was in the château kitchen chopping an onion. When the knife slipped, in her typical no-nonsense fashion Virginia tightly wrapped her hand, held her arm over her head, and said with her classic southern drawl, "Ma'am, I've cut off the tip of my thumb." When I convinced her to show me, I said, "Well now, this calls for a shot of Cognac"—in such events the heart tends to slow, and Cognac will kick it into gear. Virginia's southern specialties, fried chicken, peach pie, and popcorn okra, have long been favorites; she and I have taught happily together many times. Today Virginia has a string of cookbooks to her credit as well as a career in television. Jonathan Waxman was a thirty-six-week student very early at La Varenne in Paris and went on to become a celebrity chef of Jams and then Barbuto, among the most sought-after restaurants in New York. His genial, slightly teddy-bear personality made him a favorite among the judges of the *Top Chef* contests. Ana Sortun, another early student, earned well-deserved fame with her own Cambridge restaurant, Oleana, where she fused her talent for French cooking with a passion for Mediterranean spices. Amanda Hesser won the IACP Julia Child Award for her very first cookbook and also created our indispensable herb garden at Château du Feÿ. Amanda somehow pierced Milbert's shell, enabling her to write *The Cook and the Gardener*, chronicling a year in the life of our kitchen garden.

Cynthia Nims began with us in Paris and more or less moved with us to Burgundy, calling it an escapade. Cynthia was one of the pillars of the *Look & Cook* series and has written a half dozen of her own successful cookbooks. I do remember Cynthia and a group of trainees from the Northwest piqued my curiosity when they received an emergency delivery of Starbucks coffee. "What's Starbucks?" I asked. They shared their stash, though I secretly thought our French coffee was much better. Now and then a trainee might complain. Handsome, talented Laura Calder carped bitterly about the grunt work when she first arrived and was quick to point out she had come with two advanced degrees and much cooking experience. She had imagined all her time at the château would be in the kitchen, and she was terribly unhappy. But since then, as a star on several television series with three cookbooks to her credit, she has told me how grateful she is for all she learned. Laura had a gift for words; her headline "The Slippery Subject of Variety Meats" was a classic, and she was one of three beautiful trainees at the château one particularly hot summer when I let some of my stricter rules go by the wayside and allowed the girls to wear shorts. There was a flutter of attention when they turned around in their long aprons and revealed those long, bare legs.

That same hot summer we had a serious bee problem and we called the fire department. When the firemen climbed out of the truck, Martha Holmberg walked outside to greet them and explain the problem. They were standing in the front courtyard discussing what to do when a door opened and out walked another of the beautiful stagiaires. The firemen stared as she walked toward the garden to pick flowers and another door opened and out came two more lovely girls in shorts. Martha laughed as she described her realization that the firemen were wondering what exactly this place was with all these beauties pouring out of its many rooms.

Many days we had ten or more people around the table at the château and one of the trainee's jobs—one so many young Americans at first found incomprehensible—was to transform anything leftover at dinner into the next day's lunch. Americans tended to say, "But everything should be new and fresh," while the French said, "Americans are wasteful." We nearly always wound up with delicious things—lovely rice pilafs and gratins, chopped salads in summer, and soups in the winter cold. Thus Chambrette's most classic skill was carried to kitchens around the world. When one day he came in from the garden clutching his apron filled with windfall apples—those everyone else had left to rot on the ground—he prepared one of his specialties from way back before he joined La Varenne. We had made tarte Tatin at La Varenne for years, but it took Chef Chambrette to transform routine apple tart into a gastronomic masterpiece.

At Château du Feÿ, tarte Tatin became the house specialty; appropriately enough its birthplace was not so far away in an obscure country town called Lamotte-Beuvron. The story goes that in the nineteenth century two maiden ladies were left penniless when their father died. Luckily, they lived just opposite the railroad station and would revive travelers with the crusty dark apple tart their father had loved so much. The Hotel Tatin is there to this day. When I visited ten years ago, they still served their version of tarte Tatin.

TARTE DES DEMOISELLES TATIN (UPSIDE-DOWN CARAMELIZED APPLE TART)

Chef Chambrette's tarte Tatin is a virtuoso performance. First of all, you must be choosy about the apples, which have to hold their shape during cooking and be slightly acidic. In France *reine de reinettes* were perfect; in the United States I look for Granny Smiths or Cortlands. The apples are peeled, halved, and cored in advance. Then the sugar is toasted with an astonishing amount of butter to a deep, almost smoking caramel in the characteristic copper Tatin pan lined with tin—mine has accompanied me around the world at least once (I've lately found that a heavy cast-iron skillet works quite well, too). Then, while the caramel is still scalding hot, the apple halves are perched upright in concentric circles and packed as tightly as possible. Lengthy simmering on the stove reduces—almost preserves—the apples to a dark mahogany. Finally, the tart is baked with a flat crust of puff pastry (yet more butter) before being turned out to serve while still warm, with a bowl of the thickest possible crème fraîche.

Serves 8 to 10

About 5 pounds/2–2.5 kg firm apples
½ cup/110 g butter
1½ cups/300 g sugar
¾ pound/330 g prepared butter puff pastry

10–11 inch/25–28 cm Tatin mold or skillet

Peel and halve the apples; scoop out the cores with a melon baller or the point of a paring knife. Melt the butter in the Tatin mold and stir in the sugar with a wooden spoon. Cook over medium heat, without stirring, until the sugar starts to brown and caramelize. Stir gently, then continue cooking until the caramel is deep golden brown, 6 to 8 minutes total. The caramel at this stage is very hot, so let it cool in the pan for 3 to 5 minutes; the butter will separate, but this does not matter.

Arrange the apples in the mold in concentric circles with the cut sides standing vertically—the caramel will help to anchor them and the wooden spoon is a useful prop. Pack the apples as tightly as possible, as they will shrink during cooking. Cook over medium heat until the juice starts to run from the apples, about 8 minutes. Raise the heat and cook them as fast as possible until the underside is caramelized to a deep gold and most of the juice has evaporated, 15 to 25 minutes. With a two-pronged fork, turn the apples one by one so the upper sides are now down in the caramel. Continue cooking until this second side is brown also, the apples are tender, and almost all the juice has evaporated, 10 to 20 minutes more. Cooking times will vary with the variety and ripeness of the apples and can take up to an hour in total—long cooking is important so the apple juices caramelize as well as the sugar. Let the apples cool to tepid while heating the oven to 400°F/200°C.

Roll out the pastry dough to a round just larger than the mold and prick it all over with a fork so it does not puff in the oven. Wrap the dough around the rolling pin and transfer it to cover the apples. Tuck the edges down around the apples, working quickly so their warmth does not melt the dough. Poke a hole in the center so steam can escape. Bake the tart until the pastry is firm and browned, 20 to 25 minutes. Take the tart from the oven and let it cool at least 10 minutes, or until tepid. Tarte Tatin may be made up to 12 hours ahead and kept in the mold in the refrigerator (if you use a cast-iron skillet, the tart must be turned out immediately).

To finish, if necessary, warm the tart in the mold on the stove top before you turn it out, to soften the caramel and loosen the apples. Select a flat platter with a lip to catch any juices; invert the platter on top of the tart pan and flip the tart onto the platter. Be careful, because you can be splashed with hot juice. Cut the tart in wedges to serve.

As our La Varenne classes continued to flourish, Julia came every year to teach at The Greenbrier.

Chapter Fifteen

....

AT HOME IN THE KITCHEN

One's destination is never a place, but a new way of seeing things.

—Henry Miller

As château cooking programs were expanding, the children, who spent summers there and gathered with Mark and me at Christmas, were growing up. Simon had gone to Vassar, where all went well. Despite an acceptance at Princeton, Emma decided on Brown. At first her choice rather startled me, but it turned out to be the perfect place. Not only did she love the school; it was at Brown that she met Todd Schulkin, who would eventually become our son-in-law. In the spring of 1993 Emma graduated from Brown and went to intern first with the World Bank, then with the State Department in Morocco while Todd moved into our apartment in Washington. Their romance did not bloom until later, when Emma returned to the States to attend Johns Hopkins School of Advanced International Studies.

Simon had graduated from Vassar a year earlier and was living in Paris, taking odd jobs. To our delight one of our former trainees, Lisa Dobbs, offered him a challenge. Lisa's husband, Michael, had been posted to Moscow as bureau chief of *The Washington Post* right at the start of perestroika. Since there were no restaurants in Moscow at the time, Lisa had decided to change all that and started a catering business that did terrifically well. When it was time for Michael to be dispatched elsewhere, Lisa was looking around and Simon had a basic qualification: he spoke Russian. When Simon was enrolling at Vassar, Mark had said, "Russia is opening up, and you're good at languages," and so it proved. Mark and I visited Simon in Moscow during perestroika. It was a time when apartments, heating, and light were still free, but everything else was crazy and Russians were selling everything they had to make a little bit of money—the knobs off their doors, the coats off their backs. People were opening tiny, hole-in-the-wall places, paying off the local cops, and anyone who had a car was operating a taxi system. One of the first eating places we went to was run by monks in a monastery, as they could get hold of anything. The Moscow Catering Company was a natural for Simon, who loves food, and after all had learned the basics of cooking from me!

Mark and I were with Simon in Moscow again in 1993 during the constitutional crisis and the shelling of the Russian parliament, but life otherwise continued much as usual and one evening the catering company was catering a party at the Moscow Conservatory. The young boys and girls performed magnificently. Afterward there was a reception with tables piled high with canapés, and as it began Simon whispered, "Just watch." We saw everyone was filling napkins with canapés, stuffing them into their handbags. Within five minutes, the trays were clear. "People here have never seen food like this. Whenever we cater, we keep at least double repeat trays in the back," he told us. When they brought out more trays, once again they were swept clean.

Lubov was the formidable directress of the technical school #45 where the catering company was installed and one summer we invited her to visit the château. She was a terrific cook and made *pilmenyi*, Russian ravioli, and *schii*, the robust Russian cabbage soup. She was a strong-minded woman, much like one of our talented trainees at the time, Tanya Holland, who would go on to become chef and owner of the well-known restaurant Brown

Sugar Kitchen and B-side BBQ in Oakland, California. Neither woman could speak the other's language, but it was clear neither was prepared to give in. A memorable shouting match ensued. Somehow I managed to calm the situation and everyone enjoyed the meal.

Now that the children were grown and Mark was retired, we traveled a great deal. The last time I watched *Around the World in 80 Days*, I realized Mark and I had been to every one of the places depicted in the film, with the exception of Allahabad in India. I have also taught all over the United States and on every continent except Antarctica. Every class has some things in common, including hard work, and because everyone expects to eat lunch or supper, generous tastings of half a dozen dishes are a must. I have a few standbys, such as Aunt Louie's cheese balls and hot bacon and egg salad that are a quick fix.

HOT BACON AND EGG SALAD

Hot bacon and egg salad can be a first course or a main dish if you serve it with a couple of eggs. I like to make it with smoked bacon and duck eggs (one per person) if I can find them.

Serves 4 as a main course, 8 as an appetizer

4–8 eggs
½ cup/125 ml red wine vinegar, plus more for poaching
A medium head (1 pound/450 g) of frisée or escarole
1 tablespoon/15 ml vegetable oil
8 ounces/225 g piece of smoked bacon, diced
Ground black pepper

Wok or frying pan

To poach the eggs: Bring to a boil a shallow pan of water about 2 inches/5 cm deep. Add about 2 tablespoons vinegar. Break an egg into a small bowl and with the water boiling rapidly drop the egg into a bubbling patch—the bubbles will help coat the egg yolk with the white. Repeat with the remaining eggs. Reduce the heat so the water is scarcely bubbling and poach the eggs 2 to 3 minutes until the whites are set and the yolks are still soft. Test by lifting an egg on a slotted spoon and pressing the yolk with a fingertip. Transfer the eggs to a bowl of cold water and set aside.

Discard the tough outer green leaves from the frisée or escarole and trim the root. Separate the pale center leaves and tear any large leaves into 2 or 3 pieces. Wash and dry the leaves and put them in a salad bowl.

Just before serving, transfer the eggs to a bowl of very warm water so they reheat. Heat the oil in the wok and fry the bacon until lightly browned—do not over-brown or it will be tough. Lift out the bacon with a draining spoon and sprinkle it on the greens. Discard all but about 4 tablespoons of fat from the wok, reheat briefly, and pour the hot fat over the greens, tossing so the leaves wilt slightly (a friend to toss helps here). Add the vinegar to the hot wok (stand back to avoid the fumes) and bring it to a boil, stirring to dissolve the pan juices. Cook until reduced by about half, about 1 minute, and pour the hot vinegar over the greens, tossing again, so the leaves wilt further. Sprinkle with pepper and pile in individual salad bowls. Drain the warm eggs on paper towels, set 1 or 2 eggs on top of each salad, and serve at once, while still warm.

The joy of traveling and teaching is that you never know what you will find; the audience and atmosphere in every city and country varies. But everywhere you make new friends. I have given classes in the tropical resort of Port Douglas, Australia, in a restored Victorian schoolhouse where the outdoor market was abloom with wild orchids and pineapples so fresh the stems were moist. It was there that I gathered recipes from the students, one for a chocolate macadamia torte from a nut farmer, and another for a coconut fish stew that used the tropical fish. A local cook taught me how to crack a coconut. (Tap below the eyes with the back of a large knife, rotating until a faint crack indicates the fault line. Bingo, the nut falls open.) On that same trip Mark and I explored the underworld of coral in the Great Barrier Reef, coral with names like Asparagus and Pumpkin, a marine lookalike of their edible counterparts on land. As fish flashed past, I learned from the guide that the brighter their color, the more toxic they were likely to be. At Ayers Rock, the sacred red mountain in the Outback, I was introduced to bush ingredients, curious little fruits and nuts and dark chewy emu and gamey kangaroo. Our meal there, under the starlight, with someone playing a didgeridoo, was eerie and unforgettable. When we visited Sydney we stopped in to see our former stagiaire Robert Carmack and his partner, Morrison Polkinghorne, who always asked us to dinner. I'll never forget one extraordinary meal Robert served that included seaweed that looked exactly like pubic hair (he was the first to say so).

I also made several memorable teaching journeys to the Hotel Cipriani in Venice, reputedly the most expensive hotel in the world, and headed by Natale Rusconi, whom I had first met at the Gritti Palace. Everything about the Cipriani was small and intimate, like a well-run private house. No one disturbed you unless you wished to engage in conversation. Amidst this blissful peace I explored Venetian cooking from the inside, visiting the Rialto fish market to select the freshest catch only a half hour away in the lagoon. Fresh pasta was made in the morning for lunch and in the afternoon for dinner. The cheese vendor was Natale Rusconi's special contact, who reserved for him the luscious Caciocavallo of fresh cheese enclosing a ball of butter. One year Natale entertained the whole class with his Venetian friends at the Palazzo Pisani Moretta on the Grand Canal, where we danced beneath a dozen huge chandeliers twinkling with real candles.

I was at the Cipriani, as elsewhere, to teach French cooking, but every year a strikingly handsome Italian, a Venetian and good friend of Natale's, joined us to give a class, too. Carlo Maria Rocco told me he had always wanted to be a count. One day Natale had simply said, "Look, why don't you just call yourself a count," and since that day he had. The count's set piece was minestrone, repeated every year to the delight of returning students. His deep-flavored vegetable mélange was almost a stew, and worlds away from the familiar light broth most of us think of as minestrone.

Every time I watched, mesmerized, as he poured generous amounts of olive oil into a large copper pot and said, "Now you add all the vegetables you can find except eggplant and bell peppers." He began to pile in vegetables, and as they began to cook he made conversation. He smiled in my direction. "You have a cup of coffee; we have a glass of wine," he said. "That is the difference in our cultures." He sprinkled prosciutto on top ("use the fatty part") and tucked a couple of crusts of Parmesan cheese into the vegetable mass. He added Lamon beans—legend has it that the thin-skinned, speckled kidney beans from the New World were given by Pope Clement III to the town of Lamon and have been famous ever since.

"Black pepper is important in dishes with many onions," Count Rocco continued as he added generous amounts. I was astonished when he added so little water, popped on the lid, and fiddled with the knobs on the stove. When nothing happened he sighed, "Ah, Italy—a nice country but disorganized!" Later that evening he invited us to his palazzo with its Tiepolo fresco and display of eighteenth-century porcelain and served us his thick, fragrant, intense rustic soup as a first course before risotto, and then beef braised for five hours in Chianti red wine. I noticed he ate only a small portion. "A cook has dinner before he sits down," he said. The next day was my turn at the stove, but I always knew the count would be a hard act to follow.

COUNT ROCCO'S MINESTRONE

The flavor intensity of Carlo Maria's vegetarian minestrone is astonishing. Please don't be tempted to thin it to a pourable soup—it should be so thick that "a spoon stands up in it." To simplify the recipe, use fewer ingredients, but increase quantities in proportion. Basil and grated Parmesan cheese are added just before serving.

Serves 8 to 10 as a main course

1 cup/200 g dried white kidney beans
2 medium tomatoes
3 bay leaves
Medium bunch of thyme
¼ cup/60 ml olive oil
2 medium onions, cut in ½-inch/1.25-cm chunks
1 medium carrot, cut in ½-inch/1.25-cm chunks
2 stalks celery, cut in ½-inch/1.25-cm chunks
2 medium zucchini, cut in ½-inch/1.25-cm chunks with the skin
20–28 green beans, trimmed and cut in ¾-inch/2-cm sticks
1 potato, peeled and cut in medium dice
3–4 leaves Savoy cabbage or kale, finely shredded
2 cups fresh or frozen peas
8 cloves garlic, peeled
Salt and pepper
2–3 pieces of rind from Parmesan cheese
2 cups/500 ml water, more if needed

To finish

Bunch of basil
½ cup/60 g grated Parmesan cheese
¼ cup/60 ml olive oil, more for drizzling if desired

Soak the beans overnight in cold water, then drain them. Heat the oven to 325°F/160°C (Count Rocco cooked his soup on the stove top, thus needing a constant watch, but the oven is the easy way out). To prepare the tomatoes, core them and score a cross on each flower end. Immerse them in a pan of boiling water until the cross opens, 8 to 15 seconds. Transfer to cold water and peel them. Cut them crosswise, squeeze the halves in your fist so the seeds pop out, then chop the flesh. Tie the bay leaves and thyme in a bundle with string.

Heat the oil in a soup pot, add the onions, and sauté gently until very tender but not browned, 10 to 12 minutes. Stir in the beans, tomatoes, carrot, celery, zucchini, green beans, potato, cabbage or kale, peas, and garlic. Add a little salt and plenty of pepper, and tuck in the herb bundle and cheese rinds. Add the water to generate steam when cooking begins.

Cover the pot and transfer it to the oven. Cook, stirring occasionally, until the vegetables are very tender and falling apart so the flavor is concentrated, 3 to 4 hours. The minestrone should be the consistency of soft risotto. During cooking, add more water if the vegetables seem dry. Discard Parmesan rinds, taste the minestrone, and adjust the seasoning. It will mellow if you keep it a day or two in the refrigerator.

To finish: Reheat the minestrone. Coarsely shred leaves from the basil, reserving sprigs for decoration. Stir the shredded basil and grated Parmesan with a generous drizzle of olive oil into the minestrone. Taste again and adjust seasoning, particularly with pepper. Serve the minestrone in bowls, topped with a basil sprig. If you like, pass a bottle of your favorite virgin olive oil to drizzle on top.

One year on the way home from Venice Mark and I decided to stop at another Michelin wonder restaurant on Lake Annecy. We arrived quite late at night and encountered the chef clad in a shepherd's smock and floppy hat lurking in the lobby. We were skeptical about what was in store. The next morning when we called down for breakfast, Lapsang souchong tea was *pas de problème,* but the wait was interminable. We had a spectacular view of snowcapped peaks and a sunlit lake, but we were hungry. At last we heard the heavy steps, the knock on the door, and two maids stepped inside with trays. We blinked as they spread a white cloth on the balcony table and set down teapot and hot water. There was also café au lait, in case we changed our minds, and bucket-sized cups. The bread basket held warm brioches, toasted crusty country bread, a *ficelle* (a skinny baguette), a pound cake laden with candied cherries, a wafer of almond tart with golden and red raspberries, sweet and salted butter, and three preserves—chunky apricot, rhubarb purée, and black raspberry. At least a dozen other little dishes followed, including mountain sausage and five different aged cheeses.

As we tucked into this feast, I came to understand why the chef wore such a curious outfit. Marc Veyrat had been raised in the mountains and loved to extract the essential essence of the local fruits and herbs—his freshly pressed juice of mixed berries was flavored with bitter root of gentian (the mountain plant used in Angostura bitters). It must be the first and only time I've been served ice cream for breakfast, this one scarcely sweetened and intensely flavored with herbs. That idealized image of Gargantua's breakfast has lingered forever.

HERB ICE CREAM

I, too, like to make ice cream with an intensely flavored herb such as lemon verbena, rose geranium, or common spearmint. When infusing the milk with herbs it's a good idea to taste along the way, as overcooked herbs can be bitter. As a clue to flavor, I like to top the pale mocha-colored scoops of ice cream with fresh herb sprigs, adding a cookie on the side.

Makes 1 quart/1 liter ice cream

1 large bunch (about 1 ounce/30 g) fresh herb leaves
2 cups/500 ml milk
Pinch of salt
7 egg yolks
½ cup/100 g brown sugar

1½ cups/375 ml heavy cream
Herb sprigs (for serving)

Ice-cream maker

To make the custard: Coarsely chop the fresh herb leaves and put them in a saucepan with the milk and salt. Cover and bring the milk almost to a boil over low heat. Leave over very low heat to infuse for 15 to 20 minutes, tasting occasionally to judge the intensity of flavor. In a separate bowl, whisk the egg yolks with the brown sugar until thick and light, 1 to 2 minutes. Strain the hot milk into the egg mixture and stir to mix. Pour the custard back into the pan and cook over medium heat, stirring with a wooden spoon until it thickens lightly, 2 to 3 minutes; if you draw a finger across the back of the spoon, it should leave a clear trail. Do not overcook the custard or it will curdle.

Take the pan from the heat as soon as the custard has thickened, strain it into a bowl, and set the bowl over ice. Chill the custard, stirring occasionally. Also chill the cream and a container to hold the ice cream after freezing.

Freeze the custard in the ice-cream maker until almost set. Beat the cream until it holds a soft peak, stir it into the ice cream, and continue churning until firm. Transfer it to the chilled container, cover, and store in the freezer. If storing for more than 12 hours, let the ice cream soften in the refrigerator for an hour before serving. Serve with herb sprigs.

Mark and I made regular visits to my parents in Yorkshire, and in June 1994 my father turned ninety. He said to Mark, "You know, I'm slowing down. I shan't be here much longer." Mark passed on the comment to me, which had, of course, been Daddy's intention. The day Mark and I were there and my father forgot to put out the drinks on the sideboard for a visitor, I realized it was true. My father had always been most hospitable and whenever anybody called, even if it was only the solicitor to sign a contract, my father served tea or coffee and whisky on the sideboard. At table, he sometimes lifted his wineglass in an age-old toast, "I raises my glass to thee, and likewise I looks in thine eye." I inherited that idea from him—I feel it's very important when anyone comes to the house, no matter the hour of the day, to offer hospitality.

The following winter both my father and my mother got a terrible flu and my father did not recover. He died peacefully at home. He had asked to be cremated, but I wanted to deliver his ashes to the graveyard up in Wensley-dale at Hawes where the rest of the Willan family were buried. My mother at eighty-five was too frail to make the journey, so Mark stayed with her while Simon and Emma accompanied me up to the Dales. I'll never forget the bleak grandeur of those age-old mountains covered in snow. I wept as I listened to the vicar's words: "May the angels and archangels look down upon him, peace be with him." I gripped Simon's hand, so very sad to say good-bye. My mother insisted on living on alone in the house, and every couple of months I visited her there. Each summer Mark went over to collect her and bring her for two weeks to visit us at the château.

In the mid-nineties I began to comprehend the two sides of my personal-ity. Solitude is no problem for me—I must have inherited that trait from my mother. I've always enjoyed lonely walks and burying my nose in a book. But even as a child I enjoyed conversation, particularly at table, and later that translated in my love of teaching and with it the adrenaline rush of a success-ful class. After the seventeen-volume Look & Cook series came out, I was asked to do a television series based on the books, an obvious choice since it was an immense body of work of nearly two thousand recipes to choose from. And in front of the camera, I found I could switch on easily, striding onto the set with a cheerful "welcome to my kitchen," and off we would go. Inspiration for the recipes came from all over—Cipriani, guest chefs at The Greenbrier, book tours in the United States, and of course from La Varenne and our kitchen and garden at the château.

The series was shot in Vancouver, where Mark still had dozens of rela-tions. We lived there that winter, and every morning he dropped me at the studio and picked me up at night, having spent the day with one of his many cousins. I was thrilled when Emma was able to join us, and I immersed my-self in the community that is a television shoot. Emma manned the tele-prompt machine while my producer, Marjorie Poore, stayed in the control room. Her husband, Alec, who been thrown out of his native Ukraine as a dissident, built a charismatic set, designed as if we were on the sunlit Medi-terranean, and I had my own dressing room, where we kept a Christmas fruitcake and a bottle of Gordon's gin. Whenever I needed a pick-me-up I'd have a slice of cake, but I'm proud to say I never had to resort to the gin until the cast party. I ate almost all of the cake.

The seamless appearance of good food television requires half a dozen cooks in back, organizing a succession of trays of ingredients and food at several stages of preparation. I had an invaluable, unflappable personal assistant in a former La Varenne trainee and editor, Val Cipollone, who fielded all manner of concerns from phone calls to clean aprons to lending an occasional hand in the kitchen. Television was literally trial by fire and when once a frying pan burst into flame, I looked cheerfully into the camera and said, "Don't worry; this happens often!" I most enjoyed shooting the one- or two-minute "Tips from Anne" that came at the end of each episode—how to chop an onion or whisk egg whites or melt chocolate. The *Look & Cook* series aired on PBS throughout the United States and Canada, Australia, and parts of Asia, and to my parents' delight it even made it in one or two markets in England.

But in those days cooking shows were moving away from the Julia Child approach to a different kind of show à la Nigella Lawson, with the talent providing entertainment. A year before *Look & Cook* aired, when the Food Network was founded, the idea of a television channel devoted entirely to cooking had seemed outlandish. Five years later it was an institution and its culinary director, Georgia Downard, once a student at La Varenne in Paris, was developing programs thick and fast, helping to make New York City the hub of food news and culinary personalities. When she invited me to be a guest on *Taste,* I felt immediately at home in the cheerful, zany atmosphere backstage that flowed onto the set, though rarely onto camera. Georgia and her team had a sharp eye for what worked best for television. As she explained, "The perfect dish is colorful, spectacular, requires a minimum of ingredients and equipment, and takes two minutes, leaving plenty of time to talk." Of course Georgia knew that in real life such a dish didn't exist, although in one spot I did a Fifteen-Minute Firepot that came close.

But live television can be precarious. In 1996 when Sara Moulton launched her show *Cooking Live,* I appeared quite often. One day Sara said, "Let's do *frites* on the show." It never occurred to me she would not have a thermostatically controlled deep fryer, but we improvised, half-filling a deep saucepan with oil. We turned on the heat underneath and had begun having an animated discussion about the potatoes when I realized the oil was smoking away. We hastily turned off the heat, smiled, waited a minute, and then, gingerly, lowered in sticks of potato. If we had lowered the damp potatoes into fat that was too hot, the oil would have exploded into sheets of flame. Thankfully, we were lucky.

Performance was also involved in another aspect of my life—this time with the IACP Foundation, now the Culinary Trust. I had been disappointed over the years with the shows for the annual fund-raiser, and when I took over as foundation treasurer in the late 1990s I was determined things would change. I developed the Culinary Concerts and for three years organized funny, inspiring shows featuring stars like Emeril Lagasse, whom I had met with Julia very early in his career when he had just opened his first restaurant, Emeril's, in New Orleans. Back then he was young and shy and completely devoted to Julia. By the time we were doing the Culinary Concerts, he had learned to switch on a personality with his famous "Bim! Bam!" and when he and Julia shared a stage it was magical. Martin Yan's virtuosity in boning a chicken in eighteen seconds astounded the audience every time. And everyone loved charismatic Chef Patrick O'Connell, the outstanding innkeeper at The Inn at Little Washington in Virginia.

In October 1995, not long after I'd been elected a Grande Dame of another culinary organization, Les Dames d'Escoffier International, Mark and I were in Cape Town, South Africa. The trip had been part teaching, part travel. I was looking out at the beautiful view of Table Mountain, with the cloud dripping just like a tablecloth down over the mountain, and fiddling to put on a necklace, when I felt a lump in my neck. It didn't hurt, but because we had already planned to go to the American Hospital in Paris for Mark, who had been having some bouts with skin melanoma, and because there was cancer in my family on both sides, I decided to have the lump checked when we were back in France. With just a touch of his fingers the doctor diagnosed suspected lymphatic cancer. I was totally surprised but after some discussion I asked, "What are the chances of this being the curable kind of cancer?"—I meant Hodgkin's disease. He told me I had a 40 percent chance, and after five awful days of waiting in limbo for biopsy results I learned it was indeed Hodgkin's. Once again I was lucky—the cancer seemed not to have spread—but I knew I had to tell my mother and went to see her. As always, like a good Yorkshire woman, she was stoic and strong.

I launched into radiation treatment in Paris, four days a week for six weeks, then two weeks off before it all started again. In the clinic in the boring 16th Arrondissement I would wait my turn in a room filled with people. There's always a bright side. The doors to the cubicles where we changed had no locks, and I remember one little old man who looked through the cracks in the doors at the naked women. When I was lying on the slab, I counted down the fifty-seven seconds with my toes in different languages, switching from English to Spanish to French to Italian—*un, deux, trois,* one, two, three, *uno, dos, tres*—the point being to get the timing right. By the end of the treatments I could usually hit fifty-seven right on the dot. It was just a silly system but worked to keep my mind off what was happening. I still use it when I have an MRI.

I took a nap every day the first week, and the next week I was a bit more tired. By the end my throat was so scorched I had to give up alcoholic drinks— even the tiniest sip hurt to swallow. I was off it for four months, a record for me! By the end I was on fluids and ice cream. I was always exhausted and had huge painful burns, but luckily we weren't doing classes and I had just one little book going to bed at the publishers', *In & Out of the Kitchen in 15 Minutes or Less.* During those six months I saw almost no one, not even the children—Emma and Todd had moved together to California, and Simon was working in Russia. Dear Mark never left me alone. Each day he and I planned an activity, an exhibit, a visit to the cinema, though my usual consolation of a good meal was impossible. Every now and then we took a short walk through the Paris streets with George Wanklyn.

Gradually, happily, I recovered, but the experience taught me a lot about myself. I learned that I could not just breeze through life, going my own way without thinking of the people I loved, Mark, the children, my mother. Always before I had brushed off everyone with an, "I'll be fine," but for the first time in my life I wasn't. A stranger I had met somewhere on the teaching road wrote to me about her experience with cancer, and it helped me a lot. I began to realize the fragility of the status quo, how easily it could be shattered. And I became, I hope, more outgoing and more sympathetic with the troubles of others.

As the children grew older, Mark began to organize more and more exotic trips for us to take as a family at Christmas. As always, he was good at finding outstanding places to stay and sights to see, and one of the most memorable moments was, remarkably, not a meal. We were in Spain when Mark happened to notice a little card on the concierge's desk: "Alhambra open for the full moon." Arab architecture being one of Mark's enthusiasms, he jumped at the opportunity to see this palace and fortress constructed during the fourteenth century by Moorish rulers. The Alhambra stands atop the hill of the Assabica on the southeastern border of Granada. For centuries it had been allowed to fall into disrepair, but in the nineteenth century European scholars and travelers began its restoration.

That evening as we all walked up the hill I could see why the Alhambra not only is considered one of the most significant examples of Islamic architecture but also has inspired so many stories and songs—"a pearl set in emeralds," as Moorish poets called it. We could smell the orange trees and hear the nightingale's song and water in the fountains and cascades. The light came from lanterns—no electricity—and beneath that full moon I experienced a moment of such beauty and serenity I'll never forget it. Some great artworks transcend time and place—I think for instance of that wonderful moment in the film *Out of Africa* when someone puts on an early disc of Mozart and the Bushmen are instantly enthralled. For me, being at the Alhambra was like that, a moment when all the activity and projects and personalities stilled and there was utter peace.

Emma and Todd's wedding at Le Feÿ—just one of our glorious celebrations that lasted late into the night.

Chapter Sixteen

....

BOARS' HEADS, BUNKERS, AND BUBBLY

When we no longer have good cooking in the world, we will have no literature, nor high and sharp intelligence, nor friendly gatherings.

—Antonin Carême

By now our children, raised to travel, were doing some of their own wandering. Simon left the Moscow Catering Company to attend INSEAD, an international business school in France, at Fontainebleau. But Russia beckoned—Simon says he has always felt Russian. After he received his MBA he returned to Moscow to run Eliseevsky Gastronom, the top gourmet grocery where the oligarch owner parked his bulletproof car in a bomb-secured garage beside the store. Eliseevsky Gastronom was at least as famous for its belle epoque ceiling as for its truffles and ten different kinds of caviar. In our family it remains famous for being the place where Simon fell in love with the store's marketing director, Katya, a beautiful, affectionate woman whom he'd been the one to hire and who would become his wife.

Emma finished her master's degree at Johns Hopkins School of Advanced International Studies in Washington, D.C., and moved to L.A. to join Todd, who had decided the lure of the Hollywood media business was irresistible. He worked at Innovative Artists, while Emma took a job at the not-for-profit Pacific Council on International Policy, confirming her interest in international affairs. Always in pursuit of knowledge, in her spare time, Emma took courses in accounting, bartending, and pistol shooting. With my link to Southern California through my column for the Los Angeles Times Syndicate, visits were an excuse to mix work and pleasure.

Despite a varied life, family was always first. In 1997 my mother was diagnosed with inoperable lung cancer and doctors warned us she would live only a few months. Typically, she continued to work in the garden, and in December was felled by pneumonia. I flew to be with her in the hospital and sitting by her bedside, I noticed that her window had a distant view of the Highlands, my childhood home. We had planned to spend Christmas, as always, with the children at the château, but it was clear she would not last long. In despair I called Mark, and he and the children, who had flown to France for the holiday, piled into the car to head to Yorkshire.

On the day they were to arrive, I was driving my mother's vintage BMW when a hundred yards from the hospital the car died. I stood out in the cold awaiting the tow truck, frustrated and terribly sad. When the mechanic opened the hood, he discovered a squirrel's nest in the engine—the car had sat idle for too long. The symbolism confirmed what I already knew—that Mummy was going to die and this would be the saddest Christmas of my life. Two days later she passed away.

But in the midst of our sorrow, we also received happy news. Todd had been planning to propose over New Year's in Paris, but when he learned they must drive to my mother's deathbed he wasn't sure what to do. One day in Hurworth Emma came home with a tearstained face after visiting my mother. Emma told Todd her grandmother was concerned about her future. He took that as an omen and proposed, and the next day, when Emma told my mother, she was thrilled. I am sure she was at peace when she died that very night.

Todd and Emma's news delighted all of us. They selected a date, July 4, 1998, and Emma announced her "non-negotiable" wedding plans. She must have at least seven friends as bridesmaids, and they would wear trendy black. There would be at least two hundred guests, and Dad would wear a top hat. Emma had always been a sweet and easy child, but she was also terrifically strong willed. (When Mark and I had complained about her willfulness to my parents, they smiled knowingly, for they were familiar with the problem.) That evening she proved yet again that she had inherited my obstinacy. Emma wanted it all, and gradually she won us over to her vision.

I conceded that we could find room for at least twenty guests to sleep somewhere on the property for several days before the wedding, and Mark seized the upcoming occasion as an excuse to install yet another bathroom, our eighteenth. Emma agreed a country buffet would be nice, and dinner plans revolved around the garden where in July there would be strawberries and raspberries and all of the currant family, buckets of baby green beans, zucchini, garlic, new potatoes. Chef Claude Godard prepared a wonderful spread—chicken galantine with pistachios and foie gras, a pâté of confit leg of lamb, poached salmon, assorted sausages and a diversity of salads, and the main course, guinea hen in a rich cream sauce. Madame Milbert promised extras of *tilleul* from the dried lime blossoms of the avenue trees that make a soothing tea. I knew I would need plenty of that.

Mark scouted everywhere for a conveyance to deliver him and Emma to the ceremony and at last found Antoine Frombach, once the village baker. He lived in a fortified farmhouse and kept a hidden collection of old carriages in his barns, and when Mark and I went to see him he proudly showed me one of the earliest commercial mixers, still fitted with its balloon whisk and giant copper bowl for beating egg whites. As we were climbing into the car to leave, he rushed out with a treasure—a *banneton*, one of the linen-lined wicker bread baskets used to shape long French baguettes. "This one is for loaves of one kilo," he said. "It's for you."

The extended château family was all involved. By this time Monsieur Milbert had been officially retired for years, though they both were involved in preparations. Christine Corby, a cheerful young woman from the village whom Mark and I eventually asked to move into the gardener's cottage to take Milbert's place as *guardienne* of the property, was helping out. Portuguese Fernanda, who had taken over as housekeeper when Maria retired, had Maria's gift for running things. Fernanda had the additional talent of being a wonderful dressmaker and florist—she brought in flowers, berries, and green leaves from the garden in every season, arranging them with imagination, never the same twice. She was in charge of flowers for the wedding.

A few days ahead, people began to arrive. The large American contingent was anchored by Todd's parents, Bonnie and Carl Schulkin, and supplemented by Emma and Todd's college friends. Many came from England and Paris for the weekend. As they appeared the water heater gave up, but no one complained. *"C'est la vie de château,"* we all agreed. The festive, joyful spirit of the wedding had begun. The ceremony and reception in the front courtyard passed in a haze for me, though I do vividly remember small things—Simon holding my hand as we walked in procession to the steps, Zigzag, our Dalmatian, performing his hereditary act as carriage dog trotting behind Emma and Mark in the carriage drawn by magnificent matched Comtois horses. In his wedding speech Mark repeated my father's words to him at the party celebrating our marriage thirty-two years earlier: "I always think that the most important quality in a husband, or wife, is really a kindly nature. If there is genuine kindness, so many other things flow from it, you can't go far wrong." I almost became the classic weeping mother of the bride.

Toward sunset I began to register more normally and wondered why half the tables were without wine, why the terrace candles weren't lit, who would serve the coffee. Simon calmed me and led me to the microphone, where I donned a La Varenne apron and announced the arrival of Chef Randall Price's grandiose *pièce montée,* a great fantasy wedding cake evoking the style of the Middle Ages, with pound cake flavored with white chocolate and pistachio, imbibed with lemon syrup and Scotch whisky as base, and atop that layer after layer filled with lemon and raspberry curd and our own fresh raspberries. Randall had spent days making the cake and had even gathered blossoms of white lilac and candied them with egg white and fine sugar to a crisp, ethereal white. The assembly of this masterpiece was a feat of engineering. He and a helper marched gingerly up the ramp bearing the five-tiered cake on a huge plank irresistibly nicknamed "the bier." With bravado, Simon sabered the neck of a bottle of Champagne with a scimitar from Morocco, and we all happily toasted the bride and groom. After the cake cutting came the fireworks and dancing. Even in high heels, which I never wear, once I began to dance, I couldn't stop. Oblivious to time, we danced beyond dawn, on until the sun rose high into the sky, pure happiness.

At the end of the next year the whole family was gathering again at Château du Feÿ for another big party—this one to celebrate the millennium. We started out with traditional Christmas dinner with the family, including Todd's parents, who normally celebrated the Jewish holidays and bravely tried everything on our multi-national menu: from smoked salmon followed by roast goose and all the trimmings—caramelized onions, glazed wild chestnuts from the alley of trees at the gate, Brussels sprouts from the garden, mashed Milbert potatoes with gravy—to a dessert of pecan pie with crème fraîche to cut the sweetness. Mark brought out our best local wines, a ten-year-old Chablis Grand Cru and a fine old Beaune. We all departed happily to bed without a glance at the weather forecast. But at Le Feÿ we were always in the eye of any storm. The following morning Mark and I were awoken by a screaming wind and I looked out from our little bathroom window to see the great pyramid oaks, rare trees older and taller than the château itself, swirling in the gale. I'd never seen them like that. A few moments later, the lights went out.

Milbert came up to the house to announce that a huge windstorm had blown up without warning. Early that morning the nurse had been driving up the avenue to see Madame Milbert when one of the giant trees fell just in front of her car. She'd turned around and fled, but now there were more trees down, so there was no getting out. We called the gardener for help, and soon Denis arrived with two friends and spent nearly the whole day sawing apart two vast linden trees, releasing us. We walked out into the woods, where we found fifty fallen oak trees, many of them lying across the rides so that we literally had to climb over trunks several feet thick. The sight was both awe inspiring and heartrending. By the time we had finished our walk, we were speechless. Thankfully, the ancient pyramid oaks with their vast roots still stood beside the house.

No electricity meant we had no water or heat, so we built up the fire in the library. Luckily the old water cistern on the terrace held a good supply, and Todd, Mark, Simon, and Carl carried in buckets of water for washing and cooking. When the sun set, we lit candles and sat around the fire. In the silence without phones or computers, only the ticking of the 250-year-old grandfather clock, we clustered around the fire and talked, just as people had done two hundred years before. Eventually we spotted lights across the river and realized someone had power, so we drove out to find some supper at the only place open, a Chinese restaurant. Later we learned that the storm had been a tornado, virtually unknown in our part of the world, and had twirled the roots of the trees right out of the ground. It became known as the Millennium storm.

The next morning, no sooner was our electricity restored than guests began arriving for this special New Year. We had somehow managed to find beds for forty-six, an all-time record, and we built roaring fires in the two great reception rooms. Simon and Emma's French teacher, Michel Gandolfo, had a student who had formed a jazz trio, and Michel was enthusiastic about their abilities. We were skeptical, but the group proved the hit of the evening. After a leisurely buffet dinner with plenty of wine, we moved to the salon, where Mark had set up a television linked to the BBC showing celebrations in London's Trafalgar Square. As we watched the countdown, I noticed a sudden flurry in one corner of the room and turned to see the table laden with bottles of Champagne collapse. Strong men leant their shoulders, bystanders seized bottles, and within a few minutes order was restored. In a sea of fizz midnight had come and gone, and we had all missed it. That did not diminish the gaiety of the party.

Every time Mark and I visited Todd and Emma in Southern California, where she had become deputy director of the California Committee South for Human Rights Watch, we said to each other, "Well, this place is surprisingly agreeable." Despite its reputation, L.A. turned out to hold much more than Hollywood hype and beautiful weather. I always stopped in to talk with Russ Parsons and Jim Burns, my *LA Times* editors, who gave me the inside track on food news—the craze for tapas and small tastings was just beginning.

The column got me out and about, exploring aspects of cooks and cooking I otherwise might not have done. At the Santa Monica Farmers' Market I talked to the vendors and visited their farms. The market was leading the way to an explosion of outdoor produce markets throughout Southern California. Besides the fact that it had opened only in 1978 and was, therefore, new compared to the centuries-old market back home in Joigny, there were other contrasts. Santa Monica had no charcuterie stands and little cheese, whereas in Burgundy a single market stall might have a hundred or more types of cheese, and charcuterie stands lined the walls. In Santa Monica it was the salad greens that caught my eye—leaf lettuce, arugula, cress, multi-colored chard, and a dozen Asian greens that were novelties to me. One spring I caught sight of the season's first fresh garlic, perfect for the garlic sauce I'd found in Languedoc, served with duck breast.

DUCK BREAST WITH GARLIC AND WALNUT RELISH

Magret, the breast of a duck, has become the upmarket steak, and it behaves very much the same way. When pleasantly pink, the meat is rich and juicy, but be warned that overcooked *magret* is tough as leather. The pungent *aillade,* more relish than sauce, comes from the French *ail,* meaning "garlic," and is fragant with walnuts. In general, a *magret* serves one person, but they can be very large, so here I am suggesting three *magrets* to serve four. A roasted root vegetable such as turnip, root celery, or a jacket potato is the best accompaniment.

Serves 4

3 duck *magrets* (2¼ pounds/about 1 kg total)
Salt and pepper

For the aillade sauce
½ cup/60 g walnut pieces
4–5 garlic cloves, cut in pieces
Salt and pepper
¼ cup/60 ml walnut oil
¼ cup/15 g chopped fresh parsley
2 tablespoons/30 g chopped capers
Grated zest of 1 lemon (for sprinkling)
Vegetable garnish

To make the sauce: Put the walnut pieces, garlic, salt, and pepper in a food processor and pulse a few seconds until chopped. With the blades running, add the oil in a slow, steady stream to make a smooth emulsion. Transfer the mixture to a bowl and stir in the chopped parsley and capers. Taste, and adjust the seasoning. The relish can be kept, tightly covered, in the refrigerator for a day or two. Sprinkle lemon zest on top of the relish just before serving.

Shortly before serving, let the relish come to room temperature. Trim excess fat from the *magrets,* then crosshatch the skin, cutting down almost to the meat so fat can escape. Sprinkle the breasts with salt and pepper. Heat a skillet or heavy, dry frying pan over medium heat. Add the *magrets* skin side down, and fry until the skin is very brown and crisp so as much fat as possible is extracted, 5 to 7 minutes, or longer if necessary. Turn and brown the other side, 2 to 3 minutes longer. Test a *magret* by poking the center with the point of a knife to see the color of the meat. If it is too rare for your taste, continue cooking for 1 to 2 minutes, but remember it will be very tough if overcooked. When done, set the *magrets* aside, skin side up, on a carving board, cover them loosely with foil, and leave about 5 minutes for the juices to be reabsorbed.

Carve the *magrets* on the diagonal into thin slices and arrange them overlapping on serving plates. Spoon a little relish on the side of the plates, sprinkle with grated lemon zest, and add your chosen vegetable garnish. Serve the remaining relish in a small bowl, topped with more lemon zest.

It was also in the market that I ran across top chefs like Michael McCarty, Michael Voltaggio, Alain Giraud, and Jean-François Meteigner. When Mark and I later moved to Santa Monica, I invited these chefs to come and teach in my kitchen where I invariably learned some helpful tips. One of my favorite columns was a story on Fergus Henderson, London restaurateur extraordinaire and pioneer of the British back-to-meat movement, who stood in front of his California audience in very English lace-up shoes and a blue-striped butcher's apron declaring with utter seriousness, "It is unkind to animals not to use every bit. I have this sad modern image of people only eating their middles, but there's so much beyond the fillet at both ends." Indeed, Fergus launched me in new directions with his shredded pig's ears, deep-fried to resemble chitterlings. His crispy breaded pig tails were brined overnight and simmered for hours before frying. Fergus told me his animals lived in mini-Hiltons, fed on foods such as the whey from goat cheese. "Hug your butcher," was his advice. "All that knowledge is disappearing."

Fergus is one of the many English chefs who are putting London back on the gastronomic map. It is his slow-roasted pig's head that lingers in my mind—partly simmered, partly roasted, the skin mellowing to a deep polished mahogany and presented on a green pillow of arugula, it was a work of art. I was determined to publish that recipe that called for half a pig's head. You can't buy just the half, so I bought a whole one, split in two, and when we tested the recipe it came out perfectly—crackling and crisp and delicious.

For months afterward, every time I opened the freezer there was still half a pig's head winking at me.

I had another honor in the States when *Bon Appétit* named me Teacher of the Year in 2000. Barbara Fairchild, then the magazine's editor, has a wonderful sense of style and held the award ceremony, as always, at a top New York restaurant. Barbara had asked how I would feel about Julia's doing the presentation, which of course delighted me. Naturally Mark was my guest, but Todd and Emma were in New York that weekend and joined us for drinks before dinner. Forty or fifty of us were enjoying ourselves tremendously, awaiting the arrival of the top honoree so that dinner could be served. Time passed. Mark got into a conversation with Al Roker, though, having no idea who he was, asked, "What brings you here?" a comment that surprised the celebrated television weatherman. Still there was no sign of the honoree, and people were grumbling. I had been talking with Anna Wintour, who was very bright and engaging, but as the hour grew later she said, "I'm sorry, it's so late I won't be able to stay. Perhaps your daughter and son-in-law would like to take my place at dinner." And with that the evening was absolutely complete.

In September 2001 I was teaching at The Greenbrier when one of those bad flu epidemics swept the place. Everybody got it, and so eventually did I. The doctor warned me to be careful, but I took no notice since Mark and I had planned a trip to Aspen, where I was to teach. Off we went to five thousand feet. Although in Colorado I felt a little light-headed, I paid no attention. Afterward Mark flew back to France and I went on to Minneapolis, where I was scheduled to teach another class. In the middle of that class, I began to feel dreadful—I can usually rely on adrenaline to keep me going, but this time I was so faint I asked for Cognac, which revived me well enough to finish. But that night I had an acute bronchitis attack and postponed my flight back to The Greenbrier. Two days later, on Monday, I finally got myself to the airport and flew to Roanoke. By the time I reached The Greenbrier, I was again feeling so ill, I told Riki I was awfully sorry, but I simply could not teach the next day.

The next morning while I was resting, the housekeeper came to my cottage and said, "You might want to turn on the television." When I did, I saw the World Trade Center towers were under attack. I called Mark, but he was so far away in a different time zone, he couldn't quite take in the news.

When I saw the Pentagon was a target, I knew I had to be with my students and made my way to the class. Until only a few years earlier the very classroom I walked into that morning had been the auxiliary White House bunker in case of nuclear attack. Its walls were ten yards of concrete thick, but when *The Washington Post* leaked the story twenty years earlier, complete with photographs, the bunker's location became common knowledge. No one knew what to do with the hideaway, so a cooking school was installed.

I staggered in and told them what was happening, and on overhead monitors we watched, appalled, as the second tower fell. A rumor went round that the president might come to take refuge at The Greenbrier, though he did not. For the next two weeks, I was so sick I couldn't leave and everyone looked after me with great kindness, but I couldn't shake the infection. I lay in bed for weeks, watching the depressing news of 9/11. I felt that somehow the flu and the bunker and 9/11 were all bound up in the end of an era.

The next year brought another cloud over my life. In 2002 Julia turned ninety and went on a birthday tour around the country, ending with a big reception for the installation of her famous Cambridge house kitchen at the Smithsonian. Paul had died eight years earlier, but Julia was always courageous about moving on—one of the many things she taught me. "I'm not sentimental," Julia once said to me. I rather wish I were the same. I still miss the lovely places Mark and I have lived in. After Simca died in 2000, Julia, with her niece, Phila, had made one last visit to her home on Simca's property in the south of France before moving to a retirement community in Montecito, California, where she had a small ground-floor apartment with a little patio and her own specially installed kitchen. Whenever Mark and I were in California we visited.

It was during the ninetieth birthday tour that Julia's knee began to bother her (both knees had been replaced years before), and by the time she returned to California she couldn't climb the steps to the little hedgehopper airplane that would take her home. Her longtime assistant, Stephanie Hersh, drove Julia straight to the hospital in Santa Barbara, where they discovered the knee replacement had collapsed. "They opened it up and put in a bouquet garni," Julia said, classic Julia. For weeks she was treated in the hospital and Stephanie brought in her food, since the hospital food came in cardboard containers reheated in a microwave. "Nasty enough to kill anybody," Stephanie said.

Julia was allowed one visitor a day for ten minutes only. When I came to see her there, I feared it might be for the last time, but thankfully she recovered and I happily visited her several more times. The last was only a few months before she died two days before her birthday in 2004. Mark and I brought her some tangerines and a loaf of my home-baked cheese brioche, a favorite from back in our Normandy days, and the three of us sat in the garden talking while Stephanie cooked us onion soup and an omelet. Julia was nursing a slightly bad-tempered black cat that yowled every time a bird flew over. The birds knew, so they continually pestered the cat, but we drew the line when they swooped in on the brioche.

CHEESE BRIOCHE

In the cheese-producing parts of France (so nearly everywhere), cheese may be added to brioche dough for a savory loaf. An aged hard cheese such as Comté (a type of Gruyère) is preferred. Cheese brioche is particularly delicious toasted.

Makes a 1-pound/450 g loaf

1 tablespoon/7 g dry yeast
½ cup/125 ml lukewarm milk
2¾ cups/330 g flour, plus more if needed
1 tablespoon sugar
1 teaspoon/7 g salt
2 eggs, beaten to mix
Oil, for bowl
4 tablespoons/60 g butter, plus more for the pan
1 cup/100 g grated Gruyère cheese
1 egg mixed with ½ teaspoon water, for glaze

9×4×3-inch/23×10×7.5-cm loaf pan

Sprinkle the yeast over the milk in a bowl and let it stand until dissolved, about 5 minutes. Sift the flour onto a work surface, sprinkle with the sugar and salt, and make a well in the center. Add the yeast mixture and the beaten eggs to the well. With your hand, combine the yeast mixture and eggs, then gradually work in the flour to form a smooth dough; it should be quite sticky.

Knead the dough on the work surface, lifting it up and throwing it down first with one hand, then with the other, until it is very elastic and resembles chamois leather. This should take 5 to 7 minutes and the dough will gradually change texture until it pulls into a long rope when lifted. If necessary, work in a little more flour. Alternatively, mix and knead the dough in a mixer fitted with the dough hook. Transfer the dough to an oiled bowl, flip it to coat the top with oil, and cover the bowl with plastic wrap. Leave to rise in a warm place until doubled in volume, about an hour.

Butter the loaf pan. Knead the risen dough a few seconds on the work surface to knock out the air. Squeeze the butter with your fist until it is pliable. Add it to the dough and knead it, squeezing the dough and butter together with your fist until the butter is completely incorporated, 2 to 3 minutes. Add the grated cheese and work it also into the dough, reserving 2 tablespoons for topping.

Lightly flour the work surface, pat out the dough to an 8-inch/20 cm square, and roll it, pinching the folded edge to form a seam. Tuck in the ends of dough, flip so the smooth side is up, and drop it into the loaf pan. Cover loosely with plastic wrap and leave to rise in a warm place until the pan is full, 45 minutes to 1 hour. Heat the oven to 400°F/200°C and set a shelf low down.

Brush the loaf with the egg glaze and sprinkle with reserved cheese. Slash the surface of the loaf diagonally with the point of a knife and bake in the oven until browned and the loaf sounds hollow when turned out and tapped on the bottom, 25 to 35 minutes. Unmold and let the loaf cool on a rack. Even after a day or two, the brioche still toasts well.

Julia was frail by then but still alert, and as she always had, she asked about the children and how my work was progressing. Julia always thought of others, never herself. Sitting there, I remembered a day at The Greenbrier when Riki and I were in the back row watching Julia do a presentation. At one point she asked her assistant to take a casserole out of the oven. When she carried it over to Julia, who was sitting on a stool, even from the last row we could see that the pot was steaming. Suddenly we saw Julia lift the lid and we gasped, but Julia didn't even flinch. And now she still was not flinching, though each time we met I felt sad knowing it might be good-bye. "There's nothing on the other side," she once said to me firmly. This meeting, alas, was our last.

On the day Julia died, Phila called me in France. Emma was visiting, and we both burst into tears—Julia had been so like a mother to me, a grandmother to Emma, and such a tower of strength over the years. We couldn't believe she was gone. Five years later, when Emma and I attended the movie premiere of *Julie & Julia,* we cried again. We both agreed—Meryl Streep's portrayal was so close to the real Julia, it was as if she had returned.

For several years, people had been asking me to do a reprint of *French Regional Cooking,* which was long out of print. I still worked with Andrew Nurnberg in England, but I had signed on with Lisa Ekus to handle our U.S. business and with her usual enthusiasm, she jumped on the ideas we discussed. Within six weeks she sold a project Mark and I had been intermittently working on for years—the book that would eventually become *The Cookbook Library.* Two weeks after that, Lisa got us the highest offer we'd ever had from Chronicle Books for *The Country Cooking of France.* Instead of just reprinting *French Regional Cooking,* under Lisa's guidance we added dozens of new recipes, reorganized the book, and made it more personal by adding portraits of pastry chefs and cheese makers and others so essential to the spirit of regional cooking in France.

Among the many characters I talked to for the book was Claude Vauget, who had taught for us for so many years at La Varenne. Claude came from the Loire Valley, and for me this recipe of his sums up the simple good food of his home province. When he turned out his heart-shaped mold, he would surround it with a necklace of raspberries, placing each berry against the fresh white cream, with a final tiny silver ball to echo the clasp. A few years later, after the book had appeared, I demonstrated this recipe on Martha Stewart's show.

COEUR À LA CRÈME

The perfect accompaniment to berries, *coeur à la crème* is made of whipped crème fraîche lightened with meringue, then left to drain in cheesecloth, in effect a very light, fresh cheese. Special heart-shaped molds of porcelain with holes for drainage can be found in several sizes, or you can make a cheap substitute from a metal cake pan with holes poked in it with a nail and hammer. Often the *coeur* and its berries are served with more whipped cream, sweetened this time with sugar and vanilla.

Serves 6

2 cups/500 ml crème fraîche, chilled
4 egg whites
Raspberries or strawberries, for serving
Sugar, for serving

For the whipped cream
1 cup/250 ml crème fraîche
1–2 tablespoons/15–30 g sugar
½ teaspoon vanilla extract

1-quart/1 liter heart-shaped mold or 6 individual molds; cheesecloth

Line the mold(s) with cheesecloth. Whisk the cold crème fraîche in a bowl by hand or using a stand mixer fitted with the whisk attachment until the cream holds soft peaks. In another bowl, whisk the egg whites until stiff. Stir about a quarter of the egg whites into the crème fraîche to lighten it, then fold this mixture into the remaining whites. Spoon the mixture into the mold(s), filling well into the corners, and cover with plastic wrap. Set the mold(s) on a tray to catch the drips and chill for at least 8 and up to 24 hours. The longer the mold is kept, the more firmly it will set and the better it tastes.

An hour or two before serving, make the whipped cream: Beat the crème fraîche until it holds soft peaks. Add the sugar and vanilla, and continue beating until stiff. Turn the mold(s) onto a flat platter or individual plates and peel off the cheesecloth. Arrange the berries around the edge like a necklace. Serve with separate bowls of sugar and whipped cream.

Because our contract for *Country Cooking* was so big, we had to put aside the project Mark and I had dubbed *The Cookbook Book* (ultimately *The Cookbook Library*), a culmination of our decades of collecting old, sometimes rare, cookbooks. After all, a few years could not make much difference to a book that explores four centuries of printed cookbooks starting in 1474. Sheila Levine, our editor at University of California Press, sympathized with the schedule conflict and agreed to a delay, and with help from Molly Stevens and Laura Calder (who drafted much of the material in the single-subject boxes) I began to focus on *Country Cooking*. Randall Price tested over two hundred recipes, and as with all my books, Mark was the irreplaceable editor. France Ruffenach proved the perfect choice for photographer because not only was she raised in France, but she also had the unusual gift of being equally talented on location and in the studio. She made three trips to France to capture the different seasons and locations and her sensitive views of the French countryside later earned her a James Beard Award (while the text of *Country Cooking* ran away with another).

And *Country Cooking* was to be ready for the publisher just in time for the next big party at the château, this one in 2006 in honor of Katya and Simon. Early that year at the dinner table they had announced their engagement, adding the news that Katya was pregnant. After a short pause to catch our breath, Mark and I couldn't have been happier. The baby would be born in September, but the wedding couldn't wait for the Burgundian summer. Instead Mark and I flew to Moscow to attend a real Russian marriage in the Registry office, the only one in all of Russia that will marry foreigners. We all headed there in the stretch limo Simon had rented and sipped Champagne out of plastic glasses before piling out at the Registry, where at least forty couples took their turn on a grand staircase, designed for a photo opportunity while waiting around.

We lingered with the others until, at last, we were shooed up to a narrow landing where a woman noted names and papers were signed. The ceremony took place in a pillared gold-and-white hall, and for an extra charge three stout ladies played Tchaikovsky with true Russian élan—it was all a very Soviet flashback. Afterward we adjourned to Red Square and a prime view of the Kremlin for a splendid dinner of blini and caviar, *pilmenyi* and *pojarski*. There must have been a cake, though I don't remember, since by then the toasts of vodka and Champagne had taken hold.

Naturally we planned for another celebration at the château in June. Simon and Katya's party at Le Feÿ was far from a rerun of Todd and Emma's, for they invited only eighty friends and family members, including Katya's mother, Tatiana, representing Russia. Early in the evening, guests gathered beneath the tent overlooking the valley for a cocktail hour where we showed the video of the Russian wedding. Mark had invited a magician to perform, backed up by the many toasts and much laughter, with *gougères* and canapés on the side. An unusually teary-eyed Mark gave a clever toast with all sorts of Russian literary references before we sat down for a plated dinner centered on medallions of veal with morel sauce.

The cake, in fact, was my main worry. This time Randall had devised a fantasy of Arab inspiration in pistachio and many tiers, and because of the heat I could see a distinct lean developing in the frosted walls, which only accentuated as the hours passed. When the happy couple finally took a knife to it, I was mightily relieved, and afterward there were fireworks and the marvelous jazz group played until two in the morning. That night the house was again full.

On Sunday night only a few people lingered and Katya and Simon had set off for their honeymoon. On Monday Mark left for England, where he would attend a reunion at his Oxford college, Christ Church. I was tidying things up at the château, showing some friends around the place, and we were standing in the hall looking at the map of the property when our care-taker, Christine Corby, appeared in the doorway in tears. "It's Monsieur," she said. "It's the hospital. They're on the phone." Mark had collapsed with a stroke at Waterloo Station in London.

Our lives were never to be the same.

Mark did not die, but very nearly. I rushed to St. Thomas's Hospital on the first available Eurostar express, and the children joined me, Emma from California, Simon from his honeymoon in Provence. We watched in trepida-tion as each day Mark gathered a little more strength. In fact the specialist doctor said to Simon, "You nearly lost him." For a long while, Mark had no idea he had had such a narrow escape, and for six months he was in rehabili-tation in England, then France, before returning home. By then it had be-come clear that we would have to leave the château—there was no way I could continue managing it on my own. The following year of moving our possessions once again across an ocean has remained a merciful blur. Mark's long-term memory has remained as good as ever, and eventually he was able to walk far enough to go for coffee at the corner café near our new home in Santa Monica, California. Our modest house is flanked by white iceberg roses that bloom year-round and are cooled by the Pacific one mile west, and indoors we are surrounded by the beautiful old furniture, porcelain, and glasses that have survived three centuries and more—and, most important, the books. Every room in the house except the dining room is lined with cookbooks. Indeed, we had to have the floors of the house reinforced to support them.

And it is in this house that we continue to offer a few classes, to write, and to enjoy each other's company and our many friends and ever-expanding family. And it is to this house that we return from our rare but continuing travels—I'm still one day hoping to make it along the Silk Road, from China to Iran and beyond. As it does for so many people, the name itself entices my imagination.

The end of a wonderful meal for Simon's fortieth birthday at El Bulli in Spain: (left to right) Todd and seven Cherniavskys: Emma, cousin Lexi, Katya, Anne, Simon, and cousin Kate.

EPILOGUE

Even as I continue to write new books, I am surprised how many of the older ones remain vitally alive—sparking e-books and translations. In April 2012 a longtime dream for both Mark and me was fulfilled when *The Cookbook Library* was published, and we celebrated nearly fifty years of book collecting, surrounded by many old and new friends. *The Cookbook Library* went on to gather multiple honors, including the Jane Grigson Award for outstanding culinary writing from IACP and the Gourmand Cookbook Award for Best Book of the Year. In May 2013, just three months after my seventy-fifth birthday, I was inducted into the James Beard Foundation's Cookbook Hall of Fame for the body of work that I have written, joining such luminaries as Elizabeth David, Marcella Hazan, M. F. K. Fisher, Jacques Pépin, and of course dear Julia.

Each summer we set off for what has become our annual retreat to France. A few years after we moved to Santa Monica, Simon had begun renovating a farmhouse among the vines of southern Languedoc, at the foothills of the Pyrenees, snowcapped in winter. The Mediterranean is barely a mile away, and there our ever-expanding family gathers each summer. We sit outside beside an ancient olive tree, sipping the local fruity wines, reminiscing about the past and plans—always more plans and projects—for the coming year. Simon wants to install a little swimming pool for his three daughters, Sophia, Ksenia, and Nina. The girls are tri-lingual, speaking Russian at home, English with their dad, and French in school. Emma and Todd join us from their new home in London, in the curiously named Crouch End, bringing along their children, Leo and Lucy. The moment they came into our lives, they captured our hearts. And I look forward to showing all the children how to make ginger biscuits and chocolate snowballs. They must learn to stir the Christmas cake for good luck. And one day I'll teach them how to whip up the perfect soufflé.

Anne Willan's Previous Publications

....

MAIN BOOKS

The Cookbook Library: U.S., 2012

The Country Cooking of France: U.S., 2007

The Good Cook: U.S., 2004

Good Food No Fuss: U.S. and UK, 2003

Cooking with Wine: U.S. and UK, 2001

From My Château Kitchen: U.S., 2000 (published in the UK as *A Kitchen in Burgundy*)

Cook It Right: U.S., 1998 (published in the UK as *Cooked to Perfection*)

Anne Willan's Look & Cook (a 17-volume pictorial series): U.S. and UK, 1992–95 Basis for the 1994 PBS television series, syndicated internationally. 1992: *Chicken Classics, Chocolate Desserts, Meat Classics, Perfect Pasta, Main Dish Vegetables, Fruit Desserts;* 1993: *Delicious Desserts, Fish Classics, Creative Casseroles, Creative Appetizers, Superb Salads, Italian Country Cooking;* 1994: *Asian Cooking, Perfect Pies and Tarts, Splendid Soups;* 1995: *Classic Breads, French Country Cooking*

Château Cuisine (recipes from French châteaux): UK, 1992, and U.S., 1993

Great Cooks and Their Recipes: UK and U.S., 1992 (reissue of 1977 edition)

La France Gastronomique: UK and U.S., 1991

La Varenne Pratique: U.S., 1989 (published in the UK as *Reader's Digest Complete Guide to Cookery*)

The La Varenne Cooking Course: U.S., 1982 (published in the UK as *The Observer French Cookery School,* 1980)

French Regional Cooking: UK and U.S., 1981

Many of the preceding works have been recognized for awards in the United States (James Beard Foundation, IACP) and/or the UK (Glenfiddich, André Simon, Food Writers Guild).

OTHER

In & Out of the Kitchen in 15 Minutes or Less: U.S. and UK, 1995

HARDCOVERS

Anne Willan's Desserts and Pastries: UK, 1988
Real Food: UK, 1988
Classical French Cooking: UK, 1986, and U.S., 1987
La Varenne's Paris Kitchen: U.S., 1981
La Varenne's Basic French Cooking: U.S., 1980, and UK, 1983
Entertaining Menus: U.S., 1974, and UK, 1980

PAPERBACKS

Quick Fixes and Kitchen Tips: U.S., 2005
Bistro Cooking: UK, 1997
The Cooking of Burgundy: UK, 1987
Sauces, Marinades and Dressings: UK, 1985

Index

· ·